The Complete Beginner's

INSTANT POT

COOKBOOK

A Comprehensive Collection of Easy and Delicious Recipes for Novice Cooks, Designed to Enhance Your Kitchen Experience

Earl M. Levitt

TABLE OF CONTENTS

INTRODUCTION

Greetings, culinary enthusiasts, and welcome to a culinary adventure like no other! Within the pages of this cookbook lies a treasure trove of delectable recipes, thoughtfully curated to showcase the versatility and convenience of the Instant Pot.

In today's fast-paced world, finding the time to prepare delicious and nutritious meals can often feel like a daunting task. However, with the Instant Pot at your disposal, mealtime can be transformed into a seamless and enjoyable experience. Whether you're a busy professional, a busy parent, or simply someone who loves good food, the Instant Pot is here to revolutionize the way you cook.

What sets the Instant Pot apart is its multifunctional capabilities, combining the functions of several kitchen appliances into one sleek and efficient device. From pressure cooking and slow cooking to rice cooking and yogurt making, the Instant Pot does it all – and does it exceptionally well. With just the touch of a button, you can whip up a wide array of dishes, from comforting soups and stews to succulent meats and flavorful vegetarian fare.

But the Instant Pot isn't just about convenience – it's also about elevating the quality of your meals. By harnessing the power of high pressure and precise temperature control, the Instant Pot locks in flavor and nutrients, resulting in dishes that are consistently delicious and nutritious.

In this cookbook, you'll find a diverse collection of recipes that showcase the versatility and flavor-enhancing capabilities of the Instant Pot. Whether you're in the mood for a comforting bowl of chili, a flavorful curry, or a decadent dessert, we've got you covered. Each recipe is accompanied by clear and concise instructions, making it easy for even novice cooks to achieve culinary success.

But our cookbook isn't just about recipes – it's also about empowering you to become a more confident and adventurous cook. Throughout these pages, you'll find helpful tips and tricks for getting the most out of your Instant Pot, as well as suggestions for ingredient substitutions, cooking techniques, and more.

We want to extend our heartfelt gratitude to all the talented chefs, food photographers, and editors who contributed to this cookbook. Their passion and expertise have brought these recipes to life, and we're excited to share them with you.

So, whether you're a seasoned home cook or a kitchen novice, we invite you to dive into the world of the Instant Pot and discover the endless culinary possibilities that await. Happy cooking!

Chapter 1

Breakfasts

Chapter 1 Breakfasts

Cauliflower and Cheese Quiche

Prep time: 10 minutes | Cook time: 10 minutes | Serves 2

- 1 cup chopped cauliflower
- ¼ cup shredded Cheddar cheese
- 5 eggs, beaten
- 1 teaspoon butter
- 1 teaspoon dried oregano
- 1 cup water

1. Grease the instant pot baking pan with butter from inside. 2. Pour water in the instant pot. 3. Sprinkle the cauliflower with dried oregano and put it in the prepared baking pan. Flatten the vegetables gently. 4. After this, add eggs and stir the vegetables. 5. Top the quiche with shredded cheese and transfer it in the instant pot. Close and seal the lid. Cook the quiche on Manual mode (High Pressure) for 10 minutes. Make a quick pressure release.

Classic Coffee Cake

Prep time: 5 minutes | Cook time: 40 minutes | Serves 5 to 6

Base:
- 2 eggs
- 2 tablespoons salted grass-fed butter, softened
- 1 cup blanched almond flour
- 1 cup chopped pecans
- ¼ cup sour cream, at room temperature

Topping:
- 1 cup sugar-free chocolate chips
- 1 cup chopped pecans
- ½ cup Swerve, or more to

- ¼ cup full-fat cream cheese, softened
- ½ teaspoon salt
- ½ teaspoon ground cinnamon
- ½ teaspoon ground nutmeg
- ¼ teaspoon baking soda

taste
- ½ cup heavy whipping cream

1. Pour 1 cup of filtered water into the inner pot of the Instant Pot, then insert the trivet. Using an electric mixer, combine the eggs, butter, flour, pecans, sour cream, cream cheese, salt, cinnamon, nutmeg, and baking soda. Mix thoroughly. Transfer this mixture into a well-greased, Instant Pot-friendly pan (or dish). 2. Using a sling if desired, place the pan onto the trivet, and cover loosely with aluminum foil. Close the lid, set the pressure release to Sealing, and select Manual. Set the Instant Pot to 40 minutes on High Pressure and let cook. 3. While cooking, in a large bowl, mix the chocolate chips, pecans, Swerve, and whipping cream thoroughly. Set aside. 4. Once cooked, let the pressure naturally disperse from the Instant Pot for about 10 minutes, then carefully switch the pressure release to Venting. 5. Open the Instant Pot and remove the pan. Evenly sprinkle the topping mixture over the cake. Let cool, serve, and enjoy!

Chicken, Mozzarella, and Tomato Pizza

Prep time: 5 minutes | Cook time: 20 minutes | Serves 4 to 5

Crust:
- 2 eggs
- 2 tablespoons salted grass-fed butter, softened
- 1 pound (454 g) ground chicken

Topping:
- 1 (14-ounce / 397-g) can fire roasted sugar-free or low-sugar tomatoes, drained
- 2 cups shredded full-fat Mozzarella cheese
- 1 cup chopped spinach

- 1 cup grated full-fat Parmesan cheese
- ⅓ cup blanched almond flour

- ½ teaspoon dried basil
- ½ teaspoon crushed red pepper
- ½ teaspoon dried oregano
- ½ teaspoon dried cilantro

1. Pour 1 cup of filtered water into the inner pot of the Instant Pot, then insert the trivet. In a large bowl, combine the eggs, butter, chicken, cheese, and flour. Mix thoroughly. Transfer this mixture into a greased, Instant Pot-friendly dish. Cover loosely with aluminum foil. Using a sling, place this dish on top of the trivet. 2. Close the lid, set the pressure release to Sealing, and select Manual. Set the Instant Pot to 10 minutes on High Pressure and let cook. 3. Meanwhile, in a small bowl, mix together basil, red pepper, oregano, and cilantro, and set aside. 4. Once the crust is cooked, carefully switch the pressure release to Venting. Open the Instant Pot and add the tomatoes in an even layer, followed by the Mozzarella cheese and the spinach. Sprinkle the spice and herb mixture over the top of the pizza. Loosely re-cover dish with aluminum foil. 5. Close the lid to the Instant Pot, set the pressure release to Sealing, and select Manual. Set the Instant Pot to 10 minutes on High Pressure and let cook again. 6. Once cooked, let the pressure naturally disperse from the Instant Pot for about 10 minutes, then carefully switch the pressure release to Venting. 7. Open the Instant Pot, serve, and enjoy!

Kale Omelet

Prep time: 5 minutes | Cook time: 10 minutes | Serves 2

- 2 eggs
- 1 cup chopped kale
- 1 teaspoon heavy cream
- ⅔ teaspoon white pepper
- ½ teaspoon butter

1. Grease the instant pot pan with butter. 2. Beat the eggs in the separated bowl and whisk them well. 3. After this, add heavy cream and white pepper. Stir it gently. 4. Place the chopped kale in the greased pan and add the whisked eggs. 5. Pour 1 cup of water in the instant pot. 6. Place the trivet in the instant pot and transfer the egg mixture pan on the trivet. 7. Close the instant pot and set the Manual (High Pressure) program and cook the frittata for 5 minutes. Do a natural pressure release for 5 minutes.

Mexican Breakfast Beef Chili

Prep time: 5 minutes | Cook time: 45 minutes | Serves 4

- 2 tablespoons coconut oil
- 1 pound (454 g) ground grass-fed beef
- 1 (14-ounce / 397-g) can sugar-free or low-sugar diced tomatoes
- ½ cup shredded full-fat Cheddar cheese (optional)
- 1 teaspoon hot sauce
- ½ teaspoon chili powder
- ½ teaspoon crushed red pepper
- ½ teaspoon ground cumin
- ½ teaspoon kosher salt
- ½ teaspoon freshly ground black pepper

1. Set the Instant Pot to Sauté and melt the oil. 2. Pour in ½ cup of filtered water, then add the beef, tomatoes, cheese, hot sauce, chili powder, red pepper, cumin, salt, and black pepper to the Instant Pot, stirring thoroughly. 3. Close the lid, set the pressure release to Sealing, and hit Cancel to stop the current program. Select Manual, set the Instant Pot to 45 minutes on High Pressure and let cook. 4. Once cooked, let the pressure naturally disperse from the Instant Pot for about 10 minutes, then carefully switch the pressure release to Venting. 5. Open the Instant Pot, serve, and enjoy!

Bacon Egg Cups

Prep time: 5 minutes | Cook time: 7 minutes | Serves 4

- 6 large eggs
- 2 strips cooked bacon, sliced in ¼-inch wide pieces
- ½ cup Cheddar cheese, divided
- ¼ teaspoon sea salt
- ¼ teaspoon black pepper
- 1 cup water
- 1 tablespoon chopped fresh flat leaf parsley

1. In a small bowl, beat the eggs. Stir in the cooked bacon, ¼ cup

of the cheese, sea salt and pepper. Divide the egg mixture equally among four ramekins and loosely cover with aluminum foil. 2. Pour the water and place the trivet in the Instant Pot. Place two ramekins on the trivet and stack the other two on the top. 3. Lock the lid. Select the Manual mode and set the cooking time for 7 minutes at High Pressure. When the timer goes off, use a natural pressure release for 10 minutes, then release any remaining pressure. Carefully open the lid. 4. Top each ramekin with the remaining ¼ cup of the cheese. Lock the lid and melt the cheese for 2 minutes. Garnish with the chopped parsley and serve immediately.

Baked Eggs and Ham

Prep time: 5 minutes | Cook time: 5 minutes | Serves 2

- 4 large eggs, beaten
- 4 slices ham, diced
- ½ cup shredded Cheddar cheese
- ½ cup heavy cream
- ½ teaspoon sea salt
- Pinch ground black pepper

1. Grease two ramekins. 2. In a large bowl, whisk together all the ingredients. Divide the egg mixture equally between the ramekins. 3. Set a trivet in the Instant Pot and pour in 1 cup water. Place the ramekins on the trivet. 4. Lock the lid. Select the Manual mode and set the cooking time for 5 minutes on High Pressure. When the timer goes off, perform a quick pressure release. Carefully open the lid. 5. Remove the ramekins from the Instant Pot. 6. Serve immediately.

Avocado Green Power Bowl

Prep time: 10 minutes | Cook time: 10 minutes | Serves 1

- 1 cup water
- 2 eggs
- 1 tablespoon coconut oil
- 1 tablespoon butter
- 1 ounce (28 g) sliced almonds
- 1 cup fresh spinach, sliced into strips
- ½ cup kale, sliced into strips
- ½ clove garlic, minced
- ½ teaspoon salt
- ⅛ teaspoon pepper
- ½ avocado, sliced
- ⅛ teaspoon red pepper flakes

1. Pour water into Instant Pot and place steam rack on bottom. Place eggs on steam rack. Click lid closed. Press the Manual button and adjust time for 6 minutes. When timer beeps, quick-release the pressure. Set eggs aside. 2. Pour water out, clean pot, and replace. Press the Sauté button and add coconut oil, butter, and almonds. Sauté for 2 to 3 minutes until butter begins to turn golden and almonds soften. Add spinach, kale, garlic, salt, and pepper to Instant Pot. Sauté for 4 to 6 minutes until greens begin to wilt. Press the Cancel button. Place greens in bowl for serving. Peel eggs, cut in half, and add to bowl. Slice avocado and place in bowl. Sprinkle red pepper flakes over all. Serve warm.

Cinnamon Roll Fat Bombs

Prep time: 5 minutes | Cook time: 5 minutes | Serves 5 to 6

- 2 tablespoons coconut oil
- 2 cups raw coconut butter
- 1 cup sugar-free chocolate chips
- 1 cup heavy whipping cream
- ½ cup Swerve, or more to taste
- ½ teaspoon ground cinnamon, or more to taste
- ½ teaspoon vanilla extract

1. Set the Instant Pot to Sauté and melt the oil. 2. Add the butter, chocolate chips, whipping cream, Swerve, cinnamon, and vanilla to the Instant Pot and cook. Stir occasionally until the mixture reaches a smooth consistency. 3. Pour mixture into a silicone mini-muffin mold. 4. Freeze until firm. Serve, and enjoy!

Fluffy Vanilla Pancake

Prep time: 5 minutes | Cook time: 50 minutes | Serves 6

- 3 eggs, beaten
- ½ cup coconut flour
- ¼ cup heavy cream
- ¼ cup almond flour
- 3 tablespoons Swerve
- 1 teaspoon vanilla extract
- 1 teaspoon baking powder
- Cooking spray

1. In a bowl, stir together the eggs, coconut flour, heavy cream, almond flour, Swerve and vanilla extract. Whisk in the baking powder until smooth. 2. Spritz the bottom and sides of Instant Pot with cooking spray. Place the batter in the pot. 3. Set the lid in place. Select the Manual mode and set the cooking time for 50 minutes on Low Pressure. Once the timer goes off, perform a natural pressure release for 5 minutes, then release any remaining pressure. Carefully open the lid. 4. Let the pancake rest in the pot for 5 minutes before serving.

Nutty "Oatmeal"

Prep time: 5 minutes | Cook time: 4 minutes | Serves 4

- 2 tablespoons coconut oil
- 1 cup full-fat coconut milk
- 1 cup heavy whipping cream
- ½ cup macadamia nuts
- ½ cup chopped pecans
- ⅓ cup Swerve, or more to taste
- ¼ cup unsweetened coconut flakes
- 2 tablespoons chopped hazelnuts
- 2 tablespoons chia seeds
- ½ teaspoon ground cinnamon

1. Before you get started, soak the chia seeds for about 5 to 10 minutes (can be up to 20, if desired) in 1 cup of filtered water. After soaking, set the Instant Pot to Sauté and add the coconut oil. Once melted, pour in the milk, whipping cream, and 1 cup of filtered water. Then add the macadamia nuts, pecans, Swerve, coconut flakes, hazelnuts, chia seeds, and cinnamon. Mix thoroughly inside the Instant Pot. 2. Close the lid, set the pressure release to Sealing, and hit Cancel to stop the current program. Select Manual, set the Instant Pot to 4 minutes on High Pressure, and let cook. 3. Once cooked, carefully switch the pressure release to Venting. 4. Open the Instant Pot, serve, and enjoy!

Chocolate Chip Pancake

Prep time: 5 minutes | Cook time: 37 minutes | Serves 5 to 6

- 4 tablespoons salted grass-fed butter, softened
- 2 cups blanched almond flour
- ½ cup Swerve, or more to taste
- 1¼ cups full-fat coconut milk
- ¼ cup sugar-free chocolate
- chips
- ¼ cup organic coconut flour
- 2 eggs
- 1 tablespoon chopped walnuts
- ¼ teaspoon baking soda
- ½ teaspoon salt
- ½ cup dark berries, for serving (optional)

1. Grease the bottom and sides of your Instant Pot with the butter. Make sure you coat it very liberally. 2. In a large bowl, mix together the almond flour, Swerve, milk, chocolate chips, coconut flour, eggs, walnuts, baking soda, and salt. Add this mixture to the Instant Pot. Close the lid, set the pressure release to Sealing, and select Multigrain. Set the Instant Pot to 37 minutes on Low Pressure, and let cook. 3. Switch the pressure release to Venting and open the Instant Pot. Confirm your pancake is cooked, then carefully remove it using a spatula. Serve with the berries (if desired), and enjoy!

Lettuce Wrapped Chicken Sandwich

Prep time: 10 minutes | Cook time: 15 minutes | Serves 4

- 1 tablespoon butter
- 3 ounces (85 g) scallions, chopped
- 2 cups ground chicken
- ½ teaspoon ground nutmeg
- 1 tablespoon coconut flour
- 1 teaspoon salt
- 1 cup lettuce

1. Press the Sauté button on the Instant Pot and melt the butter. Add the chopped scallions, ground chicken and ground nutmeg to the pot and sauté for 4 minutes. Add the coconut flour and salt and continue to sauté for 10 minutes. 2. Fill the lettuce with the ground chicken and transfer it on the plate. Serve immediately.

Soft-Scrambled Eggs

Prep time: 5 minutes | Cook time: 7 minutes | Serves 4

- 6 eggs
- 2 tablespoons heavy cream
- 1 teaspoon salt
- ¼ teaspoon pepper
- 2 tablespoons butter
- 2 ounces (57 g) cream cheese, softened

1. In large bowl, whisk eggs, heavy cream, salt, and pepper. Press the Sauté button and then press the Adjust button to set heat to Less. 2. Gently push eggs around pot with rubber spatula. When they begin to firm up, add butter and softened cream cheese. Continue stirring slowly in a figure-8 pattern until eggs are fully cooked, approximately 7 minutes total.

Eggs Benedict

Prep time: 5 minutes | Cook time: 1 minute | Serves 3

- 1 teaspoon butter
- 3 eggs
- ¼ teaspoon salt
- ½ teaspoon ground black
- pepper
- 1 cup water
- 3 turkey bacon slices, fried

1. Grease the eggs molds with the butter and crack the eggs inside. Sprinkle with salt and ground black pepper. 2. Pour the water and insert the trivet in the Instant Pot. Put the eggs molds on the trivet. 3. Set the lid in place. Select the Manual mode and set the cooking time for 1 minute on High Pressure. When the timer goes off, do a quick pressure release. Carefully open the lid. 4. Transfer the eggs onto the plate. Top the eggs with the fried bacon slices.

Southwestern Egg Casserole

Prep time: 10 minutes | Cook time: 20 minutes | Serves 12

- 1 cup water
- 2½ cups egg substitute
- ½ cup flour
- 1 teaspoon baking powder
- ⅛ teaspoon salt
- ⅛ teaspoon pepper
- 2 cups fat-free cottage
- cheese
- 1½ cups shredded 75%-less-fat sharp cheddar cheese
- ¼ cup no-trans-fat tub margarine, melted
- 2 (4-ounce) cans chopped green chilies

1. Place the steaming rack into the bottom of the inner pot and pour in 1 cup of water. 2. Grease a round springform pan that will fit into the inner pot of the Instant Pot. 3. Combine the egg substitute, flour, baking powder, salt and pepper in a mixing bowl. It will be lumpy. 4. Stir in the cheese, margarine, and green chilies then pour into the springform pan. 5. Place the springform pan onto the steaming rack, close the lid, and secure to the locking position. Be sure the vent is turned to sealing. Set for 20 minutes on Manual at high pressure. 6. Let the pressure release naturally. 7. Carefully remove the springform pan with the handles of the steaming rack and allow to stand 10 minutes before cutting and serving.

Breakfast Millet with Nuts and Strawberries

Prep time: 0 minutes | Cook time: 30 minutes | Serves 8

- 2 tablespoons coconut oil or unsalted butter
- 1½ cups millet
- 2⅔ cups water
- ½ teaspoon fine sea salt
- 1 cup unsweetened almond milk or other nondairy milk
- 1 cup chopped toasted pecans, almonds, or peanuts
- 4 cups sliced strawberries

1. Select the Sauté setting on the Instant Pot and melt the oil. Add the millet and cook for 4 minutes, until aromatic. Stir in the water and salt, making sure all of the grains are submerged in the liquid. 2. Secure the lid and set the Pressure Release to Sealing. Press the Cancel button to reset the cooking program, then select the Porridge, Pressure Cook, or Manual setting and set the cooking time for 12 minutes at high pressure. (The pot will take about 10 minutes to come up to pressure before the cooking program begins.) 3. When the cooking program ends, let the pressure release naturally for 10 minutes, then move the Pressure Release to Venting to release any remaining steam. Open the pot and use a fork to fluff and stir the millet. 4. Spoon the millet into bowls and top each serving with 2 tablespoons of the almond milk, then sprinkle with the nuts and top with the strawberries. Serve warm.

Mini Chocolate Chip Muffins

Prep time: 5 minutes | Cook time: 20 minutes | Serves 7

- 1 cup blanched almond flour
- 2 eggs
- ¾ cup sugar-free chocolate chips
- 1 tablespoon vanilla extract
- ½ cup Swerve, or more to
- taste
- 2 tablespoons salted grass-fed butter, softened
- ½ teaspoon salt
- ¼ teaspoon baking soda

1. Pour 1 cup of filtered water into the inner pot of the Instant Pot, then insert the trivet. Using an electric mixer, combine flour, eggs, chocolate chips, vanilla, Swerve, butter, salt, and baking soda. Mix thoroughly. Transfer this mixture into a well-greased Instant Pot-friendly muffin (or egg bites) mold. 2. Using a sling if desired, place the pan onto the trivet and cover loosely with aluminum foil. Close the lid, set the pressure release to Sealing, and select Manual. Set the Instant Pot to 20 minutes on High Pressure and let cook. 3. Once cooked, let the pressure naturally disperse from the Instant Pot for about 10 minutes, then carefully switch the pressure release to Venting. 4. Open the Instant Pot and remove the pan. Let cool, serve, and enjoy!

Egg Ham Muffins

Prep time: 10 minutes | Cook time: 6 minutes | Serves 2

- 2 eggs, beaten
- 4 ounces (113 g) ham, chopped
- ½ teaspoon avocado oil
- 1 cup water, for cooking

1. Pour water in the instant pot. 2. Then brush the muffin molds with avocado oil from inside. 3. In the mixing bowl, mix up ham and beaten eggs. 4. After this, pour the mixture into the muffin molds. 5. Place the muffins in the instant pot. Close and seal the lid. Cook the meal on Manual mode (High Pressure) for 6 minutes. Then make a quick pressure release and remove the muffins.

Bacon Cheddar Bites

Prep time: 15 minutes | Cook time: 3 minutes | Serves 2

- 2 tablespoons coconut flour
- ½ cup shredded Cheddar cheese
- 2 teaspoons coconut cream
- 2 bacon slices, cooked
- ½ teaspoon dried parsley
- 1 cup water, for cooking

1. In the mixing bowl, mix up coconut flour, Cheddar cheese, coconut cream, and dried parsley. 2. Then chop the cooked bacon and add it in the mixture. 3. Stir it well. 4. Pour water and insert the trivet in the instant pot. 5. Line the trivet with baking paper. 6. After this, make the small balls (bites) from the cheese mixture and put them on the prepared trivet. 7. Cook the meal for 3 minutes on Manual mode (High Pressure). 8. Then make a quick pressure release and cool the cooked meal well.

Mini Spinach Quiche

Prep time: 5 minutes | Cook time: 15 minutes | Serves 1

- 2 eggs
- 1 tablespoon heavy cream
- 1 tablespoon diced green pepper
- 1 tablespoon diced red onion
- ¼ cup chopped fresh spinach
- ½ teaspoon salt
- ¼ teaspoon pepper
- 1 cup water

1. In medium bowl whisk together all ingredients except water. Pour into 4-inch ramekin. Generally, if the ramekin is oven-safe, it is also safe to use in pressure cooking. 2. Pour water into Instant Pot. Place steam rack into pot. Carefully place ramekin onto steam rack. Click lid closed. Press the Manual button and set time for 15 minutes. When timer beeps, quick-release the pressure. Serve warm.

Keto Cabbage Hash Browns

Prep time: 5 minutes | Cook time: 8 minutes | Serves 3

- 1 cup shredded white cabbage
- 3 eggs, beaten
- ½ teaspoon ground nutmeg
- ½ teaspoon salt
- ½ teaspoon onion powder
- ½ zucchini, grated
- 1 tablespoon coconut oil

1. In a bowl, stir together all the ingredients, except for the coconut oil. Form the cabbage mixture into medium hash browns. 2. Press the Sauté button on the Instant Pot and heat the coconut oil. 3. Place the hash browns in the hot coconut oil. Cook for 4 minutes on each side, or until lightly browned. 4. Transfer the hash browns to a plate and serve warm.

Poached Eggs

Prep time: 5 minutes | Cook time: 5 minutes | Serves 4

- Nonstick cooking spray
- 4 large eggs

1. Lightly spray 4 cups of a 7-count silicone egg bite mold with nonstick cooking spray. Crack each egg into a sprayed cup. 2. Pour 1 cup of water into the electric pressure cooker. Place the egg bite mold on the wire rack and carefully lower it into the pot. 3. Close and lock the lid of the pressure cooker. Set the valve to sealing. 4. Cook on high pressure for 5 minutes. 5. When the cooking is complete, hit Cancel and quick release the pressure. 6. Once the pin drops, unlock and remove the lid. 7. Run a small rubber spatula or spoon around each egg and carefully remove it from the mold. The white should be cooked, but the yolk should be runny. 8. Serve immediately.

Pulled Pork Hash

Prep time: 10 minutes | Cook time: 15 minutes | Serves 4

- 4 eggs
- 10 ounces (283 g) pulled pork, shredded
- 1 teaspoon coconut oil
- 1 teaspoon red pepper
- 1 teaspoon chopped fresh cilantro
- 1 tomato, chopped
- ¼ cup water

1. Melt the coconut oil in the instant pot on Sauté mode. 2. Then add pulled pork, red pepper, cilantro, water, and chopped tomato. 3. Cook the ingredients for 5 minutes. 4. Then stir it well with the help of the spatula and crack the eggs over it. 5. Close the lid. 6. Cook the meal on Manual mode (High Pressure) for 7 minutes. Then make a quick pressure release.

Bacon and Spinach Eggs

Prep time: 5 minutes | Cook time: 9 minutes | Serves 4

- 2 tablespoons unsalted butter, divided
- ½ cup diced bacon
- ⅓ cup finely diced shallots
- ⅓ cup chopped spinach, leaves only
- Pinch of sea salt
- Pinch of black pepper
- ½ cup water
- ¼ cup heavy whipping cream
- 8 large eggs
- 1 tablespoon chopped fresh chives, for garnish

1. Set the Instant Pot on the Sauté mode and melt 1 tablespoon of the butter. Add the bacon to the pot and sauté for about 4 minutes, or until crispy. Using a slotted spoon, transfer the bacon bits to a bowl and set aside. 2. Add the remaining 1 tablespoon of the butter and shallots to the pot and sauté for about 2 minutes, or until tender. Add the spinach leaves and sauté for 1 minute, or until wilted. Season with sea salt and black pepper and stir. Transfer the spinach to a separate bowl and set aside. 3. Drain the oil from the pot into a bowl. Pour in the water and put the trivet inside. 4. With a paper towel, coat four ramekins with the bacon grease. In each ramekin, place 1 tablespoon of the heavy whipping cream, reserved bacon bits and sautéed spinach. Crack two eggs without breaking the yolks in each ramekin. Cover the ramekins with aluminum foil. Place two ramekins on the trivet and stack the other two on top. 5. Lock the lid. Select the Manual mode and set the cooking time for 2 minutes at Low Pressure. When the timer goes off, use a natural pressure release for 5 minutes, then release any remaining pressure. Carefully open the lid. 6. Carefully take out the ramekins and serve garnished with the chives.

Streusel Pumpkin Cake

Prep time: 10 minutes | Cook time: 30 minutes | Serves 8

- Streusel Topping:
- ¼ cup Swerve
- ¼ cup almond flour
- 2 tablespoons coconut oil or
- Cake:
- 2 large eggs, beaten
- 2 cups almond flour
- 1 cup pumpkin purée
- ¾ cup Swerve
- Glaze:
- ½ cup Swerve
- 3 tablespoons unsweetened

- unsalted butter, softened
- ½ teaspoon ground cinnamon

- 2 teaspoons pumpkin pie spice
- 2 teaspoons vanilla extract
- ½ teaspoon fine sea salt

- almond milk

1. Set a trivet in the Instant Pot and pour in 1 cup water. Line a baking pan with parchment paper. 2. In a small bowl, whisk together all the ingredients for the streusel topping with a fork. 3.

In a medium-sized bowl, stir together all the ingredients for the cake until thoroughly combined. 4. Scoop half of the batter into the prepared baking pan and sprinkle half of the streusel topping on top. Repeat with the remaining batter and topping. 5. Place the baking pan on the trivet in the Instant Pot. 6. Lock the lid, select the Manual mode and set the cooking time for 30 minutes on High Pressure. 7. Meanwhile, whisk together the Swerve and almond milk in a small bowl until it reaches a runny consistency. 8. When the timer goes off, do a natural pressure release for 10 minutes, then release any remaining pressure. Open the lid. 9. Remove the baking pan from the pot. Let cool in the pan for 10 minutes. Transfer the cake onto a plate and peel off the parchment paper. 10. Transfer the cake onto a serving platter. Spoon the glaze over the top of the cake. Serve immediately.

Parmesan Baked Eggs

Prep time: 5 minutes | Cook time: 10 minutes | Serves 1

- 1 tablespoon butter, cut into small pieces
- 2 tablespoons keto-friendly low-carb Marinara sauce
- 3 eggs
- 2 tablespoons grated Parmesan cheese
- ¼ teaspoon Italian seasoning
- 1 cup water

1. Place the butter pieces on the bottom of the oven-safe bowl. Spread the marinara sauce over the butter. Crack the eggs on top of the marinara sauce and top with the cheese and Italian seasoning. 2. Cover the bowl with aluminum foil. Pour the water and insert the trivet in the Instant Pot. Put the bowl on the trivet. 3. Set the lid in place. Select the Manual mode and set the cooking time for 10 minutes on Low Pressure. When the timer goes off, do a quick pressure release. Carefully open the lid. 4. Let the eggs cool for 5 minutes before serving.

Bell Peppers Stuffed with Eggs

Prep time: 5 minutes | Cook time: 14 minutes | Serves 2

- 2 eggs, beaten
- 1 tablespoon coconut cream
- ¼ teaspoon dried oregano
- ¼ teaspoon salt
- 1 large bell pepper, cut into halves and deseeded
- 1 cup water

1. In a bowl, stir together the eggs, coconut cream, oregano and salt. 2. Pour the egg mixture in the pepper halves. 3. Pour the water and insert the trivet in the Instant Pot. Put the stuffed pepper halves on the trivet. 4. Set the lid in place. Select the Manual mode and set the cooking time for 14 minutes on High Pressure. When the timer goes off, do a quick pressure release. Carefully open the lid. 5. Serve warm.

Traditional Porridge

Prep time: 5 minutes | Cook time: 4 minutes | Serves 4

- 2 tablespoons coconut oil
- 1 cup full-fat coconut milk
- 2 tablespoons blanched almond flour
- 2 tablespoons sugar-free chocolate chips
- 1 cup heavy whipping cream
- ½ cup chopped cashews
- ½ cup chopped pecans
- ½ teaspoon ground cinnamon
- ½ teaspoon erythritol, or more to taste
- ¼ cup unsweetened coconut flakes

1. Set the Instant Pot to Sauté and melt the coconut oil. 2. Pour in the coconut milk, 1 cup of filtered water, then combine and mix the flour, chocolate chips, whipping cream, cashews, pecans, cinnamon, erythritol, and coconut flakes, inside the Instant Pot. 3. Close the lid, set the pressure release to Sealing, and hit Cancel to stop the current program. Select Manual, set the Instant Pot to 4 minutes on High Pressure, and let cook. 4. Once cooked, perform a quick release by carefully switching the pressure valve to Venting. 5. Open the Instant Pot, serve, and enjoy!

Coddled Eggs and Smoked Salmon Toasts

Prep time: 5 minutes | Cook time: 10 minutes | Serves 4

- 2 teaspoons unsalted butter
- 4 large eggs
- 4 slices gluten-free or whole-grain rye bread
- ½ cup plain 2 percent Greek yogurt
- 4 ounces cold-smoked salmon, or 1 medium avocado, pitted, peeled, and
- sliced
- 2 radishes, thinly sliced
- 1 Persian cucumber, thinly sliced
- 1 tablespoon chopped fresh chives
- ¼ teaspoon freshly ground black pepper

1. Pour 1 cup water into the Instant Pot and place a long-handled silicone steam rack into the pot. (If you don't have the long-handled rack, use the wire metal steam rack and a homemade sling) 2. Coat each of four 4-ounce ramekins with ½ teaspoon butter. Crack an egg into each ramekin. Place the ramekins on the steam rack in the pot. 3. Secure the lid and set the Pressure Release to Sealing. Select the Steam setting and set the cooking time for 3 minutes at low pressure. (The pot will take about 5 minutes to come up to pressure before the cooking program begins.) 4. While eggs are cooking, toast the bread in a toaster until golden brown. Spread the yogurt onto the toasted slices, put the toasts onto plates, and then top each toast with the smoked salmon, radishes, and cucumber. 5. When the cooking program ends, let the pressure release naturally for 5 minutes, then move the Pressure Release to Venting to release any remaining steam. Open the pot and, wearing heat-resistant mitts, grasp the handles of the steam rack and lift it out of the pot. 6. Run a knife around the inside edge of each ramekin to loosen the egg and unmold one egg onto each toast. Sprinkle the chives and pepper on top and serve right away. 7. Note 8. The yolks of these eggs are fully cooked through. If you prefer the yolks slightly less solid, perform a quick pressure release rather than letting the pressure release naturally for 5 minutes.

Easy Quiche

Prep time: 15 minutes | Cook time: 25 minutes | Serves 6

- 1 cup water
- ¼ cup chopped onion
- ¼ cup chopped mushroom, optional
- 3 ounces 75%-less-fat cheddar cheese, shredded
- 2 tablespoons bacon bits, chopped ham or browned
- sausage
- 4 eggs
- ¼ teaspoons salt
- 1½ cups fat-free milk
- ½ cup whole wheat flour
- 1 tablespoon trans-fat-free tub margarine

1. Pour water into Instant Pot and place the steaming rack inside. 2. Spray a 6" round cake pan with nonstick spray. 3. Sprinkle the onion, mushroom, shredded cheddar, and meat around in the cake pan. 4. Combine remaining ingredients in medium bowl. Pour over meat and vegetables mixture. 5. Place the cake pan onto the steaming rack, close the lid and secure to the locking position. Be sure the vent is turned to sealing. Set for 25 minutes on Manual at high pressure. 7. Let the pressure release naturally. 8. Carefully remove the cake pan with the handles of the steaming rack and allow to stand 10 minutes before cutting and serving.

Breakfast Burrito Bowls

Prep time: 10 minutes | Cook time: 15 minutes | Serves 4

- 6 eggs
- 3 tablespoons melted butter
- 1 teaspoon salt
- ¼ teaspoon pepper
- ½ pound (227 g) cooked breakfast sausage
- ½ cup shredded sharp Cheddar cheese
- ½ cup salsa
- ½ cup sour cream
- 1 avocado, cubed
- ¼ cup diced green onion

1. In large bowl, mix eggs, melted butter, salt, and pepper. Press the Sauté button and then press the Adjust button to set the heat to Less. 2. Add eggs to Instant Pot and cook for 5 to 7 minutes while gently moving with rubber spatula. When eggs begin to firm up, add cooked breakfast sausage and cheese and continue to cook until eggs are fully cooked. Press the Cancel button. 3. Divide eggs into four bowls and top with salsa, sour cream, avocado, and green onion.

Blueberry Almond Cereal

Prep time: 5 minutes | Cook time: 2 minutes | Serves 4

- ⅓ cup crushed roasted almonds
- ¼ cup almond flour
- ¼ cup unsalted butter, softened
- ¼ cup vanilla-flavored egg
- white protein powder
- 2 tablespoons Swerve
- 1 teaspoon blueberry extract
- 1 teaspoon ground cinnamon

1. Add all the ingredients to the Instant Pot and stir to combine. 2. Lock the lid, select the Manual mode and set the cooking time for 2 minutes on High Pressure. When the timer goes off, do a natural pressure release for 10 minutes, then release any remaining pressure. Open the lid. 3. Stir well and pour the mixture onto a sheet lined with parchment paper to cool. It will be crispy when completely cool. 4. Serve the cereal in bowls.

Pecan and Walnut Granola

Prep time: 10 minutes | Cook time: 2 minutes | Serves 12

- 2 cups chopped raw pecans
- 1¾ cups vanilla-flavored egg white protein powder
- 1¼ cups unsalted butter, softened
- 1 cup sunflower seeds
- ½ cup chopped raw walnuts
- ½ cup slivered almonds
- ½ cup sesame seeds
- ½ cup Swerve
- 1 teaspoon ground cinnamon
- ½ teaspoon sea salt

1. Add all the ingredients to the Instant Pot and stir to combine. 2. Lock the lid, select the Manual mode and set the cooking time for 2 minutes on High Pressure. When the timer goes off, do a natural pressure release for 10 minutes, then release any remaining pressure. Open the lid. 3. Stir well and pour the granola onto a sheet of parchment paper to cool. It will become crispy when completely cool. Serve the granola in bowls.

Cranberry Almond Grits

Prep time: 10 minutes | Cook time: 10 minutes | Serves 5

- ¾ cup stone-ground grits or polenta (not instant)
- ½ cup unsweetened dried cranberries
- Pinch kosher salt
- 1 tablespoon unsalted butter or ghee (optional)
- 1 tablespoon half-and-half
- ¼ cup sliced almonds, toasted

1. In the electric pressure cooker, stir together the grits, cranberries, salt, and 3 cups of water. 2. Close and lock the lid. Set the valve to sealing. 3. Cook on high pressure for 10 minutes. 4. When the cooking is complete, hit Cancel and quick release the pressure. 5. Once the pin drops, unlock and remove the lid. 6. Add the butter (if using) and half-and-half. Stir until the mixture is creamy, adding more half-and-half if necessary. 7. Spoon into serving bowls and sprinkle with almonds.

Bacon Spaghetti Squash Fritters

Prep time: 20 minutes | Cook time: 15 minutes | Serves 4

- ½ cooked spaghetti squash
- 2 tablespoons cream cheese
- ½ cup shredded whole-milk Mozzarella cheese
- 1 egg
- ½ teaspoon salt
- ¼ teaspoon pepper
- 1 stalk green onion, sliced
- 4 slices cooked bacon, crumbled
- 2 tablespoons coconut oil

1. Remove seeds from cooked squash and use fork to scrape strands out of shell. Place strands into cheesecloth or kitchen towel and squeeze to remove as much excess moisture as possible. 2. Place cream cheese and Mozzarella in small bowl and microwave for 45 seconds to melt together. Mix with spoon and place in large bowl. Add all ingredients except coconut oil to bowl. Mixture will be wet like batter. 3. Press the Sauté button and then press the Adjust button to set heat to Less. Add coconut oil to Instant Pot. When fully preheated, add 2 to 3 tablespoons of batter to pot to make a fritter. Let fry until firm and completely cooked through.

Tropical Steel Cut Oats

Prep time: 5 minutes | Cook time: 5 minutes | Serves 4

- 1 cup steel cut oats
- 1 cup unsweetened almond milk
- 2 cups coconut water or water
- ¾ cup frozen chopped peaches
- ¾ cup frozen mango chunks
- 1 (2-inch) vanilla bean, scraped (seeds and pod)
- Ground cinnamon
- ¼ cup chopped unsalted macadamia nuts

1. In the electric pressure cooker, combine the oats, almond milk, coconut water, peaches, mango chunks, and vanilla bean seeds and pod. Stir well. 2. Close and lock the lid of the pressure cooker. Set the valve to sealing. 3. Cook on high pressure for 5 minutes. 4. When the cooking is complete, allow the pressure to release naturally for 10 minutes, then quick release any remaining pressure. Hit Cancel. 5. Once the pin drops, unlock and remove the lid. 6. Discard the vanilla bean pod and stir well. 7. Spoon the oats into 4 bowls. Top each serving with a sprinkle of cinnamon and 1 tablespoon of the macadamia nuts.

Chicken and Egg Sandwich

Prep time: 5 minutes | Cook time: 15 minutes | Serves 1

- 1 (6-ounce / 170-g) boneless, skinless chicken breast
- ¼ teaspoon salt
- ⅛ teaspoon pepper
- ¼ teaspoon garlic powder
- 2 tablespoons coconut oil, divided
- 1 egg
- 1 cup water
- ¼ avocado
- 2 tablespoons mayonnaise
- ¼ cup shredded white Cheddar
- Salt and pepper, to taste

1. Cut chicken breast in half lengthwise. Use meat tenderizer to pound chicken breast until thin. Sprinkle with salt, pepper, and garlic powder, and set aside. 2. Add 1 tablespoon coconut oil to Instant Pot. Press Sauté button, then press Adjust button and set temperature to Less. Once oil is hot, fry the egg, remove, and set aside. Press Cancel button. Press Sauté button, then press Adjust button to set temperature to Normal. Add second tablespoon of coconut oil to Instant Pot and sear chicken on each side for 3 to 4 minutes until golden. 3. Press the Manual button and set time for 8 minutes. While chicken cooks, use fork to mash avocado and then mix in mayo. When timer beeps, quick-release the pressure. Put chicken on plate and pat dry with paper towel. Use chicken pieces to form a sandwich with egg, cheese, and avocado mayo. Season lightly with salt and pepper.

Pumpkin Mug Muffin

Prep time: 5 minutes | Cook time: 9 minutes | Serves 1

- ½ cup Swerve
- ½ cup blanched almond flour
- 2 tablespoons organic pumpkin purée
- 1 teaspoon sugar-free chocolate chips
- 1 tablespoon organic coconut flour
- 1 egg
- 1 tablespoon coconut oil
- ½ teaspoon pumpkin pie spice
- ½ teaspoon ground nutmeg
- ½ teaspoon ground cinnamon
- ⅛ teaspoon baking soda

1. Mix the Swerve, almond flour, pumpkin purée, chocolate chips, coconut flour, egg, coconut oil, pumpkin pie spice, nutmeg, cinnamon, and baking soda in a large bowl. Transfer this mixture into a well-greased, Instant Pot-friendly mug. 2. Pour 1 cup of filtered water into the inner pot of the Instant Pot, and insert the trivet. Cover the mug in foil and place on top of the trivet. 3. Close the lid, set the pressure release to Sealing, and select Manual. Set the Instant Pot to 9 minutes on High Pressure. 4. Once cooked, release the pressure immediately by switching the valve to Venting. Be sure your muffin is done by inserting a toothpick into the cake and making sure it comes out clean, as cook times may vary. 5. Remove mug and enjoy!

Potato-Bacon Gratin

Prep time: 20 minutes | Cook time: 40 minutes | Serves 8

- 1 tablespoon olive oil
- 6 ounces bag fresh spinach
- 1 clove garlic, minced
- 4 large potatoes, peeled or unpeeled, divided
- 6 ounces Canadian bacon slices, divided
- 5 ounces reduced-fat grated Swiss cheddar, divided
- 1 cup lower-sodium, lower-fat chicken broth

1. Set the Instant Pot to Sauté and pour in the olive oil. Cook the spinach and garlic in olive oil just until spinach is wilted (5 minutes or less). Turn off the instant pot. 2. Cut potatoes into thin slices about ¼" thick. 3. In a springform pan that will fit into the inner pot of your Instant Pot, spray it with nonstick spray then layer ⅓ the potatoes, half the bacon, ⅓ the cheese, and half the wilted spinach. 4. Repeat layers ending with potatoes. Reserve ⅓ cheese for later. 5. Pour chicken broth over all. 6. Wipe the bottom of your Instant Pot to soak up any remaining oil, then add in 2 cups of water and the steaming rack. Place the springform pan on top. 7. Close the lid and secure to the locking position. Be sure the vent is turned to sealing. Set for 35 minutes on Manual at high pressure. 8. Perform a quick release. 9. Top with the remaining cheese, then allow to stand 10 minutes before removing from the Instant Pot, cutting and serving.

Chapter 2

Poultry

Chapter 2 Poultry

Chicken Escabèche

Prep time: 5 minutes | Cook time: 15 minutes | Serves 4

- 1 cup filtered water
- 1 pound (454 g) chicken, mixed pieces
- 3 garlic cloves, smashed
- 2 bay leaves
- 1 onion, chopped
- ½ cup red wine vinegar
- ½ teaspoon coriander
- ½ teaspoon ground cumin
- ½ teaspoon mint, finely chopped
- ½ teaspoon kosher salt
- ½ teaspoon freshly ground black pepper

1. Pour the water into the Instant Pot and insert the trivet. 2. Thoroughly combine the chicken, garlic, bay leaves, onion, vinegar, coriander, cumin, mint, salt, and black pepper in a large bowl. 3. Put the bowl on the trivet and cover loosely with aluminum foil. 4. Secure the lid. Select the Manual mode and set the cooking time for 15 minutes at High Pressure. 5. Once cooking is complete, do a natural pressure release for 10 minutes, then release any remaining pressure. Carefully open the lid. 6. Remove the dish from the Instant Pot and cool for 5 to 10 minutes before serving.

Unstuffed Peppers with Ground Turkey and Quinoa

Prep time: 0 minutes | Cook time: 35 minutes | Serves 8

- 2 tablespoons extra-virgin olive oil
- 1 yellow onion, diced
- 2 celery stalks, diced
- 2 garlic cloves, chopped
- 2 pounds 93 percent lean ground turkey
- 2 teaspoons Cajun seasoning blend (plus 1 teaspoon fine sea salt if using a salt-free blend)
- ½ teaspoon freshly ground black pepper
- ¼ teaspoon cayenne pepper
- 1 cup quinoa, rinsed
- 1 cup low-sodium chicken broth
- One 14½-ounce can fire-roasted diced tomatoes and their liquid
- 3 red, orange, and/or yellow bell peppers, seeded and cut into 1-inch squares
- 1 green onion, white and green parts, thinly sliced
- 1½ tablespoons chopped fresh flat-leaf parsley
- Hot sauce (such as Crystal or Frank's RedHot) for serving

1. Select the Sauté setting on the Instant Pot and heat the oil for

2 minutes. Add the onion, celery, and garlic and sauté for about 4 minutes, until the onion begins to soften. Add the turkey, Cajun seasoning, black pepper, and cayenne and sauté, using a wooden spoon or spatula to break up the meat as it cooks, for about 6 minutes, until cooked through and no streaks of pink remain. 2. Sprinkle the quinoa over the turkey in an even layer. Pour the broth and the diced tomatoes and their liquid over the quinoa, spreading the tomatoes on top. Sprinkle the bell peppers over the top in an even layer. 3. Secure the lid and set the Pressure Release to Sealing. Press the Cancel button to reset the cooking program, then select the Pressure Cook or Manual setting and set the cooking time for 8 minutes at high pressure. (The pot will take about 15 minutes to come up to pressure before the cooking program begins.) 4. When the cooking program ends, let the pressure release naturally for at least 15 minutes, then move the Pressure Release to Venting to release any remaining steam. Open the pot and sprinkle the green onion and parsley over the top in an even layer. 5. Spoon the unstuffed peppers into bowls, making sure to dig down to the bottom of the pot so each person gets an equal amount of peppers, quinoa, and meat. Serve hot, with hot sauce on the side.

Chicken and Mixed Greens Salad

Prep time: 5 minutes | Cook time: 20 minutes | Serves 4

Chicken:
- 2 tablespoons avocado oil
- 1 pound (454 g) chicken breast, cubed
- ½ cup filtered water
- ½ teaspoon ground turmeric

Salad:
- 1 avocado, mashed
- 1 cup chopped arugula
- 1 cup chopped Swiss chard
- 1 cup chopped kale

- ½ teaspoon dried parsley
- ½ teaspoon dried basil
- ½ teaspoon kosher salt
- ½ teaspoon freshly ground black pepper

- ½ cup chopped spinach
- 2 tablespoons pine nuts, toasted

1. Combine all the chicken ingredients in the Instant Pot. 2. Secure the lid. Select the Manual mode and set the cooking time for 20 minutes at High Pressure. 3. Meanwhile, toss all the salad ingredients in a large salad bowl. 4. Once cooking is complete, do a quick pressure release. Carefully open the lid. 5. Remove the chicken to the salad bowl and serve.

Chicken Fajitas with Bell Peppers

Prep time: 10 minutes | Cook time: 5 minutes | Serves 4

- 1½ pounds (680 g) boneless, skinless chicken breasts
- ¼ cup avocado oil
- 2 tablespoons water
- 1 tablespoon Mexican hot sauce
- 2 cloves garlic, minced
- 1 teaspoon lime juice
- 1 teaspoon ground cumin
- 1 teaspoon salt
- 1 teaspoon erythritol
- ¼ teaspoon chili powder
- ¼ teaspoon smoked paprika
- 5 ounces (142 g) sliced yellow bell pepper strips
- 5 ounces (142 g) sliced red bell pepper strips
- 5 ounces (142 g) sliced green bell pepper strips

1. Slice the chicken into very thin strips lengthwise. Cut each strip in half again. Imagine the thickness of restaurant fajitas when cutting. 2. In a measuring cup, whisk together the avocado oil, water, hot sauce, garlic, lime juice, cumin, salt, erythritol, chili powder, and paprika to form a marinade. Add to the pot, along with the chicken and peppers. 3. Close the lid and seal the vent. Cook on High Pressure for 5 minutes. Quick release the steam.

Chicken with Lentils and Butternut Squash

Prep time: 15 minutes | Cook time: 28 minutes | Serves 4

- 2 large shallots, halved and sliced thin, divided
- 5 teaspoons extra-virgin olive oil, divided
- ½ teaspoon grated lemon zest plus 2 teaspoons juice
- 1 teaspoon table salt, divided
- 4 (5 to 7 ounces / 142 to 198 g) bone-in chicken thighs, trimmed
- ¼ teaspoon pepper
- 2 garlic cloves, minced
- 1½ teaspoons caraway seeds
- 1 teaspoon ground coriander
- 1 teaspoon ground cumin
- ½ teaspoon paprika
- ⅛ teaspoon cayenne pepper
- 2 cups chicken broth
- 1 cup French green lentils, picked over and rinsed
- 2 pounds (907 g) butternut squash, peeled, seeded, and cut into 1½-inch pieces
- 1 cup fresh parsley or cilantro leaves

1. Combine half of shallots, 1 tablespoon oil, lemon zest and juice, and ¼ teaspoon salt in bowl; set aside. Pat chicken dry with paper towels and sprinkle with ½ teaspoon salt and pepper. Using highest sauté function, heat remaining 2 teaspoons oil in Instant Pot for 5 minutes (or until just smoking). Place chicken skin side down in pot and cook until well browned on first side, about 5 minutes; transfer to plate. 2. Add remaining shallot and remaining ¼ teaspoon salt to fat left in pot and cook, using highest sauté function, until shallot is softened, about 2 minutes. Stir in garlic, caraway, coriander, cumin,

paprika, and cayenne and cook until fragrant, about 30 seconds. Stir in broth, scraping up any browned bits, then stir in lentils. 3. Nestle chicken skin side up into lentils and add any accumulated juices. Arrange squash on top. Lock lid in place and close pressure release valve. Select high pressure cook function and cook for 15 minutes. 4. Turn off Instant Pot and quick-release pressure. Carefully remove lid, allowing steam to escape away from you. Transfer chicken to plate and discard skin, if desired. Season lentil mixture with salt and pepper to taste. Add parsley to shallot mixture and toss to combine. Serve chicken with lentil mixture, topping individual portions with shallot-parsley salad.

Lemony Chicken Thighs

Prep time: 15 minutes | Cook time: 15 minutes | Serves 3 to 5

- 1 cup low-sodium chicken bone broth
- 5 frozen bone-in chicken thighs
- 1 small onion, diced
- 5 to 6 cloves garlic, diced
- Juice of 1 lemon
- 2 tablespoons margarine, melted
- ½ teaspoon salt
- ¼ teaspoon black pepper
- 1 teaspoon True Lemon Lemon Pepper seasoning
- 1 teaspoon parsley flakes
- ¼ teaspoon oregano
- Rind of 1 lemon

1. Add the chicken bone broth into the inner pot of the Instant Pot. 2. Add the chicken thighs. 3. Add the onion and garlic. 4. Pour the fresh lemon juice in with the melted margarine. 5. Add the seasonings. 6. Lock the lid, make sure the vent is at sealing, then press the Poultry button. Set to 15 minutes. 7. When cook time is up, let the pressure naturally release for 3 to 5 minutes, then manually release the rest. 8. You can place these under the broiler for 2 to 3 minutes to brown. 9. Plate up and pour some of the sauce over top with fresh grated lemon rind.

Parmesan-Crusted Chicken

Prep time: 15 minutes | Cook time: 13 minutes | Serves 2

- 1 tomato, sliced
- 8 ounces (227 g) chicken fillets
- 2 ounces (57 g) Parmesan, sliced
- 1 teaspoon butter
- 4 tablespoons water, for sprinkling
- 1 cup water, for cooking

1. Pour water and insert the steamer rack in the instant pot. 2. Then grease the baking mold with butter. 3. Slice the chicken fillets into halves and put them in the mold. 4. Sprinkle the chicken with water and top with tomato and Parmesan. 5. Cover the baking mold with foil and place it on the rack. 6. Close and seal the lid. 7. Cook the meal in Manual mode for 13 minutes. Then allow the natural pressure release for 10 minutes.

Broccoli Chicken Divan

Prep time: 15 minutes | Cook time: 10 minutes | Serves 4

- 1 cup chopped broccoli
- 2 tablespoons cream cheese
- ½ cup heavy cream
- 1 tablespoon curry powder
- ¼ cup chicken broth
- ½ cup grated Cheddar cheese
- 6 ounces (170 g) chicken fillet, cooked and chopped

1. Mix up broccoli and curry powder and put the mixture in the instant pot. 2. Add heavy cream and cream cheese. 3. Then add chicken and mix up the ingredients. 4. Then add chicken broth and heavy cream. 5. Top the mixture with Cheddar cheese. Close and seal the lid. 6. Cook the meal on Manual mode (High Pressure) for 10 minutes. Allow the natural pressure release for 5 minutes, open the lid and cool the meal for 10 minutes.

Pulled BBQ Chicken and Texas-Style Cabbage Slaw

Prep time: 5 minutes | Cook time: 20 minutes | Serves 6

- Chicken
- 1 cup water
- ¼ teaspoon fine sea salt
- 3 garlic cloves, peeled
- 2 bay leaves
- 2 pounds boneless, skinless chicken thighs (see Note)
- Cabbage Slaw
- ½ head red or green cabbage, thinly sliced
- 1 red bell pepper, seeded and thinly sliced
- 2 jalapeño chiles, seeded and cut into narrow strips
- 2 carrots, julienned
- 1 large Fuji or Gala apple, julienned
- ½ cup chopped fresh cilantro
- 3 tablespoons fresh lime juice
- 3 tablespoons extra-virgin olive oil
- ½ teaspoon ground cumin
- ¼ teaspoon fine sea salt
- ¾ cup low-sugar or unsweetened barbecue sauce
- Cornbread, for serving

1. To make the chicken: Combine the water, salt, garlic, bay leaves, and chicken thighs in the Instant Pot, arranging the chicken in a single layer. 2. Secure the lid and set the Pressure Release to Sealing. Select the Poultry, Pressure Cook, or Manual setting and set the cooking time for 10 minutes at high pressure. (The pot will take about 10 minutes to come up to pressure before the cooking program begins.) 3. To make the slaw: While the chicken is cooking, in a large bowl, combine the cabbage, bell pepper, jalapeños, carrots, apple, cilantro, lime juice, oil, cumin, and salt and toss together until the vegetables and apples are evenly coated. 4. When the cooking program ends, perform a quick pressure release by moving the Pressure Release to Venting, or let the pressure release naturally. Open the pot and, using tongs, transfer the chicken to a cutting board. Using two forks, shred the chicken into bite-size pieces. Wearing heat-resistant mitts, lift out the inner pot and discard the cooking liquid. Return the inner pot to the housing. 5. Return the chicken to the pot and stir in the barbecue sauce. You can serve it right away or heat it for a minute or two on the Sauté setting, then return the pot to its Keep Warm setting until ready to serve. 6. Divide the chicken and slaw evenly among six plates. Serve with wedges of cornbread on the side.

Chicken Tacos with Fried Cheese Shells

Prep time: 5 minutes | Cook time: 25 minutes | Serves 6

Chicken:
- 4 (6-ounce / 170-g) boneless, skinless chicken breasts
- 1 cup chicken broth
- 1 teaspoon salt
- ¼ teaspoon pepper
- 1 tablespoon chili powder
- 2 teaspoons garlic powder
- 2 teaspoons cumin

Cheese Shells:
- 1½ cups shredded whole-milk Mozzarella cheese

1. Combine all ingredients for the chicken in the Instant Pot. 2. Secure the lid. Select the Manual mode and set the cooking time for 20 minutes at High Pressure. 3. Once cooking is complete, do a quick pressure release. Carefully open the lid. 4. Shred the chicken and serve in bowls or cheese shells. 5. Make the cheese shells: Heat a nonstick skillet over medium heat. 6. Sprinkle ¼ cup of Mozzarella cheese in the skillet and fry until golden. Flip and turn off the heat. Allow the cheese to get brown. Fill with chicken and fold. The cheese will harden as it cools. Repeat with the remaining cheese and filling. 7. Serve warm.

Parmesan Carbonara Chicken

Prep time: 15 minutes | Cook time: 25 minutes | Serves 5

- 1 pound (454 g) chicken, skinless, boneless, chopped
- 1 cup heavy cream
- 1 cup chopped spinach
- 2 ounces (57 g) Parmesan, grated
- 1 teaspoon ground black pepper
- 1 tablespoon coconut oil
- 2 ounces (57 g) bacon, chopped

1. Put the coconut oil and chopped chicken in the instant pot. 2. Sauté the chicken for 10 minutes. Stir it from time to time. 3. Then add ground black pepper, and spinach. Stir the mixture well and sauté for 5 minutes more. 4. Then add heavy cream and Parmesan. Close and seal the lid. 5. Cook the meal on Manual mode (High Pressure) for 10 minutes. Allow the natural pressure release for 10 minutes.

Chicken in Wine

Prep time: 10 minutes | Cook time: 12 minutes | Serves 6

- 2 pounds chicken breasts, trimmed of skin and fat
- 10¾-ounce can 98% fat-free, reduced-sodium cream of mushroom soup
- 10¾-ounce can French onion soup
- 1 cup dry white wine or chicken broth

1. Place the chicken into the Instant Pot. 2. Combine soups and wine. Pour over chicken. 3. Secure the lid and make sure vent is set to sealing. Cook on Manual mode for 12 minutes. 4. When cook time is up, let the pressure release naturally for 5 minutes and then release the rest manually.

Mushroom Chicken Alfredo

Prep time: 15 minutes | Cook time: 10 minutes | Serves 4

- ½ cup sliced cremini mushrooms
- ¼ cup chopped leek
- 1 tablespoon sesame oil
- 1 teaspoon chili flakes
- 1 cup heavy cream
- 1 pound (454 g) chicken fillet, chopped
- 1 teaspoon Italian seasoning
- 1 tablespoon cream cheese

1. Brush the instant pot boil with sesame oil from inside. 2. Put the chicken in the instant pot in one layer. 3. Then top it with mushrooms and leek. 4. Sprinkle the ingredients with chili flakes, heavy cream, Italian seasoning, and cream cheese. 5. Close and seal the lid. 6. Cook the meal on Manual mode (High Pressure) for 10 minutes. 7. When the time is finished, allow the natural pressure release for 10 minutes.

Orange Chicken Thighs with Bell Peppers

Prep time: 15 to 20 minutes | Cook time: 7 minutes | Serves 4 to 6

- 6 boneless skinless chicken thighs, cut into bite-sized pieces
- 2 packets crystallized True Orange flavoring
- ½ teaspoon True Orange Orange Ginger seasoning
- ½ teaspoon coconut aminos
- ¼ teaspoon Worcestershire sauce
- Olive oil or cooking spray
- 2 cups bell pepper strips,
- any color combination (I used red)
- 1 onion, chopped
- 1 tablespoon green onion, chopped fine
- 3 cloves garlic, minced or chopped
- ½ teaspoon pink salt
- ½ teaspoon black pepper
- 1 teaspoon garlic powder
- 1 teaspoon ground ginger
- ¼ to ½ teaspoon red pepper

flakes
- 2 tablespoons tomato paste
- ½ cup chicken bone broth or water
- 1 tablespoon brown sugar
- substitute (I use Sukrin Gold)
- ½ cup Seville orange spread (I use Crofter's brand)

1. Combine the chicken with the 2 packets of crystallized orange flavor, the orange ginger seasoning, the coconut aminos, and the Worcestershire sauce. Set aside. 2. Turn the Instant Pot to Sauté and add a touch of olive oil or cooking spray to the inner pot. Add in the orange ginger marinated chicken thighs. 3. Sauté until lightly browned. Add in the peppers, onion, green onion, garlic, and seasonings. Mix well. 4. Add the remaining ingredients; mix to combine. 5. Lock the lid, set the vent to sealing, set to 7 minutes. 6. Let the pressure release naturally for 2 minutes, then manually release the rest when cook time is up.

Paprika Chicken with Tomato

Prep time: 10 minutes | Cook time: 20 minutes | Serves 2

- 8 ounces (227 g) chicken fillet, sliced
- 1 tomato, chopped
- 2 tablespoons mascarpone
- 1 teaspoon coconut oil
- 1 teaspoon ground paprika
- ½ teaspoon ground turmeric
- 1 tablespoon butter

1. Rub the chicken fillet with ground paprika, ground turmeric, and paprika. 2. Put the sliced chicken in the instant pot. 3. Add tomato, mascarpone, coconut oil, and butter. 4. Close the lid and cook the meal on Sauté mode for 20 minutes. 5. Stir it every 5 minutes to avoid burning.

Chicken with Spiced Sesame Sauce

Prep time: 20 minutes | Cook time: 8 minutes | Serves 5

- 2 tablespoons tahini (sesame sauce)
- ¼ cup water
- 1 tablespoon low-sodium soy sauce
- ¼ cup chopped onion
- 1 teaspoon red wine vinegar
- 2 teaspoons minced garlic
- 1 teaspoon shredded ginger root (Microplane works best)
- 2 pounds chicken breast, chopped into 8 portions

1. Place first seven ingredients in bottom of the inner pot of the Instant Pot. 2. Add coarsely chopped chicken on top. 3. Secure the lid and make sure vent is at sealing. Set for 8 minutes using Manual setting. When cook time is up, let the pressure release naturally for 10 minutes, then perform a quick release. 4. Remove ingredients and shred chicken with fork. Combine with other ingredients in pot for a tasty sandwich filling or sauce.

Cider Chicken with Pecans

Prep time: 10 minutes | Cook time: 15 minutes | Serves 2

- 6 ounces (170 g) chicken fillet, cubed
- 2 pecans, chopped
- 1 teaspoon coconut aminos
- ½ bell pepper, chopped
- 1 tablespoon coconut oil
- ¼ cup apple cider vinegar
- ¼ cup chicken broth

1. Melt coconut oil on Sauté mode and add chicken cubes. 2. Add bell pepper, and pecans. 3. Sauté the ingredients for 10 minutes and add apple cider vinegar, chicken broth, and coconut aminos. 4. Sauté the chicken for 5 minutes more.

Sage Chicken Thighs

Prep time: 10 minutes | Cook time: 16 minutes | Serves 4

- 1 teaspoon dried sage
- 1 teaspoon ground turmeric
- 2 teaspoons avocado oil
- 4 skinless chicken thighs
- 1 cup water
- 1 teaspoon sesame oil

1. Rub the chicken thighs with dried sage, ground turmeric, sesame oil, and avocado oil. 2. Then pour water in the instant pot and insert the steamer rack. 3. Place the chicken thighs on the rack and close the lid. 4. Cook the meal on Manual (High Pressure) for 16 minutes. 5. Then make a quick pressure release and open the lid. 6. Let the cooked chicken thighs cool for 10 minutes before serving.

Barbecue Shredded Chicken

Prep time: 5 minutes | Cook time: 25 minutes | Serves 4

- 1 (5-pound / 2.2-kg) whole chicken
- 3 teaspoons salt
- 1 teaspoon pepper
- 1 teaspoon dried parsley
- 1 teaspoon garlic powder
- ½ medium onion, cut into 3 to 4 large pieces
- 1 cup water
- ½ cup sugar-free barbecue sauce, divided

1. Scatter the chicken with salt, pepper, parsley, and garlic powder. Put the onion pieces inside the chicken cavity. 2. Pour the water into the Instant Pot and insert the trivet. Place seasoned chicken on the trivet. Brush with half of the barbecue sauce. 3. Lock the lid. Select the Manual mode and set the cooking time for 25 minutes at High Pressure. 4. When the timer beeps, perform a natural pressure release for 10 minutes, then release any remaining pressure. Carefully remove the lid. 5. Using a clean brush, add the remaining half of the sauce to chicken. For crispy skin or thicker sauce, you can broil in the oven for 5 minutes until lightly browned. 6. Slice or shred the chicken and serve warm.

Chicken and Kale Sandwiches

Prep time: 10 minutes | Cook time: 10 minutes | Serves 2

- 4 ounces (113 g) kale leaves
- 8 ounces (227 g) chicken fillet
- 1 tablespoon butter
- 1 ounce (28 g) lemon
- ¼ cup water

1. Dice the chicken fillet. 2. Squeeze the lemon juice over the poultry. 3. Transfer the poultry into the instant pot; add water and butter. 4. Close the lid and cook the chicken on the Poultry mode for 10 minutes. 5. When the chicken is cooked, place it on the kale leaves to make the medium sandwiches.

Shredded Buffalo Chicken

Prep time: 10 minutes | Cook time: 20 minutes | Serves 8

- 2 tablespoons avocado oil
- ½ cup finely chopped onion
- 1 celery stalk, finely chopped
- 1 large carrot, chopped
- ⅓ cup mild hot sauce (such
- as Frank's RedHot)
- ½ tablespoon apple cider vinegar
- ¼ teaspoon garlic powder
- 2 bone-in, skin-on chicken breasts (about 2 pounds)

1. Set the electric pressure cooker to the Sauté setting. When the pot is hot, pour in the avocado oil. 2. Sauté the onion, celery, and carrot for 3 to 5 minutes or until the onion begins to soften. Hit Cancel. 3. Stir in the hot sauce, vinegar, and garlic powder. Place the chicken breasts in the sauce, meat-side down. 4. Close and lock the lid of the pressure cooker. Set the valve to sealing. 5. Cook on high pressure for 20 minutes. 6. When cooking is complete, hit Cancel and quick release the pressure. Once the pin drops, unlock and remove the lid. 7. Using tongs, transfer the chicken breasts to a cutting board. When the chicken is cool enough to handle, remove the skin, shred the chicken and return it to the pot. Let the chicken soak in the sauce for at least 5 minutes. 8. Serve immediately.

Cajun Chicken

Prep time: 15 minutes | Cook time: 25 minutes | Serves 4

- 1 teaspoon Cajun seasoning
- ¼ cup apple cider vinegar
- 1 pound (454 g) chicken
- fillet
- 1 tablespoon sesame oil
- ¼ cup water

1. Put all ingredients in the instant pot. Close and seal the lid. 2. Cook the chicken fillets on Manual mode (High Pressure) for 25 minutes. 3. Allow the natural pressure release for 10 minutes.

Crack Chicken Breasts

Prep time: 5 minutes | Cook time: 15 minutes | Serves 2

- ½ pound (227 g) boneless, skinless chicken breasts
- 2 ounces (57 g) cream cheese, softened
- ½ cup grass-fed bone broth
- ¼ cup tablespoons keto-friendly ranch dressing
- ½ cup shredded full-fat Cheddar cheese
- 3 slices bacon, cooked and chopped into small pieces

1. Combine all the ingredients except the Cheddar cheese and bacon in the Instant Pot. 2. Secure the lid. Select the Manual mode and set the cooking time for 15 minutes at High Pressure. 3. Once cooking is complete, do a quick pressure release. Carefully open the lid. 4. Add the Cheddar cheese and bacon and stir well, then serve.

Ann's Chicken Cacciatore

Prep time: 25 minutes | Cook time: 3 to 9 minutes | Serves 8

- 1 large onion, thinly sliced
- 3 pound chicken, cut up, skin removed, trimmed of fat
- 2 6-ounce cans tomato paste
- 4-ounce can sliced mushrooms, drained
- 1 teaspoon salt
- ¼ cup dry white wine
- ¼ teaspoons pepper
- 1 to 2 garlic cloves, minced
- 1 to 2 teaspoons dried oregano
- ½ teaspoon dried basil
- ½ teaspoon celery seed, optional
- 1 bay leaf

1. In the inner pot of the Instant Pot, place the onion and chicken. 2. Combine remaining ingredients and pour over the chicken. 3. Secure the lid and make sure vent is at sealing. Cook on Slow Cook mode, low 7 to 9 hours, or high 3 to 4 hours.

Pizza in a Pot

Prep time: 25 minutes | Cook time: 15 minutes | Serves 8

- 1 pound bulk lean sweet Italian turkey sausage, browned and drained
- 28 ounces can crushed tomatoes
- 15½ ounces can chili beans
- 2¼ ounces can sliced black olives, drained
- 1 medium onion, chopped
- 1 small green bell pepper, chopped
- 2 garlic cloves, minced
- ¼ cup grated Parmesan cheese
- 1 tablespoon quick-cooking tapioca
- 1 tablespoon dried basil
- 1 bay leaf

1. Set the Instant Pot to Sauté, then add the turkey sausage. Sauté until browned. 2. Add the remaining ingredients into the Instant Pot and stir. 3. Secure the lid and make sure the vent is set to sealing. Cook on Manual for 15 minutes. 4. When cook time is up, let the pressure release naturally for 5 minutes then perform a quick release. Discard bay leaf.

Classic Chicken Salad

Prep time: 5 minutes | Cook time: 12 minutes | Serves 8

- 2 pounds (907 g) chicken breasts
- 1 cup vegetable broth
- 2 sprigs fresh thyme
- 1 teaspoon granulated garlic
- 1 teaspoon onion powder
- 1 bay leaf
- ½ teaspoon ground black pepper
- 1 cup mayonnaise
- 2 stalks celery, chopped
- 2 tablespoons chopped fresh chives
- 1 teaspoon fresh lemon juice
- 1 teaspoon Dijon mustard
- ½ teaspoon coarse sea salt

1. Combine the chicken, broth, thyme, garlic, onion powder, bay leaf, and black pepper in the Instant Pot. 2. Lock the lid. Select the Poultry mode and set the cooking time for 12 minutes at High Pressure. 3. When the timer beeps, perform a natural pressure release for 10 minutes, then release any remaining pressure. Carefully remove the lid. 4. Remove the chicken from the Instant Pot and let rest for a few minutes until cooled slightly. 5. Slice the chicken breasts into strips and place in a salad bowl. Add the remaining ingredients and gently stir until well combined. Serve immediately.

Tangy Meatballs

Prep time: 10 minutes | Cook time: 10 minutes | Makes 20 meatballs

- 1 pound (454 g) ground chicken
- 1 egg, lightly beaten
- ½ medium onion, diced

Sauce:
- 2 teaspoons erythritol
- 1 teaspoon rice vinegar
- 1 teaspoon garlic powder
- 1 teaspoon pepper
- 1 teaspoon salt
- 1 cup water
- ½ teaspoon sriracha

1. Stir together the ground chicken, beaten egg, onion, garlic powder, salt, and pepper in a large bowl. Shape into bite-sized balls with your hands. 2. Pour the water into Instant Pot and insert a steamer basket. Put the meatballs in the basket. 3. Secure the lid. Select the Manual mode and set the cooking time for 10 minutes at High Pressure. 4. Meanwhile, whisk together all ingredients for the sauce in a separate bowl. 5. Once cooking is complete, do a quick pressure release. Carefully open the lid. 6. Toss the meatballs in the prepared sauce and serve.

Chicken and Scallions Stuffed Peppers

Prep time: 5 minutes | Cook time: 20 minutes | Serves 5

- 1 tablespoon butter, at room temperature
- ½ cup scallions, chopped
- 1 pound (454 g) ground chicken
- ½ teaspoon sea salt
- ½ teaspoon chili powder
- ⅓ teaspoon paprika
- ⅓ teaspoon ground cumin
- ¼ teaspoon shallot powder
- 6 ounces (170 g) goat cheese, crumbled
- 1½ cups water
- 5 bell peppers, tops, membrane, and seeds removed
- ½ cup sour cream

1. Set your Instant Pot to Sauté and melt the butter. 2. Add the scallions and chicken and sauté for 2 to 3 minutes. 3. Stir in the sea salt, chili powder, paprika, cumin, and shallot powder. Add the crumbled goat cheese, stir, and reserve the mixture in a bowl. 4. Clean your Instant Pot. Pour the water into the Instant Pot and insert the trivet. 5. Stuff the bell peppers with enough of the chicken mixture, and don't pack the peppers too tightly. Put the peppers on the trivet. 6. Lock the lid. Select the Poultry mode and set the cooking time for 15 minutes at High Pressure. 7. When the timer beeps, perform a natural pressure release for 10 minutes, then release any remaining pressure. Carefully remove the lid. 8. Remove from the Instant Pot and serve with the sour cream.

Mexican Chicken with Red Salsa

Prep time: 10 minutes | Cook time: 20 minutes | Serves 8

- 2 pounds (907 g) boneless, skinless chicken thighs, cut into bite-size pieces
- 1½ tablespoons ground cumin
- 1½ tablespoons chili powder
- 1 tablespoon salt
- 2 tablespoons vegetable oil
- 1 (14½ ounces / 411 g) can
- diced tomatoes, undrained
- 1 (5 ounces / 142 g) can sugar-free tomato paste
- 1 small onion, chopped
- 3 garlic cloves, minced
- 2 ounces (57 g) pickled jalapeños from a can, with juice
- ½ cup sour cream

1. Preheat the Instant Pot by selecting Sauté and adjusting to high heat. 2. In a medium bowl, coat the chicken with the cumin, chili powder, and salt. 3. Put the oil in the inner cooking pot. When it is shimmering, add the coated chicken pieces. (This step lets the spices bloom a bit to get their full flavor.) Cook the chicken for 4 to 5 minutes. 4. Add the tomatoes, tomato paste, onion, garlic, and jalapeños. 5. Lock the lid into place. Select Manual and adjust the pressure to High. Cook for 15 minutes. When the cooking is complete, let the pressure release naturally for 10 minutes, then

quick-release any remaining pressure. Unlock and remove the lid. 6. Use two forks to shred the chicken. Serve topped with the sour cream. This dish is good with mashed cauliflower, steamed vegetables, or a salad.

Chicken Curry with Eggplant

Prep time: 15 minutes | Cook time: 12 minutes | Serves 4

- 1 eggplant, chopped
- ¼ cup chopped fresh cilantro
- 1 teaspoon curry powder
- 1 cup coconut cream
- 1 teaspoon coconut oil
- 1 pound (454 g) chicken breast, skinless, boneless, cubed

1. Put the coconut oil and chicken breast in the instant pot. 2. Sauté the ingredients on Sauté mode for 5 minutes. 3. Then stir well and add cilantro, eggplant, coconut cream, and curry powder. 4. Close and seal the lid. 5. Cook the meal on Manual mode (High Pressure) for 7 minutes. 6. Make a quick pressure release and transfer the cooked chicken in the serving bowls.

Lemony Chicken with Fingerling Potatoes and Olives

Prep time: 20 minutes | Cook time: 21 minutes | Serves 4

- 4 (5- to 7-ounce / 142- to 198-g) bone-in chicken thighs, trimmed
- ½ teaspoon table salt
- ¼ teaspoon pepper
- 2 teaspoons extra-virgin olive oil, plus extra for drizzling
- 4 garlic cloves, peeled and smashed
- ½ cup chicken broth
- 1 small lemon, sliced thin
- 1½ pounds (680 g) fingerling potatoes, unpeeled
- ¼ cup pitted brine-cured green or black olives, halved
- 2 tablespoons coarsely chopped fresh parsley

1. Pat chicken dry with paper towels and sprinkle with salt and pepper. Using highest sauté function, heat oil in Instant Pot for 5 minutes (or until just smoking). Place chicken skin side down in pot and cook until well browned on first side, about 5 minutes; transfer to plate. 2. Add garlic to fat left in pot and cook, using highest sauté function, until golden and fragrant, about 2 minutes. Stir in broth and lemon, scraping up any browned bits. Return chicken skin side up to pot and add any accumulated juices. Arrange potatoes on top. Lock lid in place and close pressure release valve. Select high pressure cook function and cook for 9 minutes. 3. Turn off Instant Pot and quick-release pressure. Carefully remove lid, allowing steam to escape away from you. Transfer chicken to serving dish and discard skin, if desired. Stir olives and parsley into potatoes and season with salt and pepper to taste. Serve chicken with potatoes.

Chili Lime Turkey Burgers

Prep time: 10 minutes | Cook time: 3 minutes | Serves 4

Burgers:
- 2 pounds (907 g) ground turkey
- 1½ ounces (43 g) diced red onion
- 2 cloves garlic, minced
- 1½ teaspoons minced

Dipping Sauce:
- ½ cup sour cream
- 4 teaspoons sriracha
- 1 tablespoon chopped

cilantro
- 1½ teaspoons salt
- 1 teaspoon Mexican chili powder
- Juice and zest of 1 lime
- ½ cup water

cilantro, plus more for garnish
- 1 teaspoon lime juice

1. Make the burgers: In a large bowl, add the turkey, onion, garlic, cilantro, salt, chili powder, and lime juice and zest. Use a wooden spoon to mix until the ingredients are well distributed. 2. Divide the meat into four 8-ounce / 227-g balls. Use a kitchen scale to measure for accuracy. Pat the meat into thick patties, about 1 inch thick. 3. Add the water and trivet to the Instant Pot. Place the turkey patties on top of the trivet, overlapping if necessary. 4. Close the lid and seal the vent. Cook on High Pressure for 3 minutes. Quick release the steam. 5. Remove the patties from the pot. 6. Make the dipping sauce: In a small bowl, whisk together the sour cream, sriracha, cilantro, and lime juice. 7. Top each patty with 2 tablespoons of the sauce and garnish with fresh cilantro.

Chicken and Bacon Ranch Casserole

Prep time: 5 minutes | Cook time: 30 minutes | Serves 4

- 4 slices bacon
- 4 (6-ounce / 170-g) boneless, skinless chicken breasts, cut into 1-inch cubes
- ½ teaspoon salt
- ¼ teaspoon pepper

- 1 tablespoon coconut oil
- ½ cup chicken broth
- ½ cup ranch dressing
- ½ cup shredded Cheddar cheese
- 2 ounces (57 g) cream cheese

1. Press the Sauté button to heat your Instant Pot. 2. Add the bacon slices and cook for about 7 minutes until crisp, flipping occasionally. 3. Remove from the pot and place on a paper towel to drain. Set aside. 4. Season the chicken cubes with salt and pepper. 5. Set your Instant Pot to Sauté and melt the coconut oil. 6. Add the chicken cubes and brown for 3 to 4 minutes until golden brown. 7. Stir in the broth and ranch dressing. 8. Secure the lid. Select the Manual mode and set the cooking time for 20 minutes at High Pressure. 9. Once cooking is complete, do a quick pressure release. Carefully open the lid. 10. Stir in the Cheddar and cream cheese. Crumble the cooked bacon and scatter on top. Serve immediately.

Mexican Turkey Tenderloin

Prep time: 5 minutes | Cook time: 8 minutes | Serves 6

- 1 cup Low-Sodium Salsa or bottled salsa
- 1 teaspoon chili powder
- ½ teaspoon ground cumin
- ¼ teaspoon dried oregano
- 1½ pounds unseasoned turkey tenderloin or

boneless turkey breast, cut into 6 pieces
- Freshly ground black pepper
- ½ cup shredded Monterey Jack cheese or Mexican cheese blend

1. In a small bowl or measuring cup, combine the salsa, chili powder, cumin, and oregano. Pour half of the mixture into the electric pressure cooker. 2. Nestle the turkey into the sauce. Grind some pepper onto each piece of turkey. Pour the remaining salsa mixture on top. 3. Close and lock the lid of the pressure cooker. Set the valve to sealing. 4. Cook on high pressure for 8 minutes. 5. When the cooking is complete, hit Cancel. Allow the pressure to release naturally for 10 minutes, then quick release any remaining pressure. 6. Once the pin drops, unlock and remove the lid. 7. Sprinkle the cheese on top, and put the lid back on for a few minutes to let the cheese melt. 8. Serve immediately.

Pesto Chicken

Prep time: 5 minutes | Cook time: 25 minutes | Serves 2

- 2 (6-ounce / 170-g) boneless, skinless chicken breasts, butterflied
- ½ teaspoon salt
- ¼ teaspoon pepper
- ¼ teaspoon dried parsley
- ¼ teaspoon garlic powder
- 2 tablespoons coconut oil

- 1 cup water
- ¼ cup whole-milk ricotta cheese
- ¼ cup pesto
- ¼ cup shredded whole-milk Mozzarella cheese
- Chopped parsley, for garnish (optional)

1. Sprinkle the chicken breasts with salt, pepper, parsley, and garlic powder. 2. Set your Instant Pot to Sauté and melt the coconut oil. 3. Add the chicken and brown for 3 to 5 minutes. Remove the chicken from the pot to a 7-cup glass bowl. 4. Pour the water into the Instant Pot and use a wooden spoon or rubber spatula to make sure no seasoning is stuck to bottom of pot. 5. Scatter the ricotta cheese on top of the chicken. Pour the pesto over chicken, and sprinkle the Mozzarella cheese over chicken. Cover with aluminum foil. Add the trivet to the Instant Pot and place the bowl on the trivet. 6. Secure the lid. Select the Manual mode and set the cooking time for 20 minutes at High Pressure. 7. Once cooking is complete, do a natural pressure release for 10 minutes, then release any remaining pressure. Carefully open the lid. 8. Serve the chicken garnished with the chopped parsley, if desired.

Smoky Whole Chicken

Prep time: 20 minutes | Cook time: 21 minutes | Serves 6

- 2 tablespoons extra-virgin olive oil
- 1 tablespoon kosher salt
- 1½ teaspoons smoked paprika
- 1 teaspoon freshly ground black pepper
- ½ teaspoon herbes de Provence
- ¼ teaspoon cayenne pepper
- 1 (3½ pounds) whole chicken, rinsed and patted dry, giblets removed
- 1 large lemon, halved
- 6 garlic cloves, peeled and crushed with the flat side of a knife
- 1 large onion, cut into 8 wedges, divided
- 1 cup Chicken Bone Broth, low-sodium store-bought chicken broth, or water
- 2 large carrots, each cut into 4 pieces
- 2 celery stalks, each cut into 4 pieces

1. In a small bowl, combine the olive oil, salt, paprika, pepper, herbes de Provence, and cayenne. 2. Place the chicken on a cutting board and rub the olive oil mixture under the skin and all over the outside. Stuff the cavity with the lemon halves, garlic cloves, and 3 to 4 wedges of onion. 3. Pour the broth into the electric pressure cooker. Add the remaining onion wedges, carrots, and celery. Insert a wire rack or trivet on top of the vegetables. 4. Place the chicken, breast-side up, on the rack. 5. Close and lock the lid of the pressure cooker. Set the valve to sealing. 6. Cook on high pressure for 21 minutes. 7. When the cooking is complete, hit Cancel and allow the pressure to release naturally for 15 minutes, then quick release any remaining pressure. 8. Once the pin drops, unlock and remove the lid. 9. Carefully remove the chicken to a clean cutting board. Remove the skin and cut the chicken into pieces or shred/chop the meat, and serve.

BBQ Turkey Meat Loaf

Prep time: 5 minutes | Cook time: 40 minutes | Serves 6

- 1 pound 93 percent lean ground turkey
- ⅓ cup low-sugar or unsweetened barbecue sauce, plus 2 tablespoons
- ⅓ cup gluten-free panko (Japanese bread crumbs)
- 1 large egg
- ½ small yellow onion, finely diced
- 1 garlic clove, minced
- ½ teaspoon fine sea salt
- ½ teaspoon freshly ground black pepper
- Cooked cauliflower "rice" or brown rice for serving

1. Pour 1 cup water into the Instant Pot. Lightly grease a 7 by 3-inch round cake pan or a 5½ by 3-inch loaf pan with olive oil or coat with nonstick cooking spray. 2. In a medium bowl, combine the turkey, ⅓ cup barbecue sauce, panko, egg, onion, garlic, salt, and pepper and mix well with your hands until all of the ingredients are evenly distributed. Transfer the mixture to the prepared pan, pressing it into an even layer. Cover the pan tightly with aluminum foil. Place the pan on a long-handled silicone steam rack, then, holding the handles of the steam rack, lower it into the pot. (If you don't have the long-handled rack, use the wire metal steam rack and a homemade sling) 3. Secure the lid and set the Pressure Release to Sealing. Select the Pressure Cook or Manual setting and set the cooking time for 25 minutes at high pressure if using a 7-inch round cake pan, or for 35 minutes at high pressure if using a 5½ by 3-inch loaf pan. (The pot will take about 10 minutes to come up to pressure before the cooking program begins.) 4. Preheat a toaster oven or position an oven rack 4 to 6 inches below the heat source and preheat the broiler. 5. When the cooking program ends, perform a quick pressure release by moving the Pressure Release to Venting. Open the pot and, wearing heat-resistant mitts, grasp the handles of the steam rack and lift it out of the pot. Uncover the pan, taking care not to get burned by the steam or to drip condensation onto the meat loaf. Brush the remaining 2 tablespoons barbecue sauce on top of the meat loaf. 6. Broil the meat loaf for a few minutes, just until the glaze becomes bubbly and browned. Cut the meat loaf into slices and serve hot, with the cauliflower "rice" alongside.

Mild Chicken Curry with Coconut Milk

Prep time: 10 minutes | Cook time: 14 minutes | Serves 4 to 6

- 1 large onion, diced
- 6 cloves garlic, crushed
- ¼ cup coconut oil
- ½ teaspoon black pepper
- ½ teaspoon turmeric
- ½ teaspoon paprika
- ¼ teaspoon cinnamon
- ¼ teaspoon cloves
- ¼ teaspoon cumin
- ¼ teaspoon ginger
- ½ teaspoon salt
- 1 tablespoon curry powder (more if you like more
- flavor)
- ½ teaspoon chili powder
- 24-ounce can of low-sodium diced or crushed tomatoes
- 13½-ounce can of light coconut milk (I prefer a brand that has no unwanted ingredients, like guar gum or sugar)
- 4 pounds boneless skinless chicken breasts, cut into chunks

1. Sauté onion and garlic in the coconut oil, either with Sauté setting in the inner pot of the Instant Pot or on stove top, then add to pot. 2. Combine spices in a small bowl, then add to the inner pot. 3. Add tomatoes and coconut milk and stir. 4. Add chicken, and stir to coat the pieces with the sauce. 5. Secure the lid and make sure vent is at sealing. Set to Manual mode (or Pressure Cook on newer models) for 14 minutes. 6. Let pressure release naturally (if you're crunched for time, you can do a quick release). 7. Serve with your favorite sides, and enjoy!

Chicken and Spiced Freekeh with Cilantro and Preserved Lemon

Prep time: 20 minutes | Cook time: 11 minutes | Serves 4

- 2 tablespoons extra-virgin olive oil, plus extra for drizzling
- 1 onion, chopped fine
- 4 garlic cloves, minced
- 1½ teaspoons smoked paprika
- ¼ teaspoon ground cardamom
- ¼ teaspoon red pepper flakes
- 2¼ cups chicken broth
- 1½ cups cracked freekeh, rinsed

- 2 (12-ounce / 340-g) bone-in split chicken breasts, halved crosswise and trimmed
- ½ teaspoon table salt
- ¼ teaspoon pepper
- ¼ cup chopped fresh cilantro
- 2 tablespoons sesame seeds, toasted
- ½ preserved lemon, pulp and white pith removed, rind rinsed and minced (2 tablespoons)

1. Using highest sauté function, heat oil in Instant Pot until shimmering. Add onion and cook until softened, about 5 minutes. Stir in garlic, paprika, cardamom, and pepper flakes and cook until fragrant, about 30 seconds. Stir in broth and freekeh. Sprinkle chicken with salt and pepper. Nestle skin side up into freekeh mixture. Lock lid in place and close pressure release valve. Select high pressure cook function and cook for 5 minutes. 2. Turn off Instant Pot and quick-release pressure. Carefully remove lid, allowing steam to escape away from you. Transfer chicken to serving dish and discard skin, if desired. Tent with aluminum foil and let rest while finishing freekeh. 3. Gently fluff freekeh with fork. Lay clean dish towel over pot, replace lid, and let sit for 5 minutes. Season with salt and pepper to taste. Transfer freekeh to serving dish with chicken and sprinkle with cilantro, sesame seeds, and preserved lemon. Drizzle with extra oil and serve.

Paprika Chicken Wings

Prep time: 10 minutes | Cook time: 13 minutes | Serves 4

- 1 pound (454 g) boneless chicken wings
- 1 teaspoon ground paprika
- 1 teaspoon avocado oil

- ¼ teaspoon minced garlic
- ¾ cup beef broth

1. Pour the avocado oil in the instant pot. 2. Rub the chicken wings with ground paprika and minced garlic and put them in the instant pot. 3. Cook the chicken on Sauté mode for 4 minutes from each side. 4. Then add beef broth and close the lid. 5. Sauté the meal for 5 minutes more.

Chapter 3

Beef, Pork, and Lamb

Chapter 3 Beef, Pork, and Lamb

Blue Pork

Prep time: 5 minutes | Cook time: 20 minutes | Serves 2

- 1 teaspoon coconut oil
- 2 pork chops
- 2 ounces (57 g) blue cheese,
- crumbled
- 1 teaspoon lemon juice
- ¼ cup heavy cream

1. Heat the coconut oil in the Instant Pot on Sauté mode. 2. Put the pork chops in the Instant Pot and cook on Sauté mode for 5 minutes on each side. 3. Add the lemon juice and crumbled cheese. Stir to mix well. 4. Add heavy cream and close the lid. 5. Select Manual mode and set cooking time for 10 minutes on High Pressure. 6. When timer beeps, perform a natural pressure release for 5 minutes, then release any remaining pressure. Open the lid. 7. Serve immediately.

Beef Cheeseburger Pie

Prep time: 15 minutes | Cook time: 30 minutes | Serves 6

- 1 tablespoon olive oil
- 1 pound (454 g) ground beef
- 3 eggs (1 beaten)
- ½ cup unsweetened tomato purée
- 2 tablespoons golden flaxseed meal
- 1 garlic clove, minced
- ½ teaspoon Italian seasoning blend
- ½ teaspoon sea salt
- ½ teaspoon smoked paprika
- ½ teaspoon onion powder
- 2 tablespoons heavy cream
- ½ teaspoon ground mustard
- ¼ teaspoon ground black pepper
- 2 cups water
- ½ cup grated Cheddar cheese

1. Coat a round cake pan with the olive oil. 2. Select Sauté mode. Once the pot is hot, add the ground beef and sauté for 5 minutes or until the beef is browned. 3. Transfer the beef to a large bowl. 4. Add the 1 beaten egg, tomato purée, flaxseed meal, garlic, Italian seasoning, sea salt, smoked paprika, and onion powder to the bowl. Mix until well combined. 5. Transfer the meat mixture to the prepared cake pan and use a knife to spread the mixture into an even layer. Set aside. 6. In a separate medium bowl, combine the 2 remaining eggs, heavy cream, ground mustard, and black pepper. Whisk until combined. 7. Pour the egg mixture over the meat mixture. Tightly cover the pan with a sheet of aluminum foil. 8. Place the trivet in the Instant Pot and add the water to the bottom of the pot. Place the pan on the trivet. 9. Lock the lid. Select Manual mode and set cooking time for 20 minutes on High Pressure. 10.

When cooking is complete, allow the pressure to release naturally for 10 minutes and then release the remaining pressure. Allow the pie to rest in the pot for 5 minutes. 11. Preheat the oven broiler to 450°F (235°C). 12. Open the lid, remove the pan from the pot. Remove the foil and sprinkle the Cheddar over top of the pie. 13. Place the pie in the oven and broil for 2 minutes or until the cheese is melted and the top becomes golden brown. Slice into six equal-sized wedges. Serve hot.

Easy Pot Roast and Vegetables

Prep time: 20 minutes | Cook time: 35 minutes | Serves 6

- 3–4 pound chuck roast, trimmed of fat and cut into serving-sized chunks
- 4 medium potatoes, cubed, unpeeled
- 4 medium carrots, sliced, or
- 1 pound baby carrots
- 2 celery ribs, sliced thin
- 1 envelope dry onion soup mix
- 3 cups water

1. Place the pot roast chunks and vegetables into the Instant Pot along with the potatoes, carrots and celery. 2. Mix together the onion soup mix and water and pour over the contents of the Instant Pot. 3. Secure the lid and make sure the vent is set to sealing. Set the Instant Pot to Manual mode for 35 minutes. Let pressure release naturally when cook time is up.

Stuffed Meatballs with Mozzarella

Prep time: 10 minutes | Cook time: 20 minutes | Serves 6

- 1 pound (454 g) ground pork
- 1 teaspoon chili flakes
- ½ teaspoon salt
- ⅓ cup shredded Mozzarella
- cheese
- 1 tablespoon butter
- ¼ cup chicken broth
- ½ teaspoon garlic powder

1. Mix up ground pork, chili flakes, salt, and garlic powder. 2. Then make the meatballs with the help of the fingertips. 3. Make the mini balls from the cheese. 4. Fill the meatballs with the mini cheese balls. 5. Toss the butter in the instant pot. 6. Heat it up on Sauté mode and add the prepared meatballs. 7. Cook the on Sauté mode for 3 minutes from each side. 8. Then add chicken broth and close the lid. 9. Cook the meal on Meat/Stew mode for 10 minutes.

Chili Pork Loin

Prep time: 10 minutes | Cook time: 20 minutes | Serves 2

- 10 ounces (283 g) pork loin
- ¼ cup water
- 1 teaspoon chili paste
- ½ teaspoon ground black pepper
- ½ teaspoon salt

1. Chop the pork loin into the medium pieces. 2. Sprinkle the meat with the salt and ground black pepper. 3. add chili paste in the meat. 4. Mix up the meat mixture with the help of the hands. 5. Pour water in the instant pot bowl and add meat mixture. 6. Close the lid and set the Meat/Stew mode. Cook the meal for 25 minutes. 7. Then chill the meat until warm.

Pork Meatballs with Thyme

Prep time: 15 minutes | Cook time: 16 minutes | Serves 8

- 2 cups ground pork
- 1 teaspoon dried thyme
- ½ teaspoon chili flakes
- ½ teaspoon garlic powder
- 1 tablespoon coconut oil
- ¼ teaspoon ground ginger
- 3 tablespoons almond flour
- ¼ cup water

1. In the mixing bowl, mix up ground pork, dried thyme, chili flakes, garlic powder, ground ginger, and almond flour. 2. Make the meatballs. 3. Melt the coconut oil in the instant pot on Sauté mode. 4. Arrange the meatballs in the instant pot in one layer and cook them for 3 minutes from each side. 5. Then add water and cook the meatballs for 10 minutes.

Wine-Braised Short Ribs with Potatoes

Prep time: 20 minutes | Cook time: 1 hour 20 minutes | Serves 4

- 2 pounds (907 g) bone-in English-style beef short ribs, trimmed
- ¾ teaspoon table salt, divided
- ¼ teaspoon pepper
- 1 tablespoon extra-virgin olive oil
- 1 onion, chopped fine
- 6 garlic cloves, minced
- 2 tablespoons tomato paste
- 1 tablespoon minced fresh oregano or 1 teaspoon dried
- 1 (14½-ounce / 411-g) can whole peeled tomatoes, drained with ¼ cup juice reserved, chopped coarse
- ½ cup dry red wine
- 1 pound (454 g) small red potatoes, unpeeled, halved
- 2 tablespoons minced fresh parsley

1. Pat short ribs dry with paper towels and sprinkle with ½ teaspoon salt and pepper. Using highest sauté function, heat oil in Instant Pot for 5 minutes (or until just smoking). Brown short ribs on all sides, 6 to 8 minutes; transfer to plate. 2. Add onion and remaining ¼ teaspoon salt to fat left in pot and cook, using highest sauté function, until onion is softened, about 3 minutes. Stir in garlic, tomato paste, and oregano and cook until fragrant, about 30 seconds. Stir in tomatoes and reserved juice and wine, scraping up any browned bits. Nestle short ribs meat side down into pot and add any accumulated juices. Lock lid in place and close pressure release valve. Select high pressure cook function and cook for 60 minutes. 3. Turn off Instant Pot and let pressure release naturally for 15 minutes. Quick-release any remaining pressure, then carefully remove lid, allowing steam to escape away from you. Transfer short ribs to serving dish, tent with aluminum foil, and let rest while preparing potatoes. 4. Strain braising liquid through fine-mesh strainer into fat separator; transfer solids to now-empty pot. Let braising liquid settle for 5 minutes, then pour 1½ cups defatted liquid and any accumulated juices into pot with solids; discard remaining liquid. Add potatoes. Lock lid in place and close pressure release valve. Select high pressure cook function and cook for 4 minutes. Turn off Instant Pot and quick-release pressure. Carefully remove lid, allowing steam to escape away from you. 5. Using slotted spoon, transfer potatoes to serving dish. Season sauce with salt and pepper to taste. Spoon sauce over short ribs and potatoes and sprinkle with parsley. Serve.

5-Ingredient Mexican Lasagna

Prep time: 15 minutes | Cook time: 15 minutes | Serves 4

- Nonstick cooking spray
- ½ (15 ounces) can light red kidney beans, rinsed and drained
- 4 (6-inch) gluten-free corn tortillas
- 1½ cups cooked shredded beef, pork, or chicken
- 1⅓ cups salsa
- 1⅓ cups shredded Mexican cheese blend

1. Spray a 6-inch springform pan with nonstick spray. Wrap the bottom in foil. 2. In a medium bowl, mash the beans with a fork. 3. Place 1 tortilla in the bottom of the pan. Add about ⅓ of the beans, ½ cup of meat, ⅓ cup of salsa, and ⅓ cup of cheese. Press down. Repeat for 2 more layers. Add the remaining tortilla and press down. Top with the remaining salsa and cheese. There are no beans or meat on the top layer. 4. Tear off a piece of foil big enough to cover the pan, and spray it with nonstick spray. Line the pan with the foil, sprayed-side down. 5. Pour 1 cup of water into the electric pressure cooker. 6. Place the pan on the wire rack and carefully lower it into the pot. Close and lock the lid of the pressure cooker. Set the valve to sealing. 7. Cook on high pressure for 15 minutes. 8. When the cooking is complete, hit Cancel. Allow the pressure to release naturally for 10 minutes, then quick release any remaining pressure. 9. Once the pin drops, unlock and remove the lid. 10. Using the handles of the wire rack, carefully remove the pan from the pot. Let the lasagna sit for 5 minutes. Carefully remove the ring. 11. Slice into quarters and serve.

Cilantro Pork

Prep time: 10 minutes | Cook time: 85 minutes | Serves 4

- 1 pound (454 g) boneless pork shoulder
- ¼ cup chopped fresh cilantro
- 1 cup water
- 1 teaspoon salt
- 1 teaspoon coconut oil
- ½ teaspoon mustard seeds

1. Pour water in the instant pot. 2. Add pork shoulder, fresh cilantro, salt, coconut oil, and mustard seeds. 3. Close and seal the lid. Cook the meat on High Pressure (Manual mode) for 85 minutes. 4. Then make a quick pressure release and open the lid. 5. The cooked meat has to be served with the remaining liquid from the instant pot.

Almond Butter Beef Stew

Prep time: 10 minutes | Cook time: 60 minutes | Serves 3

- 10 ounces (283 g) beef chuck roast, chopped
- ½ cup almond butter
- ½ teaspoon cayenne pepper
- ½ teaspoon salt
- 1 teaspoon dried basil
- 1 cup water

1. Place the almond butter in the instant pot and start to preheat it on the Sauté mode. 2. Meanwhile, mix up together the cayenne pepper, salt, and dried basil. 3. Sprinkle the beef with the spices and transfer the meat in the melted almond butter. 4. Close the instant pot lid and lock it. 5. Set the Manual mode and put a timer on 60 minutes (Low Pressure).

Aromatic Pork Steak Curry

Prep time: 15 minutes | Cook time: 8 minutes | Serves 6

- ½ teaspoon mustard seeds
- 1 teaspoon fennel seeds
- 1 teaspoon cumin seeds
- 2 chili peppers, deseeded and minced
- ½ teaspoon ground bay leaf
- 1 teaspoon mixed peppercorns
- 1 tablespoon sesame oil
- 1½ pounds (680 g) pork steak, sliced
- 2 cloves garlic, finely minced
- 2 tablespoons scallions,
- chopped
- 1 teaspoon fresh ginger, grated
- 1 teaspoon curry powder
- 1 cup chicken broth
- 2 tablespoons balsamic vinegar
- 3 tablespoons coconut cream
- ¼ teaspoon red pepper flakes, crushed
- Sea salt, to taste
- ¼ teaspoon ground black pepper

1. Heat a skillet over medium-high heat. Once hot, roast the mustard seeds, fennel seeds, cumin seeds, chili peppers, ground bay leaf, and peppercorns for 1 or 2 minutes or until aromatic. 2. Press the Sauté button to heat up the Instant Pot. Heat the sesame oil until sizzling. Sear pork steak for 5 minutes or until browned. 3. Add the remaining ingredients, including roasted seasonings. Stir to mix well. 4. Secure the lid. Choose the Manual mode and set cooking time for 8 minutes on High pressure. 5. Once cooking is complete, use a quick pressure release. Carefully remove the lid. Serve immediately.

Korean Short Rib Lettuce Wraps

Prep time: 7 minutes | Cook time: 25 minutes | Serves 4

- ¼ cup coconut aminos, or 1 tablespoon wheat-free tamari
- 2 tablespoons coconut vinegar
- 2 tablespoons sesame oil
- 3 green onions, thinly sliced, plus more for garnish
- 2 teaspoons peeled and
- grated fresh ginger
- 2 teaspoons minced garlic
- ½ teaspoon fine sea salt
- ½ teaspoon red pepper flakes, plus more for garnish
- 1 pound (454 g) boneless beef short ribs, sliced ½ inch thick

For Serving:
- 1 head radicchio, thinly sliced
- Butter lettuce leaves

1. Place the coconut aminos, vinegar, sesame oil, green onions, ginger, garlic, salt, and red pepper flakes in the Instant Pot and stir to combine. Add the short ribs and toss to coat well. 2. Seal the lid, press Manual, and set the timer for 20 minutes. Once finished, let the pressure release naturally. 3. Remove the ribs from the Instant Pot and set aside on a warm plate, leaving the sauce in the pot. 4. Press Sauté and cook the sauce, whisking often, until thickened to your liking, about 5 minutes. 5. Put the sliced radicchio on a serving platter, then lay the short ribs on top. Pour the thickened sauce over the ribs. Garnish with more sliced green onions and red pepper flakes. Serve wrapped in lettuce leaves.

Oregano Beef

Prep time: 10 minutes | Cook time: 15 minutes | Serves 2

- 1 cup water
- ¼ cup coconut milk
- 14 ounces (397 g) beef
- sirloin, chopped
- 1 teaspoon dried oregano

1. Put all ingredients in the instant pot. Close and seal the lid. 2. Cook the meal on Manual mode (High Pressure) for 15 minutes. 3. Use the quick pressure release.

Cuban Pork Shoulder

Prep time: 20 minutes | Cook time: 35 minutes | Serves 3

- 9 ounces (255 g) pork shoulder, boneless, chopped
- 1 tablespoon avocado oil
- 1 teaspoon ground cumin
- ½ teaspoon ground black pepper
- ¼ cup apple cider vinegar
- 1 cup water

1. In the mixing bowl, mix up avocado oil, ground cumin, ground black pepper, and apple cider vinegar. 2. Mix up pork shoulder and spice mixture together and transfer on the foil. Wrap the meat mixture. 3. Pour water and insert the steamer rack in the instant pot. 4. Put the wrapped pork shoulder on the rack. Close and seal the lid. 5. Cook the Cuban pork for 35 minutes. 6. Then allow the natural pressure release for 10 minutes.

Creamy Pork Liver

Prep time: 5 minutes | Cook time: 7 minutes | Serves 3

- 14 ounces (397 g) pork liver, chopped
- 1 teaspoon salt
- 1 teaspoon butter
- ½ cup heavy cream
- 3 tablespoons scallions, chopped

1. Rub the liver with the salt on a clean work surface. 2. Put the butter in the Instant Pot and melt on the Sauté mode. 3. Add the heavy cream, scallions, and liver. 4. Stir and close the lid. Select Manual mode and set cooking time for 12 minutes on High Pressure. 5. When timer beeps, perform a natural pressure release for 5 minutes, then release any remaining pressure. Open the lid. 6. Serve immediately.

Beef Tenderloin with Red Wine Sauce

Prep time: 30 minutes | Cook time: 10 minutes | Serves 5

- 2 pounds (907 g) beef tenderloin
- Salt and black pepper, to taste
- 2 tablespoons avocado oil
- ½ cup beef broth
- ½ cup dry red wine
- 2 cloves garlic, minced
- 1 teaspoon Worcestershire sauce
- 1½ teaspoons dried rosemary
- ¼ teaspoon xanthan gum
- Chopped fresh rosemary, for garnish (optional)

1. Thirty minutes prior to cooking, take the tenderloin out of the fridge and let it come to room temperature. Crust the outside of the tenderloin in salt and pepper. 2. Turn the pot to Sauté mode and add the avocado oil. Once hot, add the tenderloin and sear on all sides, about 5 minutes. Press Cancel. 3. Add the broth, wine, garlic, Worcestershire sauce, and rosemary to the pot around the beef. 4. Close the lid and seal the vent. Cook on High Pressure for 8 minutes. Quick release the steam. 5. Remove the tenderloin to a platter, tent with aluminum foil, and let it rest for 10 minutes. Press Cancel. 6. Turn the pot to Sauté mode. Once the broth has begun a low boil, add the xanthan gum and whisk until a thin sauce has formed, 2 to 3 minutes. 7. Slice the tenderloin against the grain into thin rounds. Top each slice with the red wine glaze. Garnish with rosemary, if desired.

Rosemary Lamb Chops

Prep time: 25 minutes | Cook time: 2 minutes | Serves 4

- 1½ pounds lamb chops (4 small chops)
- 1 teaspoon kosher salt
- Leaves from 1 (6-inch) rosemary sprig
- 2 tablespoons avocado oil
- 1 shallot, peeled and cut in quarters
- 1 tablespoon tomato paste
- 1 cup beef broth

1. Place the lamb chops on a cutting board. Press the salt and rosemary leaves into both sides of the chops. Let rest at room temperature for 15 to 30 minutes. 2. Set the electric pressure cooker to Sauté/More setting. When hot, add the avocado oil. 3. Brown the lamb chops, about 2 minutes per side. (If they don't all fit in a single layer, brown them in batches.) 4. Transfer the chops to a plate. In the pot, combine the shallot, tomato paste, and broth. Cook for about a minute, scraping up the brown bits from the bottom. Hit Cancel. 5. Add the chops and any accumulated juices back to the pot. 6. Close and lock the lid of the pressure cooker. Set the valve to sealing. 7. Cook on high pressure for 2 minutes. 8. When the cooking is complete, hit Cancel and quick release the pressure. 9. Once the pin drops, unlock and remove the lid. 10. Place the lamb chops on plates and serve immediately.

Pork Mushroom Stroganoff

Prep time: 10 minutes | Cook time: 25 minutes | Serves 4

- ½ cup chopped cremini mushrooms
- 1 teaspoon dried oregano
- ½ teaspoon ground nutmeg
- ½ cup coconut milk
- 1 cup ground pork
- ½ teaspoon salt
- 2 tablespoons butter

1. Heat up butter on Sauté mode for 3 minutes. 2. Add mushrooms. Sauté the vegetables for 5 minutes. 3. Then stir them and add salt, ground pork, ground nutmeg, and dried oregano. 4. Stir the ingredients and cook for 5 minutes more. 5. Add coconut milk and close the lid. 6. Sauté the stroganoff for 15 minutes. Stir it from time to time to avoid burning.

Blue Cheese Stuffed Steak Roll-Ups

Prep time: 5 minutes | Cook time: 15 minutes | Serves 6

- 1 (1½-pound / 680-g) beef round tip roast, sliced into 6 steaks of equal thickness
- 6 ounces (170 g) blue cheese, crumbled
- ½ cup beef broth
- ¼ cup coconut aminos, or
- 1 tablespoon wheat-free tamari
- 4 cloves garlic, minced
- Chopped fresh Italian parsley, for garnish
- Cracked black pepper, for garnish

1. Place each steak in a resealable plastic bag and pound with a rolling pin or meat mallet until it is ½ inch thick. Lay the pounded steaks flat on a cutting board or other work surface. 2. Divide the blue cheese evenly among the steaks, placing the cheese on one side. Roll up each steak, starting at a shorter end, and secure with toothpicks. 3. Combine the broth, coconut aminos, and garlic in the Instant Pot. Add the steak roll-ups to the broth mixture. 4. Seal the lid, press Manual, and set the timer for 15 minutes. Once finished, turn the valve to venting for a quick release. 5. Remove the toothpicks from the steak roll-ups before serving. Garnish the roll-ups with chopped parsley and cracked black pepper.

Albóndigas Sinaloenses

Prep time: 15 minutes | Cook time: 10 minutes | Serves 6

- 1 pound (454 g) ground pork
- ½ pound (227 g) Italian sausage, crumbled
- 2 tablespoons yellow onion, finely chopped
- ½ teaspoon dried oregano
- 1 sprig fresh mint, finely minced
- ½ teaspoon ground cumin
- 2 garlic cloves, finely minced
- ¼ teaspoon fresh ginger, grated
- Seasoned salt and ground black pepper, to taste
- 1 tablespoon olive oil
- ½ cup yellow onions, finely chopped
- 2 chipotle chilies in adobo
- 2 tomatoes, puréed
- 2 tablespoons tomato passata
- 1 cup chicken broth

1. In a mixing bowl, combine the pork, sausage, 2 tablespoons of yellow onion, oregano, mint, cumin, garlic, ginger, salt, and black pepper. 2. Roll the mixture into meatballs and reserve. 3. Press the Sauté button to heat up the Instant Pot. Heat the olive oil and cook the meatballs for 4 minutes, stirring continuously. 4. Stir in ½ cup of yellow onions, chilies in adobo, tomatoes passata, and broth. Add reserved meatballs. 5. Secure the lid. Choose the Manual mode and set cooking time for 6 minutes at High pressure. 6. Once cooking is complete, use a quick pressure release. Carefully remove the lid. 7. Serve immediately.

Braised Lamb Shanks with Bell Pepper and Harissa

Prep time: 10 minutes | Cook time: 1 hour 20 minutes | Serves 4

- 4 (10- to 12-ounce/ 283- to 340-g) lamb shanks, trimmed
- ¾ teaspoon salt, divided
- 1 tablespoon extra-virgin olive oil
- 1 onion, chopped
- 1 red bell pepper, stemmed, seeded, and cut into 1-inch
- pieces
- ¼ cup harissa, divided
- 4 garlic cloves, minced
- 1 tablespoon tomato paste
- ½ cup chicken broth
- 1 bay leaf
- 2 tablespoons chopped fresh mint

1. Pat lamb shanks dry with paper towels and sprinkle with ½ teaspoon salt. Using highest sauté function, heat oil in Instant Pot for 5 minutes (or until just smoking). Brown 2 shanks on all sides, 8 to 10 minutes; transfer to plate. Repeat with remaining shanks; transfer to plate. 2. Add onion, bell pepper, and remaining ¼ teaspoon salt to fat left in pot and cook, using highest sauté function, until vegetables are softened, about 5 minutes. Stir in 2 tablespoons harissa, garlic, and tomato paste and cook until fragrant, about 30 seconds. Stir in broth and bay leaf, scraping up any browned bits. Nestle shanks into pot and add any accumulated juices. Lock lid in place and close pressure release valve. Select high pressure cook function and cook for 60 minutes. 3. Turn off Instant Pot and let pressure release naturally for 15 minutes. Quick-release any remaining pressure, then carefully remove lid, allowing steam to escape away from you. Transfer shanks to serving dish, tent with aluminum foil, and let rest while finishing sauce. 4. Strain braising liquid through fine-mesh strainer into fat separator. Discard bay leaf and transfer solids to blender. Let braising liquid settle for 5 minutes, then pour ¾ cup defatted liquid into blender with solids; discard remaining liquid. Add remaining 2 tablespoons harissa and process until smooth, about 1 minute. Season with salt and pepper to taste. Pour portion of sauce over shanks and sprinkle with mint. Serve, passing remaining sauce separately.

Marjoram Beef Ribs

Prep time: 10 minutes | Cook time: 40 minutes | Serves 2

- 10 ounces (283 g) beef ribs
- ¾ cup water
- 2 tablespoons coconut oil
- 1 teaspoon dried marjoram
- ½ teaspoon salt
- ½ cup chicken broth

1. Rub the beef ribs with the dried marjoram and salt. 2. Place the beef ribs in the instant pot bowl. 3. Add chicken broth and water. 4. Then add coconut oil. 5. Close the lid and set the Meat/Stew mode. Cook the ribs for 40 minutes.

Braised Pork Belly

Prep time: 15 minutes | Cook time: 37 minutes | Serves 4

- 1 pound (454 g) pork belly
- 1 tablespoon olive oil
- Salt and ground black pepper to taste
- 1 clove garlic, minced
- 1 cup dry white wine
- Rosemary sprig

1. Select the Sauté mode on the Instant Pot and heat the oil. 2. Add the pork belly and sauté for 2 minutes per side, until starting to brown. 3. Season the meat with salt and pepper, add the garlic. 4. Pour in the wine and add the rosemary sprig. Bring to a boil. 5. Select the Manual mode and set the cooking time for 35 minutes at High pressure. 6. Once cooking is complete, use a natural pressure release for 10 minutes, then release any remaining pressure. Open the lid. 7. Slice the meat and serve.

Apple and Pumpkin Ham

Prep time: 10 minutes | Cook time: 10 minutes | Serves 6

- 1 cup apple cider vinegar
- 1 pound (454 g) ham, cooked
- 2 tablespoons erythritol
- 1 tablespoon avocado oil
- 2 tablespoons butter
- ½ teaspoon pumpkin pie spices

1. Pour apple cider vinegar in the Instant Pot and insert the trivet. 2. Rub the ham with erythritol avocado oil,, butter, and pumpkin pie spices. 3. Put the ham on the trivet. Close the lid. 4. Select Manual mode and set cooking time for 10 minutes on High Pressure. 5. When timer beeps, use a natural pressure release for 5 minutes, then release any remaining pressure and open the lid. 6. Slice the ham and serve.

Beef Chili with Kale

Prep time: 10 minutes | Cook time: 10 minutes | Serves 6

- 2 tablespoons olive oil
- 1½ pounds (680 g) ground chuck
- 1 green bell pepper, chopped
- 1 red bell pepper, chopped
- 2 red chilies, minced
- 1 red onion
- 2 garlic cloves, smashed
- 1 teaspoon cumin
- 1 teaspoon Mexican oregano
- 1 teaspoon cayenne pepper
- 1 teaspoon smoked paprika
- Salt and freshly ground black pepper, to taste
- 1½ cups puréed tomatoes
- 4 cups fresh kale

1. Press the Sauté button to heat up the Instant Pot. Then, heat the oil; once hot, cook the ground chuck for 2 minutes, crumbling it with a fork or a wide spatula. 2. Add the pepper, onions, and garlic;

cook an additional 2 minutes or until fragrant. Stir in the remaining ingredients, minus kale leaves. 3. Choose the Manual setting and cook for 6 minutes at High Pressure. Once cooking is complete, use a natural pressure release; carefully remove the lid. 4. Add kale, cover with the lid and allow the kale leaves to wilt completely. Bon appétit!

Pork Taco Casserole

Prep time: 15 minutes | Cook time: 30 minutes | Serves 6

- ½ cup water
- 2 eggs
- 3 ounces (85 g) Cottage cheese, at room temperature
- ¼ cup heavy cream
- 1 teaspoon taco seasoning
- 6 ounces (170 g) Cotija cheese, crumbled
- ¾ pound (340 g) ground pork
- ½ cup tomatoes, puréed
- 1 tablespoon taco seasoning
- 3 ounces (85 g) chopped green chilies
- 6 ounces (170 g) Queso Manchego cheese, shredded

1. Add the water in the Instant Pot and place in the trivet. 2. In a mixing bowl, combine the eggs, Cottage cheese, heavy cream, and taco seasoning. 3. Lightly grease a casserole dish. Spread the Cotija cheese over the bottom. Stir in the egg mixture. 4. Lower the casserole dish onto the trivet. 5. Secure the lid. Choose Manual mode and set cooking time for 20 minutes on High Pressure. 6. Once cooking is complete, use a quick pressure release. Carefully remove the lid. 7. In the meantime, heat a skillet over a medium-high heat. Brown the ground pork, crumbling with a fork. 8. Add the tomato purée, taco seasoning, and green chilies. Spread the mixture over the prepared cheese crust. 9. Top with shredded Queso Manchego. 10. Secure the lid. Choose Manual mode and set cooking time for 10 minutes on High Pressure. 11. Once cooking is complete, use a quick pressure release. Carefully remove the lid. Serve immediately.

Basil and Thyme Pork Loin

Prep time: 10 minutes | Cook time: 17 minutes | Serves 4

- 1 pound (454 g) pork loin
- 1 teaspoon dried basil
- 1 tablespoon avocado oil
- 1 teaspoon dried thyme
- ½ teaspoon salt
- 2 tablespoons apple cider vinegar
- 1 cup water, for cooking

1. In the shallow bowl, mix up dried basil, avocado oil, thyme, salt, and apple cider vinegar. 2. Then rub the pork loin with the spice mixture and leave the meat for 10 minutes to marinate. 3. Wrap the meat in foil and put on the steamer rack. 4. Pour water and transfer the steamer rack with meat in the instant pot. 5. Close and seal the lid. Cook the meat on Manual (High Pressure) for 20 minutes. Allow the natural pressure release for 5 minutes. 6. Slice the cooked pork loin.

Coconut Pork Muffins

Prep time: 5 minutes | Cook time: 9 minutes | Serves 2

- 1 egg, beaten
- 2 tablespoons coconut flour
- 1 teaspoon parsley
- ¼ teaspoon salt
- 1 tablespoon coconut cream
- 4 ounces (113 g) ground pork, fried
- 1 cup water

1. Whisk together the egg, coconut flour, parsley, salt, and coconut cream. Add the fried ground pork. Mix the the mixture until homogenous. 2. Pour the mixture into a muffin pan. 3. Pour the water in the Instant Pot and place in the trivet. 4. Lower the muffin pan on the trivet and close the Instant Pot lid. 5. Set the Manual mode and set cooking time for 4 minutes on High Pressure. 6. When timer beeps, perform a natural pressure release for 5 minutes, then release any remaining pressure. Open the lid. 7. Serve warm.

Filipino Pork Loin

Prep time: 10 minutes | Cook time: 40 minutes | Serves 4

- 1 pound (454 g) pork loin, chopped
- ½ cup apple cider vinegar
- 1 cup chicken broth
- 1 chili pepper, chopped
- 1 tablespoon coconut oil
- 1 teaspoon salt

1. Melt the coconut oil on Sauté mode. 2. When it is hot, and chili pepper and cook it for 2 minutes. Stir it. 3. Add chopped pork loin and salt. Cook the ingredients for 5 minutes. 4. After this, add apple cider vinegar and chicken broth. 5. Close and seal the lid and cook the Filipino pork for 30 minutes on High Pressure (Manual mode). Then make a quick pressure release.

Beef Shoulder Roast

Prep time: 15 minutes | Cook time: 46 minutes | Serves 6

- 2 tablespoons peanut oil
- 2 pounds (907 g) shoulder roast
- ¼ cup coconut aminos
- 1 teaspoon porcini powder
- 1 teaspoon garlic powder
- 1 cup beef broth
- 2 cloves garlic, minced
- 2 tablespoons champagne vinegar
- ½ teaspoon hot sauce
- 1 teaspoon celery seeds
- 1 cup purple onions, cut into wedges
- 1 tablespoon flaxseed meal, plus 2 tablespoons water

1. Press the Sauté button to heat up the Instant Pot. Then, heat the peanut oil and cook the beef shoulder roast for 3 minutes on each side. 2. In a mixing dish, combine coconut aminos, porcini powder, garlic powder, broth, garlic, vinegar, hot sauce, and celery seeds. 3. Pour the broth mixture into the Instant Pot. Add the onions to the top. 4. Secure the lid. Choose Meat/Stew mode and set cooking time for 40 minutes on High Pressure. 5. Once cooking is complete, use a natural pressure release for 15 minutes, then release any remaining pressure. Carefully remove the lid. 6. Make the slurry by mixing flaxseed meal with 2 tablespoons of water. Add the slurry to the Instant Pot. 7. Press the Sauté button and allow it to cook until the cooking liquid is reduced and thickened slightly. Serve warm.

Beery Boston-Style Butt

Prep time: 10 minutes | Cook time: 1 hour 1 minutes | Serves 4

- 1 tablespoon butter
- 1 pound (454 g) Boston-style butt
- ½ cup leeks, chopped
- ¼ cup beer
- ½ cup chicken stock
- Pinch of grated nutmeg
- Sea salt, to taste
- ¼ teaspoon ground black pepper
- ¼ cup water

1. Press the Sauté button to heat up the Instant Pot. Once hot, melt the butter. 2. Cook the Boston-style butt for 3 minutes on each side. Remove from the pot and reserve. 3. Sauté the leeks for 5 minutes or until fragrant. Add the remaining ingredients and stir to combine. 4. Secure the lid. Choose the Manual mode and set cooking time for 50 minutes on High pressure. 5. Once cooking is complete, use a natural pressure release for 20 minutes, then release any remaining pressure. Carefully remove the lid. 6. Serve immediately.

Bacon Cheddar Cheese Stuffed Burgers

Prep time: 10 minutes | Cook time: 9 minutes | Serves 4

- 1 pound (454 g) ground beef
- 6 ounces (170 g) shredded Cheddar cheese
- 5 slices bacon, coarsely chopped
- 2 teaspoons Worcestershire
- sauce
- 1 teaspoon salt
- ½ teaspoon liquid smoke
- ½ teaspoon black pepper
- ½ teaspoon garlic powder
- 1 cup water

1. In a large bowl, add the beef, cheese, bacon, Worcestershire sauce, salt, liquid smoke, pepper, and garlic powder. Gently work everything into the meat. Do not overwork the meat, or it will become tough when it cooks. 2. Separate the meat into four equal portions. Use a food scale to measure evenly. 3. Shape each piece into a ball. Use your thumb to make a crater in the middle of the patty but make sure the round shape is retained. 4. Wrap each patty loosely in aluminum foil. Place them on top of the trivet in the pot. They will overlap. 5. Add the water to the bottom of the pot. Close the lid and seal the vent. Cook on High Pressure for 9 minutes. Quick release the steam. Remove the foil packets from the pot and set them on a large plate. Carefully unwrap the burgers. There will be juices in the bottom of the foil.

Greek Lamb Leg

Prep time: 10 minutes | Cook time: 50 minutes | Serves 4

- ♦ 1 pound (454 g) lamb leg
- ♦ ½ teaspoon dried thyme
- ♦ 1 teaspoon paprika powder
- ♦ ¼ teaspoon cumin seeds
- ♦ 1 tablespoon softened butter
- ♦ 2 garlic cloves
- ♦ ¼ cup water

1. Rub the lamb leg with dried thyme, paprika powder, and cumin seeds on a clean work surface. 2. Brush the leg with softened butter and transfer to the Instant Pot. Add garlic cloves and water. 3. Close the lid. Select Manual mode and set cooking time for 50 minutes on High Pressure. 4. When timer beeps, use a quick pressure release. Open the lid. 5. Serve warm.

Low Carb Pork Tenderloin

Prep time: 15 minutes | Cook time: 30 minutes | Serves 2

- ♦ 9 ounces (255 g) pork tenderloin
- ♦ 1 teaspoon erythritol
- ♦ ½ teaspoon dried dill
- ♦ ½ teaspoon white pepper
- ♦ 1 garlic clove, minced
- ♦ 3 tablespoons butter
- ♦ ¼ cup water

1. Rub the pork tenderloin with erythritol, dried dill, white pepper, and minced garlic. 2. Then melt the butter in the instant pot on Sauté mode. 3. Add pork tenderloin and cook it for 8 minutes from each side (use Sauté mode). 4. Then add water and close the lid. 5. Cook the meat on Sauté mode for 10 minutes. 6. Cool the cooked tenderloin for 10 to 15 minutes and slice.

Red Wine Pot Roast with Winter Vegetables

Prep time: 10 minutes | Cook time: 1 hour 35 minutes | Serves 6

- ♦ One 3-pound boneless beef chuck roast or bottom round roast (see Note)
- ♦ 2 teaspoons fine sea salt
- ♦ 1 teaspoon freshly ground black pepper
- ♦ 1 tablespoon cold-pressed avocado oil
- ♦ 4 large shallots, quartered
- ♦ 4 garlic cloves, minced
- ♦ 1 cup dry red wine
- ♦ 2 tablespoons Dijon mustard
- ♦ 2 teaspoons chopped fresh rosemary
- ♦ 1 pound parsnips or turnips, cut into ½-inch pieces
- ♦ 1 pound carrots, cut into ½-inch pieces
- ♦ 4 celery stalks, cut into ½-inch pieces

1. Put the beef onto a plate, pat it dry with paper towels, and then season all over with the salt and pepper. 2. Select the Sauté setting on the Instant Pot and heat the oil for 2 minutes. Using tongs, lower the roast into the pot and sear for about 4 minutes, until browned on the first side. Flip the roast and sear for about 4 minutes more, until browned on the second side. Return the roast to the plate. 3. Add the shallots to the pot and sauté for about 2 minutes, until they begin to soften. Add the garlic and sauté for about 1 minute more. Stir in the wine, mustard, and rosemary, using a wooden spoon to nudge any browned bits from the bottom of the pot. Return the roast to the pot, then spoon some of the cooking liquid over the top. 4. Secure the lid and set the Pressure Release to Sealing. Press the Cancel button to reset the cooking program, then select the Meat/Stew setting and set the cooking time for 1 hour 5 minutes at high pressure. (The pot will take about 5 minutes to come up to pressure before the cooking program begins.) 5. When the cooking program ends, let the pressure release naturally for at least 15 minutes, then move the Pressure Release to Venting to release any remaining steam. Open the pot and, using tongs, carefully transfer the pot roast to a cutting board. Tent with aluminum foil to keep warm. 6. Add the parsnips, carrots, and celery to the pot. 7. Secure the lid and set the Pressure Release to Sealing. Press the Cancel button to reset the cooking program, then select the Pressure Cook or Manual setting and set the cooking time for 3 minutes at low pressure. (The pot will take about 10 minutes to come up to pressure before the cooking program begins.) 8. When the cooking program ends, perform a quick pressure release by moving the Pressure Release to Venting. Open the pot and, using a slotted spoon, transfer the vegetables to a serving dish. Wearing heat-resistant mitts, lift out the inner pot and pour the cooking liquid into a gravy boat or other serving vessel with a spout. (If you like, use a fat separator to remove the fat from the liquid before serving.) 9. If the roast was tied, snip the string and discard. Carve the roast against the grain into ½-inch-thick slices and arrange them on the dish with the vegetables. Pour some cooking liquid over the roast and serve, passing the remaining cooking liquid on the side.

Classic Sunday Pot Roast

Prep time: 5 minutes | Cook time: 65 minutes | Serves 6

- ♦ 1 pound (454 g) radishes, rinsed and trimmed
- ♦ 2 cups beef broth
- ♦ 2 bay leaves
- ♦ 2 pounds (907 g) chuck roast
- ♦ 2 tablespoons dried onion
- ♦ 2 teaspoons garlic powder
- ♦ 2 teaspoons salt
- ♦ 1 teaspoon black pepper
- ♦ 4 tablespoons butter

1. Place the radishes in the pot and cover with the broth. Add the bay leaves. 2. Place the roast on top of the radishes. Sprinkle the dried onion, garlic powder, salt, and pepper on top of the roast. Top with the butter. 3. Close the lid and seal the vent. Cook on High Pressure for 50 minutes. Let the steam naturally release for 15 minutes before Manually releasing. 4. Carefully remove the roast and place it on a cutting board. Use two forks to shred the meat. Serve with the radishes.

BBQ Ribs and Broccoli Slaw

Prep time: 10 minutes | Cook time: 50 minutes | Serves 6

- BBQ Ribs
- 4 pounds baby back ribs
- 1 teaspoon fine sea salt
- 1 teaspoon freshly ground black pepper
- Broccoli Slaw
- ½ cup plain 2 percent Greek yogurt
- 1 tablespoon olive oil
- 1 tablespoon fresh lemon juice
- ½ teaspoon fine sea salt

- ¼ teaspoon freshly ground black pepper
- 1 pound broccoli florets (or florets from 2 large crowns), chopped
- 10 radishes, halved and thinly sliced
- 1 red bell pepper, seeded and cut lengthwise into narrow strips
- 1 large apple (such as Fuji, Jonagold, or Gala), thinly sliced
- ½ red onion, thinly sliced
- ¾ cup low-sugar or unsweetened barbecue sauce

1. To make the ribs: Pat the ribs dry with paper towels, then cut the racks into six sections (three to five ribs per section, depending on how big the racks are). Season the ribs all over with the salt and pepper. 2. Pour 1 cup water into the Instant Pot and place the wire metal steam rack into the pot. Place the ribs on top of the wire rack (it's fine to stack them up). 3. Secure the lid and set the Pressure Release to Sealing. Select the Pressure Cook or Manual setting and set the cooking time for 20 minutes at high pressure. (The pot will take about 15 minutes to come up to pressure before the cooking program begins.) 4. To make the broccoli slaw: While the ribs are cooking, in a small bowl, stir together the yogurt, oil, lemon juice, salt, and pepper, mixing well. In a large bowl, combine the broccoli, radishes, bell pepper, apple, and onion. Drizzle with the yogurt mixture and toss until evenly coated. 5. When the ribs have about 10 minutes left in their cooking time, preheat the oven to 400°F. Line a sheet pan with aluminum foil. 6. When the cooking program ends, perform a quick pressure release by moving the Pressure Release to Venting. Open the pot and, using tongs, transfer the ribs in a single layer to the prepared sheet pan. Brush the barbecue sauce onto both sides of the ribs, using 2 tablespoons of sauce per section of ribs. Bake, meaty-side up, for 15 to 20 minutes, until lightly browned. 7. Serve the ribs warm, with the slaw on the side.

Pot Roast with Gravy and Vegetables

Prep time: 30 minutes | Cook time: 1 hour 15 minutes | Serves 6

- 1 tablespoon olive oil
- 3–4 pound bottom round, rump, or arm roast, trimmed of fat
- ¼ teaspoon salt
- 2–3 teaspoons pepper
- 2 tablespoons flour
- 1 cup cold water
- 1 teaspoon Kitchen Bouquet, or gravy browning seasoning

sauce
- 1 garlic clove, minced
- 2 medium onions, cut in wedges
- 4 medium potatoes, cubed, unpeeled
- 2 carrots, quartered
- 1 green bell pepper, sliced

1. Press the Sauté button on the Instant Pot and pour the oil inside, letting it heat up. Sprinkle each side of the roast with salt and pepper, then brown it for 5 minutes on each side inside the pot. 2. Mix together the flour, water and Kitchen Bouquet and spread over roast. 3. Add garlic, onions, potatoes, carrots, and green pepper. 4. Secure the lid and make sure the vent is set to sealing. Press Manual and set the Instant Pot for 1 hour and 15 minutes. 5. When cook time is up, let the pressure release naturally.

Korean Beef and Pickled Vegetable Bowls

Prep time: 15 minutes | Cook time: 10 minutes | Serves 6

- 1 tablespoon vegetable oil
- 5 garlic cloves, thinly sliced
- 1 tablespoon julienned fresh ginger
- 2 dried red chiles
- 1 cup sliced onions
- 1 pound (454 g) 80% lean ground beef
- 1 tablespoon gochujang, adjusted to taste
- 1 cup fresh basil leaves, divided

For the Pickled Vegetables:

- 1 cucumber, peeled, coarsely grated
- 1 turnip, coarsely grated
- ¼ cup white vinegar

- 1 tablespoon coconut aminos
- 1 teaspoon Swerve
- 2 tablespoons freshly squeezed lime juice
- 1 teaspoon salt
- 1 teaspoon freshly ground pepper
- ¼ cup water
- 1 teaspoon sesame oil

- ½ teaspoon salt
- ½ teaspoon Swerve

1. Select Sauté mode of the Instant Pot. When the pot is hot, add the oil and heat until it is shimmering. 2. Add the garlic, ginger, and chiles and sauté for 1 minute. 3. Add the onions and sauté for 1 minute. 4. Add the ground beef and cooking for 4 minutes.. 5. Add the gochujang, ½ cup of basil, coconut aminos, sweetener, lime juice, salt, pepper, water, and sesame oil, and stir to combine. 6. Lock the lid. Select Manual mode. Set the time for 4 minutes on High Pressure. 7. When cooking is complete, let the pressure release naturally for 5 minutes, then release any remaining pressure. Unlock the lid and stir in the remaining ½ cup of basil. 8. Meanwhile, put the cucumber and turnip in a medium bowl and mix with the vinegar, salt, and sweetener. To serve, portion the basil beef into individual bowls and serve with the pickled salad.

Pork Butt Roast

Prep time: 10 minutes | Cook time: 9 minutes | Serves 6 to 8

- 3 to 4 pounds pork butt roast
- 2 to 3 tablespoons of your favorite rub

- 2 cups water

1. Place pork in the inner pot of the Instant Pot. 2. Sprinkle in the rub all over the roast and add the water, being careful not to wash off the rub. 3. Secure the lid and set the vent to sealing. Cook for 9 minutes on the Manual setting. 4. Let the pressure release naturally.

Chapter
4

Fish and Seafood

Chapter 4 Fish and Seafood

Trout Casserole

Prep time: 5 minutes | Cook time: 10 minutes | Serves 3

- 1½ cups water
- 1½ tablespoons olive oil
- 3 plum tomatoes, sliced
- ½ teaspoon dried oregano
- 1 teaspoon dried basil
- 3 trout fillets
- ½ teaspoon cayenne pepper,
- or more to taste
- ⅓ teaspoon black pepper
- Salt, to taste
- 1 bay leaf
- 1 cup shredded Pepper Jack cheese

1. Pour the water into your Instant Pot and insert a trivet. 2. Grease a baking dish with the olive oil. Add the tomatoes slices to the baking dish and sprinkle with the oregano and basil. 3. Add the fish fillets and season with the cayenne pepper, black pepper, and salt. Add the bay leaf. Lower the baking dish onto the trivet. 4. Lock the lid. Select the Manual mode and set the cooking time for 10 minutes at High Pressure. 5. When the timer beeps, perform a quick pressure release. Carefully remove the lid. 6. Scatter the Pepper Jack cheese on top, lock the lid, and allow the cheese to melt. 7. Serve warm.

Salmon with Lemon-Garlic Mashed Cauliflower

Prep time: 15 minutes | Cook time: 10 minutes | Serves 4

- 2 tablespoons extra-virgin olive oil
- 4 garlic cloves, peeled and smashed
- ½ cup chicken or vegetable broth
- ¾ teaspoon table salt, divided
- 1 large head cauliflower (3 pounds / 1.4 kg), cored and
- cut into 2-inch florets
- 4 (6-ounce / 170-g) skinless salmon fillets, 1½ inches thick
- ½ teaspoon ras el hanout
- ½ teaspoon grated lemon zest
- 3 scallions, sliced thin
- 1 tablespoon sesame seeds, toasted

1. Using highest sauté function, cook oil and garlic in Instant Pot until garlic is fragrant and light golden brown, about 3 minutes. Turn off Instant Pot, then stir in broth and ¼ teaspoon salt. Arrange cauliflower in pot in even layer. 2. Fold sheet of aluminum foil into 16 by 6-inch sling. Sprinkle flesh side of salmon with ras el hanout and remaining ½ teaspoon salt, then arrange skinned side down in center of sling. Using sling, lower salmon into Instant Pot on top of cauliflower; allow narrow edges of sling to rest along sides of insert. Lock lid in place and close pressure release valve. Select high pressure cook function and cook for 2 minutes. 3. Turn off Instant Pot and quick-release pressure. Carefully remove lid, allowing steam to escape away from you. Using sling, transfer salmon to large plate. Tent with foil and let rest while finishing cauliflower. 4. Using potato masher, mash cauliflower mixture until no large chunks remain. Using highest sauté function, cook cauliflower, stirring often, until slightly thickened, about 3 minutes. Stir in lemon zest and season with salt and pepper to taste. Serve salmon with cauliflower, sprinkling individual portions with scallions and sesame seeds.

Dill Salmon Cakes

Prep time: 15 minutes | Cook time: 10 minutes | Serves 4

- 1 pound (454 g) salmon fillet, chopped
- 1 tablespoon chopped dill
- 2 eggs, beaten
- ½ cup almond flour
- 1 tablespoon coconut oil

1. Put the chopped salmon, dill, eggs, and almond flour in the food processor. 2. Blend the mixture until it is smooth. 3. Then make the small balls (cakes) from the salmon mixture. 4. After this, heat up the coconut oil on Sauté mode for 3 minutes. 5. Put the salmon cakes in the instant pot in one layer and cook them on Sauté mode for 2 minutes from each side or until they are light brown.

Tuna Stuffed Poblano Peppers

Prep time: 15 minutes | Cook time: 12 minutes | Serves 4

- 7 ounces (198 g) canned tuna, shredded
- 1 teaspoon cream cheese
- ¼ teaspoon minced garlic
- 2 ounces (57 g) Provolone cheese, grated
- 4 poblano pepper
- 1 cup water, for cooking

1. Remove the seeds from poblano peppers. 2. In the mixing bowl, mix up shredded tuna, cream cheese, minced garlic, and grated cheese. 3. Then fill the peppers with tuna mixture and put it in the baking pan. 4. Pour water and insert the baking pan in the instant pot. 5. Cook the meal on Manual mode (High Pressure) for 12 minutes. Then make a quick pressure release.

Ginger Cod

Prep time: 10 minutes | Cook time: 20 minutes | Serves 2

- 1 teaspoon ginger paste
- 8 ounces (227 g) cod fillet, chopped
- 1 tablespoon coconut oil
- ¼ cup coconut milk

1. Melt the coconut oil in the instant pot on Sauté mode. 2. Then add ginger paste and coconut milk and bring the mixture to boil. 3. Add chopped cod and sauté the meal for 12 minutes. Stir the fish cubes with the help of the spatula from time to time.

Tuna Spinach Cakes

Prep time: 15 minutes | Cook time: 8 minutes | Serves 4

- 10 ounces (283 g) tuna, shredded
- 1 cup spinach
- 1 egg, beaten
- 1 teaspoon ground coriander
- 2 tablespoon coconut flakes
- 1 tablespoon avocado oil

1. Blend the spinach in the blender until smooth. 2. Then transfer it in the mixing bowl and add tuna, egg, and ground coriander. 3. Add coconut flakes and stir the mass with the help of the spoon. 4. Heat up avocado oil in the instant pot on Sauté mode for 2 minutes. 5. Then make the medium size cakes from the tuna mixture and place them in the hot oil. 6. Cook the tuna cakes on Sauté mode for 3 minutes. Then flip the on another side and cook for 3 minutes more or until they are light brown.

Braised Striped Bass with Zucchini and Tomatoes

Prep time: 20 minutes | Cook time: 16 minutes | Serves 4

- 2 tablespoons extra-virgin olive oil, divided, plus extra for drizzling
- 3 zucchini (8 ounces / 227 g each), halved lengthwise and sliced ¼ inch thick
- 1 onion, chopped
- ¾ teaspoon table salt, divided
- 3 garlic cloves, minced
- 1 teaspoon minced fresh oregano or ¼ teaspoon dried
- ¼ teaspoon red pepper
- flakes
- 1 (28-ounce / 794-g) can whole peeled tomatoes, drained with juice reserved, halved
- 1½ pounds (680 g) skinless striped bass, 1½ inches thick, cut into 2-inch pieces
- ¼ teaspoon pepper
- 2 tablespoons chopped pitted kalamata olives
- 2 tablespoons shredded fresh mint

1. Using highest sauté function, heat 1 tablespoon oil in Instant Pot for 5 minutes (or until just smoking). Add zucchini and cook until tender, about 5 minutes; transfer to bowl and set aside. 2. Add remaining 1 tablespoon oil, onion, and ¼ teaspoon salt to now-empty pot and cook, using highest sauté function, until onion is softened, about 5 minutes. Stir in garlic, oregano, and pepper flakes and cook until fragrant, about 30 seconds. Stir in tomatoes and reserved juice. 3. Sprinkle bass with remaining ½ teaspoon salt and pepper. Nestle bass into tomato mixture and spoon some of cooking liquid on top of pieces. Lock lid in place and close pressure release valve. Select high pressure cook function and set cook time for 0 minutes. Once Instant Pot has reached pressure, immediately turn off pot and quick-release pressure. Carefully remove lid, allowing steam to escape away from you. 4. Transfer bass to plate, tent with aluminum foil, and let rest while finishing vegetables. Stir zucchini into pot and let sit until heated through, about 5 minutes. Stir in olives and season with salt and pepper to taste. Serve bass with vegetables, sprinkling individual portions with mint and drizzling with extra oil.

Salmon Steaks with Garlicky Yogurt

Prep time: 2 minutes | Cook time: 4 minutes | Serves 4

- 1 cup water
- 2 tablespoons olive oil
- 4 salmon steaks

Garlicky Yogurt:
- 1 (8-ounce / 227-g) container full-fat Greek yogurt
- Coarse sea salt and ground black pepper, to taste
- 2 cloves garlic, minced
- 2 tablespoons mayonnaise
- ⅓ teaspoon Dijon mustard

1. Pour the water into the Instant Pot and insert a trivet. 2. Rub the olive oil into the fish and sprinkle with the salt and black pepper on all sides. Put the fish on the trivet. 3. Lock the lid. Select the Manual mode and set the cooking time for 4 minutes at High Pressure. 4. When the timer beeps, perform a quick pressure release. Carefully remove the lid. 5. Meanwhile, stir together all the ingredients for the garlicky yogurt in a bowl. 6. Serve the salmon steaks alongside the garlicky yogurt.

Cayenne Cod

Prep time: 10 minutes | Cook time: 10 minutes | Serves 2

- 2 cod fillets
- ¼ teaspoon chili powder
- ½ teaspoon cayenne pepper
- ½ teaspoon dried oregano
- 1 tablespoon lime juice
- 2 tablespoons avocado oil

1. Rub the cod fillets with chili powder, cayenne pepper, dried oregano, and sprinkle with lime juice. 2. Then pour the avocado oil in the instant pot and heat it up on Sauté mode for 2 minutes. 3. Put the cod fillets in the hot oil and cook for 5 minutes. 4. Then flip the fish on another side and cook for 5 minutes more.

Steamed Halibut with Lemon

Prep time: 10 minutes | Cook time: 9 minutes | Serves 3

- 3 halibut fillet
- ½ lemon, sliced
- ½ teaspoon white pepper
- ½ teaspoon ground
- coriander
- 1 tablespoon avocado oil
- 1 cup water, for cooking

1. Pour water and insert the steamer rack in the instant pot. 2. Rub the fish fillets with white pepper, ground coriander, and avocado oil. 3. Place the fillets in the steamer rack. 4. Then top the halibut with sliced lemon. Close and seal the lid. 5. Cook the meal on High Pressure for 9 minutes. Make a quick pressure release.

Foil-Pack Haddock with Spinach

Prep time: 15 minutes | Cook time: 15 minutes | Serves 4

- 12 ounces (340 g) haddock fillet
- 1 cup spinach
- 1 tablespoon avocado oil
- 1 teaspoon minced garlic
- ½ teaspoon ground coriander
- 1 cup water, for cooking

1. Blend the spinach until smooth and mix up with avocado oil, ground coriander, and minced garlic. 2. Then cut the haddock into 4 fillets and place on the foil. 3. Top the fish fillets with spinach mixture and place them on the rack. 4. Pour water and insert the rack in the instant pot. 5. Close and seal the lid and cook the haddock on Manual (High Pressure) for 15 minutes. 6. Do a quick pressure release.

Mackerel and Broccoli Casserole

Prep time: 15 minutes | Cook time: 15 minutes | Serves 5

- 1 cup shredded broccoli
- 10 ounces (283 g) mackerel, chopped
- ½ cup shredded Cheddar
- cheese
- 1 cup coconut milk
- 1 teaspoon ground cumin
- 1 teaspoon salt

1. Sprinkle the chopped mackerel with ground cumin and salt and transfer in the instant pot. 2. Top the fish with shredded broccoli and Cheddar cheese, 3. Then add coconut milk. Close and seal the lid. 4. Cook the casserole on Manual mode (High Pressure) for 15 minutes. 5. Allow the natural pressure release for 10 minutes and open the lid.

Greek Shrimp with Tomatoes and Feta

Prep time: 10 minutes | Cook time: 2 minutes | Serves 6

- 3 tablespoons unsalted butter
- 1 tablespoon garlic
- ½ teaspoon red pepper flakes, or more as needed
- 1½ cups chopped onion
- 1 (14½-ounce / 411-g) can diced tomatoes, undrained
- 1 teaspoon dried oregano
- 1 teaspoon salt
- 1 pound (454 g) frozen shrimp, peeled
- 1 cup crumbled feta cheese
- ½ cup sliced black olives
- ¼ cup chopped parsley

1. Preheat the Instant Pot by selecting Sauté and adjusting to high heat. When the inner cooking pot is hot, add the butter and heat until it foams. Add the garlic and red pepper flakes, and cook just until fragrant, about 1 minute. 2. Add the onion, tomatoes, oregano, and salt, and stir to combine. 3. Add the frozen shrimp. 4. Lock the lid into place. Select Manual and adjust the pressure to Low. Cook for 1 minute. When the cooking is complete, quick-release the pressure. Unlock the lid. 5. Mix the shrimp in with the lovely tomato broth. 6. Allow the mixture to cool slightly. Right before serving, sprinkle with the feta cheese, olives, and parsley. This dish makes a soupy broth, so it's great over mashed cauliflower.

Fish Bake with Veggies

Prep time: 10 minutes | Cook time: 5 minutes | Serves 4

- 1½ cups water
- Cooking spray
- 2 ripe tomatoes, sliced
- 2 cloves garlic, minced
- 1 teaspoon dried oregano
- 1 teaspoon dried basil
- ½ teaspoon dried rosemary
- 1 red onion, sliced
- 1 head cauliflower, cut into
- florets
- 1 pound (454 g) tilapia fillets, sliced
- Sea salt, to taste
- 1 tablespoon olive oil
- 1 cup crumbled feta cheese
- ⅓ cup Kalamata olives, pitted and halved

1. Pour the water into your Instant Pot and insert a trivet. 2. Spritz a casserole dish with cooking spray. Add the tomato slices to the dish. Scatter the top with the garlic, oregano, basil, and rosemary. 3. Mix in the onion and cauliflower. Arrange the fish fillets on top. Sprinkle with the salt and drizzle with the olive oil. 4. Place the feta cheese and Kalamata olives on top. Lower the dish onto the trivet. 5. Lock the lid. Select the Manual mode and set the cooking time for 5 minutes at High Pressure. 6. When the timer beeps, perform a quick pressure release. Carefully remove the lid. 7. Allow to cool for 5 minutes before serving.

Salmon Fillets and Bok Choy

Prep time: 5 minutes | Cook time: 8 minutes | Serves 4

- 1½ cups water
- 2 tablespoons unsalted butter
- 4 (1-inch thick) salmon fillets
- ½ teaspoon cayenne pepper
- Sea salt and freshly ground
- pepper, to taste
- 2 cups Bok choy, sliced
- 1 cup chicken broth
- 3 cloves garlic, minced
- 1 teaspoon grated lemon zest
- ½ teaspoon dried dill weed

1. Pour the water into your Instant Pot and insert a trivet. 2. Brush the salmon with the melted butter and season with the cayenne pepper, salt, and black pepper on all sides. 3. Lock the lid. Select the Manual mode and set the cooking time for 3 minutes at Low Pressure. 4. When the timer beeps, perform a quick pressure release. Carefully remove the lid. 5. Add the remaining ingredients. 6. Lock the lid. Select the Manual mode and set the cooking time for 5 minutes at High Pressure. 7. When the timer beeps, perform a quick pressure release. Carefully remove the lid. 8. Serve the poached salmon with the veggies on the side.

Almond Milk Curried Fish

Prep time: 10 minutes | Cook time: 3 minutes | Serves 2

- 8 ounces (227 g) cod fillet, chopped
- 1 teaspoon curry paste
- 1 cup organic almond milk

1. Mix up curry paste and almond milk and pour the liquid in the instant pot. 2. Add chopped cod fillet and close the lid. 3. Cook the fish curry on Manual mode (High Pressure) for 3 minutes. 4. Then make the quick pressure release for 5 minutes.

Lemon Pepper Tilapia with Broccoli and Carrots

Prep time: 0 minutes | Cook time: 15 minutes | Serves 4

- 1 pound tilapia fillets
- 1 teaspoon lemon pepper seasoning
- ¼ teaspoon fine sea salt
- 2 tablespoons extra-virgin olive oil
- 2 garlic cloves, minced
- 1 small yellow onion, sliced
- ½ cup low-sodium vegetable broth
- 2 tablespoons fresh lemon juice
- 1 pound broccoli crowns, cut into bite-size florets
- 8 ounces carrots, cut into ¼-inch thick rounds

1. Sprinkle the tilapia fillets all over with the lemon pepper seasoning and salt. 2. Select the Sauté setting on the Instant Pot and heat the oil and garlic for 2 minutes, until the garlic is bubbling but not browned. Add the onion and sauté for about 3 minutes more, until it begins to soften. 3. Pour in the broth and lemon juice, then use a wooden spoon to nudge any browned bits from the bottom of the pot. Using tongs, add the fish fillets to the pot in a single layer; it's fine if they overlap slightly. Place the broccoli and carrots on top. 4. Secure the lid and set the Pressure Release to Sealing. Press the Cancel button to reset the cooking program, then select the Pressure Cook or Manual setting and set the cooking time for 1 minute at low pressure. (The pot will take about 10 minutes to come up to pressure before the cooking program begins.) 5. When the cooking program ends, let the pressure release naturally for 10 minutes (don't open the pot before the 10 minutes are up, even if the float valve has gone down), then move the Pressure Release to Venting to release any remaining steam. Open the pot. Use a fish spatula to transfer the vegetables and fillets to plates. Serve right away.

Perch Fillets with Red Curry

Prep time: 5 minutes | Cook time: 6 minutes | Serves 4

- 1 cup water
- 2 sprigs rosemary
- 1 large-sized lemon, sliced
- 1 pound (454 g) perch fillets
- 1 teaspoon cayenne pepper
- Sea salt and ground black pepper, to taste
- 1 tablespoon red curry paste
- 1 tablespoons butter

1. Add the water, rosemary, and lemon slices to the Instant Pot and insert a trivet. 2. Season the perch fillets with the cayenne pepper, salt, and black pepper. Spread the red curry paste and butter over the fillets. 3. Arrange the fish fillets on the trivet. 4. Lock the lid. Select the Manual mode and set the cooking time for 6 minutes at Low Pressure. 5. When the timer beeps, perform a quick pressure release. Carefully remove the lid. Serve with your favorite keto sides.

Shrimp Zoodle Alfredo

Prep time: 10 minutes | Cook time: 10 minutes | Serves 4

- 10 ounces (283 g) salmon fillet (2 fillets)
- 4 ounces (113 g) Mozzarella, sliced
- 4 cherry tomatoes, sliced
- 1 teaspoon erythritol
- 1 teaspoon dried basil
- ½ teaspoon ground black pepper
- 1 tablespoon apple cider vinegar
- 1 tablespoon butter
- 1 cup water, for cooking

1. Melt the butter on Sauté mode and add shrimp. 2. Sprinkle them with seafood seasoning and sauté then for 2 minutes. 3. After this, spiralizer the zucchini with the help of the spiralizer and add in the shrimp. 4. Add coconut cream and close the lid. Cook the meal on Sauté mode for 8 minutes.

Caprese Salmon

Prep time: 10 minutes | Cook time: 15 minutes | Serves 2

- 10 ounces (283 g) salmon fillet (2 fillets)
- 4 ounces (113 g) Mozzarella, sliced
- 4 cherry tomatoes, sliced
- 1 teaspoon erythritol
- 1 teaspoon dried basil
- ½ teaspoon ground black pepper
- 1 tablespoon apple cider vinegar
- 1 tablespoon butter
- 1 cup water, for cooking

1. Grease the mold with butter and put the salmon inside. 2. Sprinkle the fish with erythritol, dried basil, ground black pepper, and apple cider vinegar. 3. Then top the salmon with tomatoes and Mozzarella. 4. Pour water and insert the steamer rack in the instant pot. 5. Put the fish on the rack. 6. Close and seal the lid. 7. Cook the meal on Manual mode at High Pressure for 15 minutes. Make a quick pressure release.

Louisiana Shrimp Gumbo

Prep time: 10 minutes | Cook time: 4 minutes | Serves 6

- 1 pound (454 g) shrimp
- ¼ cup chopped celery stalk
- 1 chili pepper, chopped
- ¼ cup chopped okra
- 1 tablespoon coconut oil
- 2 cups chicken broth
- 1 teaspoon sugar-free tomato paste

1. Put all ingredients in the instant pot and stir until you get a light red color. 2. Then close and seal the lid. 3. Cook the meal on Manual mode (High Pressure) for 4 minutes. 4. When the time is finished, allow the natural pressure release for 10 minutes.

Foil-Packet Salmon

Prep time: 2 minutes | Cook time: 7 minutes | Serves 2

- 2 (3-ounce / 85-g) salmon fillets
- ¼ teaspoon garlic powder
- 1 teaspoon salt
- ¼ teaspoon pepper
- ¼ teaspoon dried dill
- ½ lemon
- 1 cup water

1. Place each filet of salmon on a square of foil, skin-side down. 2. Season with garlic powder, salt, and pepper and squeeze the lemon juice over the fish. 3. Cut the lemon into four slices and place two on each filet. Close the foil packets by folding over edges. 4. Add the water to the Instant Pot and insert a trivet. Place the foil packets on the trivet. 5. Secure the lid. Select the Steam mode and set the cooking time for 7 minutes at Low Pressure. 6. Once cooking is complete, do a quick pressure release. Carefully open the lid. 7. Check the internal temperature with a meat thermometer to ensure the thickest part of the filets reached at least 145ºF (63ºC). Salmon should easily flake when fully cooked. Serve immediately.

Halibut Stew with Bacon and Cheese

Prep time: 10 minutes | Cook time: 10 minutes | Serves 4

- 1½ cups water
- Cooking spray
- 4 slices bacon, chopped
- 1 celery, chopped
- ½ cup chopped shallots
- 1 teaspoon garlic, smashed
- 1 pound (454 g) halibut
- 2 cups fish stock
- 1 tablespoon coconut oil, softened
- ¼ teaspoon ground allspice
- Sea salt and crushed black peppercorns, to taste
- 1 cup Cottage cheese, at room temperature
- 1 cup heavy cream

1. Set the Instant Pot to Sauté. Cook the bacon until crispy. 2. Add the celery, shallots, and garlic and sauté for another 2 minutes, or until the vegetables are just tender. 3. Mix in the halibut, stock, coconut oil, allspice, salt, and black peppercorns. Stir well. 4. Lock the lid. Select the Manual mode and set the cooking time for 7 minutes at Low Pressure. 5. When the timer beeps, perform a natural pressure release for 10 minutes, then release any remaining pressure. Carefully remove the lid. 6. Stir in the cheese and heavy cream. Select the Sauté mode again and let it simmer for a few minutes until heated through. Serve immediately.

Aromatic Monkfish Stew

Prep time: 5 minutes | Cook time: 6 minutes | Serves 6

- Juice of 1 lemon
- 1 tablespoon fresh basil
- 1 tablespoon fresh parsley
- 1 tablespoon olive oil
- 1 teaspoon garlic, minced
- 1½ pounds (680 g) monkfish
- 1 tablespoon butter
- 1 bell pepper, chopped
- 1 onion, sliced
- ½ teaspoon cayenne pepper
- ½ teaspoon mixed
- peppercorns
- ¼ teaspoon turmeric powder
- ¼ teaspoon ground cumin
- Sea salt and ground black pepper, to taste
- 2 cups fish stock
- ½ cup water
- ¼ cup dry white wine
- 2 bay leaves
- 1 ripe tomato, crushed

1. Stir together the lemon juice, basil, parsley, olive oil, and garlic in a ceramic dish. Add the monkfish and marinate for 30 minutes. 2. Set your Instant Pot to Sauté. Add and melt the butter. Once hot, cook the bell pepper and onion until fragrant. 3. Stir in the remaining ingredients. 4. Lock the lid. Select the Manual mode and set the cooking time for 6 minutes at High Pressure. 5. When the timer beeps, perform a quick pressure release. Carefully remove the lid. 6. Discard the bay leaves and divide your stew into serving bowls. Serve hot.

Tilapia Fillets with Arugula

Prep time: 5 minutes | Cook time: 4 minutes | Serves 4

- 1 lemon, juiced
- 1 cup water
- 1 pound (454 g) tilapia fillets
- ½ teaspoon cayenne pepper, or more to taste
- 2 teaspoons butter, melted
- Sea salt and ground black pepper, to taste
- ½ teaspoon dried basil
- 2 cups arugula

1. Pour the fresh lemon juice and water into your Instant Pot and insert a steamer basket. 2. Brush the fish fillets with the melted butter. 3. Sprinkle with the cayenne pepper, salt, and black pepper. Place the tilapia fillets in the basket. Sprinkle the dried basil on top. 4. Lock the lid. Select the Manual mode and set the cooking time for 4 minutes at Low Pressure. 5. When the timer beeps, perform a quick pressure release. Carefully remove the lid. 6. Serve with the fresh arugula.

Asian Cod with Brown Rice, Asparagus, and Mushrooms

Prep time: 5 minutes | Cook time: 25 minutes | Serves 2

- ¾ cup Minute brand brown rice
- ½ cup water
- Two 5-ounce skinless cod fillets
- 1 tablespoon soy sauce or tamari
- 1 tablespoon fresh lemon juice
- ½ teaspoon peeled and grated fresh ginger
- 1 tablespoon extra-virgin olive oil or 1 tablespoon
- unsalted butter, cut into 8 pieces
- 2 green onions, white and green parts, thinly sliced
- 12 ounces asparagus, trimmed
- 4 ounces shiitake mushrooms, stems removed and sliced
- ⅛ teaspoon fine sea salt
- ⅛ teaspoon freshly ground black pepper
- Lemon wedges for serving

1. Pour 1 cup water into the Instant Pot. Have ready two-tier stackable stainless-steel containers. 2. In one of the containers, combine the rice and ½ cup water, then gently shake the container to spread the rice into an even layer, making sure all of the grains are submerged. Place the fish fillets on top of the rice. In a small bowl, stir together the soy sauce, lemon juice, and ginger. Pour the soy sauce mixture over the fillets. Drizzle 1 teaspoon olive oil on each fillet (or top with two pieces of the butter), and sprinkle the green onions on and around the fish. 3. In the second container, arrange the asparagus in the center in as even a layer as possible. Place the mushrooms on either side of the asparagus. Drizzle with the remaining 2 teaspoons olive oil (or put the remaining six pieces butter on top of the asparagus, spacing them evenly). Sprinkle the salt and pepper evenly over the vegetables. 4. Place the container

with the rice and fish on the bottom and the vegetable container on top. Cover the top container with its lid and then latch the containers together. Grasping the handle, lower the containers into the Instant Pot. 5. Secure the lid and set the Pressure Release to Sealing. Select the Pressure Cook or Manual setting and set the cooking time for 15 minutes at high pressure. (The pot will take about 10 minutes to come up to pressure before the cooking program begins.) 6. When the cooking program ends, let the pressure release naturally for 5 minutes, then move the Pressure Release to Venting to release any remaining steam. Open the pot and, wearing heat-resistant mitts, lift out the stacked containers. Unlatch, unstack, and open the containers, taking care not to get burned by the steam. 7. Transfer the vegetables, rice, and fish to plates and serve right away, with the lemon wedges on the side.

Rosemary Baked Haddock

Prep time: 7 minutes | Cook time: 10 minutes | Serves 2

- 2 eggs, beaten
- 12 ounces (340 g) haddock fillet, chopped
- 1 tablespoon cream cheese
- ¾ teaspoon dried rosemary
- 2 ounces (57 g) Parmesan, grated
- 1 teaspoon butter

1. Whisk the beaten eggs until homogenous. Add the cream cheese, dried rosemary, and dill. 2. Grease the springform with the butter and place the haddock inside. 3. Pour the egg mixture over the fish and add sprinkle with Parmesan. 4. Set the Manual mode (High Pressure) and cook for 5 minutes. Then make a natural release pressure for 5 minutes.

Haddock and Veggie Foil Packets

Prep time: 5 minutes | Cook time: 10 minutes | Serves 4

- 1½ cups water
- 1 lemon, sliced
- 2 bell peppers, sliced
- 1 brown onion, sliced into rings
- 4 sprigs parsley
- 2 sprigs thyme
- 2 sprigs rosemary
- 4 haddock fillets
- Sea salt, to taste
- ⅓ teaspoon ground black pepper, or more to taste
- 2 tablespoons extra-virgin olive oil

1. Pour the water and lemon into your Instant Pot and insert a steamer basket. 2. Assemble the packets with large sheets of heavy-duty foil. 3. Place the peppers, onion rings, parsley, thyme, and rosemary in the center of each foil. Place the fish fillets on top of the veggies. 4. Sprinkle with the salt and black pepper and drizzle the olive oil over the fillets. Place the packets in the steamer basket. 5. Lock the lid. Select the Manual mode and set the cooking time for 10 minutes at Low Pressure. 6. When the timer beeps, perform a quick pressure release. Carefully remove the lid. 7. Serve warm.

Rainbow Trout with Mixed Greens

Prep time: 5 minutes | Cook time: 12 minutes | Serves 4

- 1 cup water
- 1½ (680 g) pounds rainbow trout fillets
- 4 tablespoons melted butter, divided
- Sea salt and ground black pepper, to taste
- 1 pound (454 g) mixed

- greens, trimmed and torn into pieces
- 1 bunch of scallions
- ½ cup chicken broth
- 1 tablespoon apple cider vinegar
- 1 teaspoon cayenne pepper

1. Pour the water into your Instant Pot and insert a steamer basket. 2. Add the fish to the basket. Drizzle with 1 tablespoon of the melted butter and season with the salt and black pepper. 3. Lock the lid. Select the Manual mode and set the cooking time for 12 minutes at Low pressure. 4. When the timer beeps, perform a quick pressure release. Carefully remove the lid. 5. Wipe down the Instant Pot with a damp cloth. 6. Add and warm the remaining 3 tablespoons of butter. Once hot, add the greens, scallions, broth, vinegar, and cayenne pepper and cook until the greens are wilted, stirring occasionally. 7. Serve the prepared trout fillets with the greens on the side.

Mediterranean Salmon with Whole-Wheat Couscous

Prep time: 5 minutes | Cook time: 30 minutes | Serves 4

Couscous
- 1 cup whole-wheat couscous
- 1 cup water
- 1 tablespoon extra-virgin olive oil
- 1 teaspoon dried basil
- ¼ teaspoon fine sea salt
Salmon
- 1 pound skinless salmon fillet
- 2 teaspoons extra-virgin olive oil
- 1 tablespoon fresh lemon juice
- 1 garlic clove, minced

- 1 pint cherry or grape tomatoes, halved
- 8 ounces zucchini, halved lengthwise, then sliced crosswise ¼ inch thick

- ¼ teaspoon dried oregano
- ¼ teaspoon fine sea salt
- ¼ teaspoon freshly ground black pepper
- 1 tablespoon capers, drained
- Lemon wedges for serving

1. Pour 1 cup water into the Instant Pot. Have ready two-tier stackable stainless-steel containers. 2. To make the couscous: In one of the containers, stir together the couscous, water, oil, basil, and salt. Sprinkle the tomatoes and zucchini over the top. 3. To make the salmon: Place the salmon fillet in the second container. In a small bowl, whisk together the oil, lemon juice, garlic, oregano,

salt, pepper, and capers. Spoon the oil mixture over the top of the salmon. 4. Place the container with the couscous and vegetables on the bottom and the salmon container on top. Cover the top container with its lid and then latch the containers together. Grasping the handle, lower the containers into the Instant Pot. 5. Secure the lid and set the Pressure Release to Sealing. Select the Pressure Cook or Manual setting and set the cooking time for 20 minutes at high pressure. (The pot will take about 10 minutes to come up to pressure before the cooking program begins.) 6. When the cooking program ends, let the pressure release naturally for 5 minutes, then move the Pressure Release to Venting to release any remaining steam. Open the pot and, wearing heat-resistant mitts, lift out the stacked containers. Unlatch, unstack, and open the containers, taking care not to get burned by the steam. 7. Using a fork, fluff the couscous and mix in the vegetables. Spoon the couscous onto plates, then use a spatula to cut the salmon into four pieces and place a piece on top of each couscous serving. Serve right away, with lemon wedges on the side.

Lemon Butter Mahi Mahi

Prep time: 10 minutes | Cook time: 9 minutes | Serves 4

- 1 pound (454 g) mahi-mahi fillet
- 1 teaspoon grated lemon zest

- 1 tablespoon lemon juice
- 1 tablespoon butter, softened
- ½ teaspoon salt
- 1 cup water, for cooking

1. Cut the fish on 4 servings and sprinkle with lemon zest, lemon juice, salt, and rub with softened butter. 2. Then put the fish in the baking pan in one layer. 3. Pour water and insert the steamer rack in the instant pot. 4. Put the mold with fish on the rack. Close and seal the lid. 5. Cook the Mahi Mahi on Manual mode (High Pressure) for 9 minutes. Make a quick pressure release.

Poached Salmon

Prep time: 10 minutes | Cook time: 5 minutes | Serves 4

- 1 lemon, sliced ¼ inch thick
- 4 (6-ounce / 170-g) skinless salmon fillets, 1½ inches

- thick
- ½ teaspoon table salt
- ¼ teaspoon pepper

1. Add ½ cup water to Instant Pot. Fold sheet of aluminum foil into 16 by 6-inch sling. Arrange lemon slices widthwise in 2 rows across center of sling. Sprinkle flesh side of salmon with salt and pepper, then arrange skinned side down on top of lemon slices. 2. Using sling, lower salmon into Instant Pot; allow narrow edges of sling to rest along sides of insert. Lock lid in place and close pressure release valve. Select high pressure cook function and cook for 3 minutes. 3. Turn off Instant Pot and quick-release pressure. Carefully remove lid, allowing steam to escape away from you. Using sling, transfer salmon to large plate. Gently lift and tilt fillets with spatula to remove lemon slices. Serve.

Dill Lemon Salmon

Prep time: 10 minutes | Cook time: 4 minutes | Serves 4

- 1 pound (454 g) salmon fillet
- 1 tablespoon butter, melted
- 2 tablespoons lemon juice
- 1 teaspoon dried dill
- 1 cup water

1. Cut the salmon fillet on 4 servings. 2. Line the instant pot baking pan with foil and put the salmon fillets inside in one layer. 3. Then sprinkle the fish with dried dill, lemon juice, and butter. 4. Pour water in the instant pot and insert the rack. 5. Place the baking pan with salmon on the rack and close the lid. 6. Cook the meal on Manual mode (High Pressure) for 4 minutes. Allow the natural pressure release for 5 minutes and remove the fish from the instant pot.

Coconut Shrimp Curry

Prep time: 10 minutes | Cook time: 4 minutes | Serves 5

- 15 ounces (425 g) shrimp, peeled
- 1 teaspoon chili powder
- 1 teaspoon garam masala
- 1 cup coconut milk
- 1 teaspoon olive oil
- ½ teaspoon minced garlic

1. Heat up the instant pot on Sauté mode for 2 minutes. 2. Then add olive oil. Cook the ingredients for 1 minute. 3. Add shrimp and sprinkle them with chili powder, garam masala, minced garlic, and coconut milk. 4. Carefully stir the ingredients and close the lid. 5. Cook the shrimp curry on Manual mode for 1 minute. Make a quick pressure release.

Chunky Fish Soup with Tomatoes

Prep time: 10 minutes | Cook time: 8 minutes | Serves 4

2 teaspoons olive oil
- 1 yellow onion, chopped
- 1 bell pepper, sliced
- 1 celery, diced
- 2 garlic cloves, minced
- 3 cups fish stock
- 2 ripe tomatoes, crushed
- ¾ pound (340 g) haddock

- fillets
- 1 cup shrimp
- 1 tablespoon sweet Hungarian paprika
- 1 teaspoon hot Hungarian paprika
- ½ teaspoon caraway seeds

1. Set the Instant Pot to Sauté. Add and heat the oil. Once hot, add the onions and sauté until soft and fragrant. 2. Add the pepper, celery, and garlic and continue to sauté until soft. 3. Stir in the remaining ingredients. 4. Lock the lid. Select the Manual mode and set the cooking time for 5 minutes at High Pressure. 5. When the timer beeps, perform a quick pressure release. Carefully remove the lid. 6. Divide into serving bowls and serve hot.

Cod Fillet with Olives

Prep time: 15 minutes | Cook time: 10 minutes | Serves 2

- 8 ounces (227 g) cod fillet
- ¼ cup sliced olives
- 1 teaspoon olive oil
- ¼ teaspoon salt
- 1 cup water, for cooking

1. Pour water and insert the steamer rack in the instant pot. 2. Then cut the cod fillet into 2 servings and sprinkle with salt and olive oil. 3. Then place the fish on the foil and top with the sliced olives. Wrap the fish and transfer it in the steamer rack. 4. Close and seal the lid. Cook the fish on Manual mode (High Pressure) for 10 minutes. 5. Allow the natural pressure release for 5 minutes.

Fish Tagine

Prep time: 25 minutes | Cook time: 12 minutes | Serves 4

- 2 tablespoons extra-virgin olive oil, plus extra for drizzling
- 1 large onion, halved and sliced ¼ inch thick
- 1 pound (454 g) carrots, peeled, halved lengthwise, and sliced ¼ inch thick
- 2 (2-inch) strips orange zest, plus 1 teaspoon grated zest
- ¾ teaspoon table salt, divided
- 2 tablespoons tomato paste
- 4 garlic cloves, minced, divided
- 1¼ teaspoons paprika
- 1 teaspoon ground cumin
- ¼ teaspoon red pepper flakes
- ¼ teaspoon saffron threads, crumbled
- 1 (8-ounce / 227-g) bottle clam juice
- 1½ pounds (680 g) skinless halibut fillets, 1½ inches thick, cut into 2-inch pieces
- ¼ cup pitted oil-cured black olives, quartered
- 2 tablespoons chopped fresh parsley
- 1 teaspoon sherry vinegar

1. Using highest sauté function, heat oil in Instant Pot until shimmering. Add onion, carrots, orange zest strips, and ¼ teaspoon salt, and cook until vegetables are softened and lightly browned, 10 to 12 minutes. Stir in tomato paste, three-quarters of garlic, paprika, cumin, pepper flakes, and saffron and cook until fragrant, about 30 seconds. Stir in clam juice, scraping up any browned bits. 2. Sprinkle halibut with remaining ½ teaspoon salt. Nestle halibut into onion mixture and spoon some of cooking liquid on top of pieces. Lock lid in place and close pressure release valve. Select high pressure cook function and set cook time for 0 minutes. Once Instant Pot has reached pressure, immediately turn off pot and quick-release pressure. 3. Discard orange zest. Gently stir in olives, parsley, vinegar, grated orange zest, and remaining garlic. Season with salt and pepper to taste. Drizzle extra oil over individual portions before serving.

Garam Masala Fish

Prep time: 10 minutes | Cook time: 10 minutes | Serves 4

- 2 tablespoons sesame oil
- ½ teaspoon cumin seeds
- ½ cup chopped leeks
- 1 teaspoon ginger-garlic paste
- 1 pound (454 g) cod fillets, boneless and sliced
- 2 ripe tomatoes, chopped
- 1½ tablespoons fresh lemon juice
- ½ teaspoon garam masala
- ½ teaspoon turmeric powder
- 1 tablespoon chopped fresh dill leaves
- 1 tablespoon chopped fresh curry leaves
- 1 tablespoon chopped fresh parsley leaves
- Coarse sea salt, to taste
- ½ teaspoon smoked cayenne pepper
- ¼ teaspoon ground black pepper, or more to taste

1. Set the Instant Pot to Sauté. Add and heat the sesame oil until hot. Sauté the cumin seeds for 30 seconds. 2. Add the leeks and cook for another 2 minutes until translucent. Add the ginger-garlic paste and cook for an additional 40 seconds. 3. Stir in the remaining ingredients. 4. Lock the lid. Select the Manual mode and set the cooking time for 6 minutes at Low Pressure. 5. When the timer beeps, perform a quick pressure release. Carefully remove the lid. 6. Serve immediately.

Fish Packets with Pesto and Cheese

Prep time: 8 minutes | Cook time: 6 minutes | Serves 4

- 1½ cups cold water.
- 4 (4-ounce / 113-g) white fish fillets, such as cod or haddock
- 1 teaspoon fine sea salt
- ½ teaspoon ground black pepper
- 1 (4-ounce / 113-g) jar pesto
- ½ cup shredded Parmesan cheese (about 2 ounces / 57 g)
- Halved cherry tomatoes, for garnish

1. Pour the water into your Instant Pot and insert a steamer basket. 2. Sprinkle the fish on all sides with the salt and pepper. Take four sheets of parchment paper and place a fillet in the center of each sheet. 3. Dollop 2 tablespoons of the pesto on top of each fillet and sprinkle with 2 tablespoons of the Parmesan cheese. 4. Wrap the fish in the parchment by folding in the edges and folding down the top like an envelope to close tightly. 5. Stack the packets in the steamer basket, seam-side down. 6. Lock the lid. Select the Manual mode and set the cooking time for 6 minutes at Low Pressure. 7. Once cooking is complete, do a natural pressure release for 10 minutes, then release any remaining pressure. Carefully open the lid. 8. Remove the fish packets from the pot. Transfer to a serving plate and garnish with the cherry tomatoes. 9. Serve immediately.

Shrimp Louie Salad with Thousand Island Dressing

Prep time: 5 minutes | Cook time: 20 minutes | Serves 4

- 2 cups water
- 1½ teaspoons fine sea salt
- 1 pound medium shrimp, peeled and deveined
- 4 large eggs
- Thousand island Dressing
- ¼ cup no-sugar-added ketchup
- ¼ cup mayonnaise
- 1 tablespoon fresh lemon juice
- 1 teaspoon Worcestershire sauce
- ⅛ teaspoon cayenne pepper
- Freshly ground black pepper
- 2 green onions, white and green parts, sliced thinly
- 2 hearts romaine lettuce or 1 head iceberg lettuce, shredded
- 1 English cucumber, sliced
- 8 radishes, sliced
- 1 cup cherry tomatoes, sliced
- 1 large avocado, pitted, peeled, and sliced

1. Combine the water and salt in the Instant Pot and stir to dissolve the salt. 2. Secure the lid and set the Pressure Release to Sealing. Select the Steam setting and set the cooking time for 0 (zero) minutes at low pressure. (The pot will take about 10 minutes to come up to pressure before the cooking program begins.) 3. Meanwhile, prepare an ice bath. 4. When the cooking program ends, perform a quick release by moving the Pressure Release to Venting. Open the pot and stir in the shrimp, using a wooden spoon to nudge them all down into the water. Cover the pot and leave the shrimp for 2 minutes on the Keep Warm setting. The shrimp will gently poach and cook through. Uncover the pot and, wearing heat-resistant mitts, lift out the inner pot and drain the shrimp in a colander. Transfer them to the ice bath to cool for 5 minutes, then drain them in the colander and set aside in the refrigerator. 5. Rinse out the inner pot and return it to the housing. Pour in 1 cup water and place the wire metal steam rack into the pot. Place the eggs on top of the steam rack. 6. Secure the lid and set the Pressure Release to Sealing. Press the Cancel button to reset the cooking program, then select the Egg, Pressure Cook, or Manual setting and set the cooking time for 5 minutes at high pressure. (The pot will take about 5 minutes to come up to pressure before the cooking program begins.) 7. While the eggs are cooking, prepare another ice bath. 8. When the cooking program ends, let the pressure release naturally for 5 minutes, then move the Pressure Release to Venting to release any remaining steam. Using tongs, transfer the eggs to the ice bath and let cool for 5 minutes. 9. To make the dressing: In a small bowl, stir together the ketchup, mayonnaise, lemon juice, Worcestershire sauce, cayenne, ¼ teaspoon black pepper, and green onions. 10. Arrange the lettuce, cucumber, radishes, tomatoes, and avocado on individual plates or in large, shallow individual bowls. Mound the cooked shrimp in the center of each salad. Peel the eggs, quarter them lengthwise, and place the quarters around the shrimp. 11. Spoon the dressing over the salads and top with additional black pepper. Serve right away.

Chapter
5
Snacks and Appetizers

Chapter 5
Snacks and Appetizers

Thyme Sauté ed Radishes

Prep time: 5 minutes | Cook time: 15 minutes | Serves 4

- 1 pound (454 g) radishes, quartered (remove leaves and ends)
- 2 tablespoons butter
- ¼ teaspoon dried thyme
- ¼ teaspoon minced garlic
- ⅛ teaspoon salt
- ⅛ teaspoon garlic powder
- ⅛ teaspoon dried rosemary

1. Press the Sauté button and then press the Adjust button to lower heat to Less. 2. Place radishes into Instant Pot with butter and seasoning. 3. Sauté, stirring occasionally until tender, about 10 to 15 minutes. Add a couple of teaspoons of water if radishes begin to stick.

Garlic Herb Butter

Prep time: 10 minutes | Cook time: 8 minutes | Serves 4

- ⅓ cup butter
- 1 teaspoon dried parsley
- 1 tablespoon dried dill
- ½ teaspoon minced garlic
- ¼ teaspoon dried thyme

1. Preheat the instant pot on Sauté mode. 2. Then add butter and melt it. 3. Add dried parsley, dill, minced garlic, and thyme. Stir the butter mixture well. 4. Transfer it in the butter mold and refrigerate until it is solid.

Deviled Eggs with Tuna

Prep time: 10 minutes | Cook time: 8 minutes | Serves 3

- 1 cup water
- 6 eggs
- 1 (5 ounces / 142 g) can tuna, drained
- 4 tablespoons mayonnaise
- 1 teaspoon lemon juice
- 1 celery stalk, diced finely
- ¼ teaspoon Dijon mustard
- ¼ teaspoon chopped fresh dill
- ¼ teaspoon salt
- ⅛ teaspoon garlic powder

1. Add water to Instant Pot. Place steam rack or steamer basket inside pot. Carefully put eggs into steamer basket. Click lid closed. Press the Manual button and adjust time for 8 minutes. 2. Add remaining ingredients to medium bowl and mix. 3. When timer beeps, quick-release the steam and remove eggs. Place in bowl of cool water for 10 minutes, then remove shells. 4. Cut eggs in half and remove hard-boiled yolks, setting whites aside. Place yolks in food processor and pulse until smooth, or mash with fork. Add yolks to bowl with tuna and mayo, mixing until smooth. 5. Spoon mixture into egg-white halves. Serve chilled.

Jalapeño Poppers with Bacon

Prep time: 10 minutes | Cook time: 3 minutes | Serves 4

- 6 jalapeños
- 4 ounces (113 g) cream cheese
- ¼ cup shredded sharp
- Cheddar cheese
- 1 cup water
- ¼ cup cooked crumbled bacon

1. Cut jalapeños lengthwise and scoop out seeds and membrane, then set aside. 2. In small bowl, mix cream cheese and Cheddar. Spoon into emptied jalapeños. Pour water into Instant Pot and place steamer basket in bottom. 3. Place stuffed jalapeños on steamer rack. Click lid closed. Press the Manual button and adjust time for 3 minutes. When timer beeps, quick-release the pressure. Serve topped with crumbled bacon.

Rosemary Chicken Wings

Prep time: 10 minutes | Cook time: 16 minutes | Serves 4

- 4 boneless chicken wings
- 1 tablespoon olive oil
- 1 teaspoon dried rosemary
- ½ teaspoon garlic powder
- ¼ teaspoon salt

1. In the mixing bowl, mix up olive oil, dried rosemary, garlic powder, and salt. 2. Then rub the chicken wings with the rosemary mixture and leave for 10 minutes to marinate. 3. After this, put the chicken wings in the instant pot, add the remaining rosemary marinade and cook them on Sauté mode for 8 minutes from each side.

Cheese Stuffed Bell Peppers

Prep time: 10 minutes | Cook time: 5 minutes | Serves 5

- 1 cup water
- 10 baby bell peppers, seeded and sliced lengthwise
- 4 ounces (113 g) Monterey Jack cheese, shredded
- 4 ounces (113 g) cream cheese
- 2 tablespoons chopped scallions
- 1 tablespoon olive oil
- 1 teaspoon minced garlic
- ½ teaspoon cayenne pepper
- ¼ teaspoon ground black pepper, or more to taste

1. Pour the water into the Instant Pot and insert a steamer basket. 2. Stir together the remaining ingredients except the bell peppers in a mixing bowl until combined. Stuff the peppers evenly with the mixture. Arrange the stuffed peppers in the basket. 3. Lock the lid. Select the Manual mode and set the cooking time for 5 minutes at High Pressure. 4. When the timer beeps, perform a quick pressure release. Carefully remove the lid. 5. Cool for 5 minutes and serve.

Ground Turkey Lettuce Cups

Prep time: 5 minutes | Cook time: 30 minutes | Serves 8

- 3 tablespoons water
- 2 tablespoons soy sauce, tamari, or coconut aminos
- 3 tablespoons fresh lime juice
- 2 teaspoons Sriracha, plus more for serving
- 2 tablespoons cold-pressed avocado oil
- 2 teaspoons toasted sesame oil
- 4 garlic cloves, minced
- 1-inch piece fresh ginger, peeled and minced
- 2 carrots, diced
- 2 celery stalks, diced
- 1 yellow onion, diced
- 2 pounds 93 percent lean ground turkey
- ½ teaspoon fine sea salt
- Two 8-ounce cans sliced water chestnuts, drained and chopped
- 1 tablespoon cornstarch
- 2 hearts romaine lettuce or 2 heads butter lettuce, leaves separated
- ½ cup roasted cashews (whole or halves and pieces), chopped
- 1 cup loosely packed fresh cilantro leaves

1. In a small bowl, combine the water, soy sauce, 2 tablespoons of the lime juice, and the Sriracha and mix well. Set aside. 2. Select the Sauté setting on the Instant Pot and heat the avocado oil, sesame oil, garlic, and ginger for 2 minutes, until the garlic is bubbling but not browned. Add the carrots, celery, and onion and sauté for about 3 minutes, until the onion begins to soften. 3. Add the turkey and salt and sauté, using a wooden spoon or spatula to break up the meat as it cooks, for about 5 minutes, until cooked through and no streaks of pink remain. Add the water chestnuts and soy sauce mixture and stir to combine, working quickly so not too much steam escapes. 4. Secure the lid and set the Pressure Release to Sealing. Press the Cancel button to reset the cooking program,

then select the Pressure Cook or Manual setting and set the cooking time for 5 minutes at high pressure. (The pot will take about 10 minutes to come up to pressure before the cooking program begins.) 5. When the cooking program ends, perform a quick pressure release by moving the Pressure Release to Venting, or let the pressure release naturally. Open the pot. 6. In a small bowl, stir together the remaining 1 tablespoon lime juice and the cornstarch, add the mixture to the pot, and stir to combine. Press the Cancel button to reset the cooking program, then select the Sauté setting. Let the mixture come to a boil and thicken, stirring often, for about 2 minutes, then press the Cancel button to turn off the pot. 7. Spoon the turkey mixture onto the lettuce leaves and sprinkle the cashews and cilantro on top. Serve right away, with additional Sriracha at the table.

Herbed Mushrooms

Prep time: 5 minutes | Cook time: 10 minutes | Serves 4

- 2 tablespoons butter
- 2 cloves garlic, minced
- 20 ounces (567 g) button mushrooms
- 1 tablespoon coconut aminos
- 1 teaspoon dried rosemary
- 1 teaspoon dried basil
- 1 teaspoon dried sage
- 1 bay leaf
- Sea salt, to taste
- ½ teaspoon freshly ground black pepper
- ½ cup chicken broth
- ½ cup water
- 1 tablespoon roughly chopped fresh parsley leaves, for garnish

1. Set your Instant Pot to Sauté and melt the butter. 2. Add the garlic and mushrooms and sauté for 3 to 4 minutes until the garlic is fragrant. 3. Add the remaining ingredients except the parsley to the Instant Pot and stir well. 4. Lock the lid. Select the Manual mode and set the cooking time for 5 minutes at High Pressure. 5. When the timer beeps, perform a quick pressure release. Carefully open the lid. 6. Remove the mushrooms from the pot to a platter. Serve garnished with the fresh parsley leaves.

Lemon Artichokes

Prep time: 5 minutes | Cook time: 5 to 15 minutes | Serves 4

- 4 artichokes
- 1 cup water
- 2 tablespoons lemon juice
- 1 teaspoon salt

1. Wash and trim artichokes by cutting off the stems flush with the bottoms of the artichokes and by cutting ¾–1 inch off the tops. Stand upright in the bottom of the inner pot of the Instant Pot. 2. Pour water, lemon juice, and salt over artichokes. 3. Secure the lid and make sure the vent is set to sealing. On Manual, set the Instant Pot for 15 minutes for large artichokes, 10 minutes for medium artichokes, or 5 minutes for small artichokes. 4. When cook time is up, perform a quick release by releasing the pressure manually.

Creamy Spinach

Prep time: 5 minutes | Cook time: 4 minutes | Serves 4

- 2 cups chopped spinach
- 2 ounces (57 g) Monterey Jack cheese, shredded
- 1 cup almond milk
- 1 tablespoon butter
- 1 teaspoon minced garlic
- ½ teaspoon salt

1. Combine all the ingredients in the Instant Pot. 2. Secure the lid. Select the Manual mode and set the cooking time for 4 minutes at High Pressure. 3. Once cooking is complete, do a quick pressure release. Carefully open the lid. 4. Give the mixture a good stir and serve warm.

Creamed Onion Spinach

Prep time: 3 minutes | Cook time: 5 minutes | Serves 6

- 4 tablespoons butter
- ¼ cup diced onion
- 8 ounces (227 g) cream cheese
- 1 (12 ounces / 340 g) bag
- frozen spinach
- ½ cup chicken broth
- 1 cup shredded whole-milk Mozzarella cheese

1. Press the Sauté button and add butter. Once butter is melted, add onion to Instant Pot and sauté for 2 minutes or until onion begins to turn translucent. 2. Break cream cheese into pieces and add to Instant Pot. Press the Cancel button. Add frozen spinach and broth. Click lid closed. Press the Manual button and adjust time for 5 minutes. When timer beeps, quick-release the pressure and stir in shredded Mozzarella. If mixture is too watery, press the Sauté button and reduce for additional 5 minutes, stirring constantly.

Hummus with Chickpeas and Tahini Sauce

Prep time: 10 minutes | Cook time: 55 minutes | Makes 4 cups

- 4 cups water
- 1 cup dried chickpeas
- 2½ teaspoons fine sea salt
- ½ cup tahini
- 3 tablespoons fresh lemon juice
- 1 garlic clove
- ¼ teaspoon ground cumin

1. Combine the water, chickpeas, and 1 teaspoon of the salt in the Instant Pot and stir to dissolve the salt. 2. Secure the lid and set the Pressure Release to Sealing. Select the Bean/Chili, Pressure Cook, or Manual setting and set the cooking time for 40 minutes at high pressure. (The pot will take about 15 minutes to come up to pressure before the cooking program begins.) 3. When the cooking program ends, let the pressure release naturally for 15 minutes, then move the Pressure Release to Venting to release any remaining

steam. 4. Place a colander over a bowl. Open the pot and, wearing heat-resistant mitts, lift out the inner pot and drain the beans in the colander. Return the chickpeas to the inner pot and place it back in the Instant Pot housing on the Keep Warm setting. Reserve the cooking liquid. 5. In a blender or food processor, combine 1 cup of the cooking liquid, the tahini, lemon juice, garlic, cumin, and 1 teaspoon salt. Blend or process on high speed, stopping to scrape down the sides of the container as needed, for about 30 seconds, until smooth and a little fluffy. Scoop out and set aside ½ cup of this sauce for the topping. 6. Set aside ½ cup of the chickpeas for the topping. Add the remaining chickpeas to the tahini sauce in the blender or food processor along with ½ cup of the cooking liquid and the remaining ½ teaspoon salt. Blend or process on high speed, stopping to scrape down the sides of the container as needed, for about 1 minute, until very smooth. 7. Transfer the hummus to a shallow serving bowl. Spoon the reserved tahini mixture over the top, then sprinkle on the reserved chickpeas. The hummus will keep in an airtight container in the refrigerator for up to 3 days. Serve at room temperature or chilled.

Coconut Cajun Shrimp

Prep time: 10 minutes | Cook time: 6 minutes | Serves 2

- 4 Royal tiger shrimps
- 3 tablespoons coconut shred
- 2 eggs, beaten
- ½ teaspoon Cajun seasoning
- 1 teaspoon olive oil

1. Heat up olive oil in the instant pot on Sauté mode. 2. Meanwhile, mix up Cajun seasoning and coconut shred. 3. Dip the shrimps in the eggs and coat in the coconut shred mixture. 4. After this, place the shrimps in the hot olive oil and cook them on Sauté mode for 3 minutes from each side.

Colby Cheese and Pepper Dip

Prep time: 5 minutes | Cook time: 5 minutes | Serves 8

- 1 tablespoon butter
- 2 red bell peppers, sliced
- 2 cups shredded Colby cheese
- 1 cup cream cheese, room temperature
- 1 cup chicken broth
- 2 garlic cloves, minced
- 1 teaspoon red Aleppo pepper flakes
- 1 teaspoon sumac
- Salt and ground black pepper, to taste

1. Set your Instant Pot to Sauté and melt the butter. 2. Add the bell peppers and sauté for about 2 minutes until just tender. 3. Add the remaining ingredients to the Instant Pot and gently stir to incorporate. 4. Lock the lid. Select the Manual mode and set the cooking time for 3 minutes at High Pressure. 5. When the timer beeps, perform a quick pressure release. Carefully remove the lid. 6. Allow to cool for 5 minutes and serve warm.

Taco Beef Bites

Prep time: 10 minutes | Cook time: 15 minutes | Serves 6

- 10 ounces (283 g) ground beef
- 3 eggs, beaten
- ⅓ cup shredded Mozzarella cheese
- 1 teaspoon taco seasoning
- 1 teaspoon sesame oil

1. In the mixing bowl mix up ground beef, eggs, Mozzarella, and taco seasoning. 2. Then make the small meat bites from the mixture. 3. Heat up sesame oil in the instant pot. 4. Put the meat bites in the hot oil and cook them for 5 minutes from each side on Sauté mode.

7-Layer Dip

Prep time: 10 minutes | Cook time: 35 minutes | Serves 6

- Cashew Sour Cream
- 1 cup raw whole cashews, soaked in water to cover for 1 to 2 hours and then drained
- ½ cup avocado oil
- ½ cup water
- ¼ cup fresh lemon juice
- 2 tablespoons nutritional yeast
- 1 teaspoon fine sea salt
- Beans
- ½ cup dried black beans
- 2 cups water
- ½ teaspoon fine sea salt
- ½ teaspoon chili powder
- ¼ teaspoon garlic powder
- ½ cup grape or cherry tomatoes, halved
- 1 avocado, diced
- ¼ cup chopped yellow onion
- 1 jalapeño chile, sliced
- 2 tablespoons chopped cilantro
- 6 ounces baked corn tortilla chips
- 1 English cucumber, sliced
- 2 carrots, sliced
- 6 celery stalks, cut into sticks

1. To make the cashew sour cream: In a blender, combine the cashews, oil, water, lemon juice, nutritional yeast, and salt. Blend on high speed, stopping to scrape down the sides of the container as needed, for about 2 minutes, until very smooth. (The sour cream can be made in advance and stored in an airtight container in the refrigerator for up to 5 days.) 2. To make the beans: Pour 1 cup water into the Instant Pot. In a 1½-quart stainless-steel bowl, combine the beans, the 2 cups water, and salt and stir to dissolve the salt. Place the bowl on a long-handled silicone steam rack, then, holding the handles of the steam rack, lower it into the Instant Pot. (If you don't have the long-handled rack, use the wire metal steam rack and a homemade sling) 3. Secure the lid and set the Pressure Release to Sealing. Select the Bean/Chili, Pressure Cook, or Manual setting and set the cooking time for 25 minutes at high pressure. (The pot will take about 10 minutes to come up to pressure before the cooking program begins.) 4. When the cooking program ends, let the pressure release naturally for at least 20 minutes, then move the Pressure Release to Venting to release any remaining steam. 5. Place a colander over a bowl. Open the pot and, wearing heat-resistant mitts, lift out the inner pot and drain the beans in the colander. Transfer the liquid captured in the bowl to a measuring cup, and pour the beans into the bowl. Add ¼ cup of the cooking liquid to the beans and, using a potato masher or fork, mash the beans to your desired consistency, adding more cooking liquid as needed. Stir in the chili powder and garlic powder. 6. Using a rubber spatula, spread the black beans in an even layer in a clear-glass serving dish. Spread the cashew sour cream in an even layer on top of the beans. Add layers of the tomatoes, avocado, onion, jalapeño, and cilantro. (At this point, you can cover and refrigerate the assembled dip for up to 1 day.) Serve accompanied with the tortilla chips, cucumber, carrots, and celery on the side.

Parmesan Zucchini Fries

Prep time: 15 minutes | Cook time: 5 minutes | Serves 4

- 1 zucchini
- 1 ounce (28 g) Parmesan, grated
- 1 tablespoon almond flour
- ½ teaspoon Italian seasoning
- 1 tablespoon coconut oil

1. Trim the zucchini and cut it into the French fries. 2. Then sprinkle them with grated Parmesan, almond flour, and Italian seasoning. 3. Put coconut oil in the instant pot and melt it on Sauté mode. 4. Put the zucchini in the hot oil in one layer and cook for 2 minutes from each side or until they are golden brown. 5. Dry the zucchini fries with paper towels.

Cauliflower Cheese Balls

Prep time: 5 minutes | Cook time: 21 minutes | Serves 8

- 1 cup water
- 1 head cauliflower, broken into florets
- 1 cup shredded Asiago cheese
- ½ cup grated Parmesan cheese
- 2 eggs, beaten
- 2 tablespoons butter
- 2 tablespoons minced fresh chives
- 1 garlic clove, minced
- ½ teaspoon cayenne pepper
- Coarse sea salt and white pepper, to taste

1. Pour the water into the Instant Pot and insert a steamer basket. Place the cauliflower in the basket. 2. Lock the lid. Select the Manual mode and set the cooking time for 3 minutes at High Pressure. 3. When the timer beeps, perform a quick pressure release. Carefully remove the lid. 4. Transfer the cauliflower to a food processor, along with the remaining ingredients. Pulse until everything is well combined. 5. Form the mixture into bite-sized balls and place them on a baking sheet. 6. Bake in the preheated oven at 400°F (205°C) for 18 minutes until golden brown. Flip the balls halfway through the cooking time. Cool for 5 minutes before serving.

Cauliflower Fritters with Cheese

Prep time: 10 minutes | Cook time: 8 minutes | Serves 4

- 1 cup cauliflower, boiled
- 2 eggs, beaten
- 2 tablespoons almond flour
- 2 ounces (57 g) Cheddar
- cheese, shredded
- ½ teaspoon garlic powder
- 1 tablespoon avocado oil

1. In a medium bowl, mash the cauliflower. Add the beaten eggs, flour, cheese, and garlic powder and stir until well incorporated. Make the fritters from the cauliflower mixture. 2. Set your Instant Pot to Sauté and heat the avocado oil. 3. Add the fritters to the hot oil and cook each side for 3 minutes until golden brown. 4. Serve hot.

Broccoli Cheese Dip

Prep time: 5 minutes | Cook time: 10 minutes | Serves 6

- 4 tablespoons butter
- ½ medium onion, diced
- 1½ cups chopped broccoli
- 8 ounces (227 g) cream cheese
- ½ cup mayonnaise
- ½ cup chicken broth
- 1 cup shredded Cheddar cheese

1. Press the Sauté button and then press the Adjust button to set heat to Less. Add butter to Instant Pot. Add onion and sauté until softened, about 5 minutes. Press the Cancel button. 2. Add broccoli, cream cheese, mayo, and broth to pot. Press the Manual button and adjust time for 4 minutes. 3. When timer beeps, quick-release the pressure and stir in Cheddar. Serve warm.

Broccoli with Garlic-Herb Cheese Sauce

Prep time: 5 minutes | Cook time: 3 minutes | Serves 4

- ½ cup water
- 1 pound (454 g) broccoli (frozen or fresh)
- ½ cup heavy cream
- 1 tablespoon butter
- ½ cup shredded Cheddar
- cheese
- 3 tablespoons garlic and herb cheese spread
- Pinch of salt
- Pinch of black pepper

1. Add the water to the pot and place the trivet inside. 2. Put the steamer basket on top of the trivet. Place the broccoli in the basket. 3. Close the lid and seal the vent. Cook on Low Pressure for 1 minute. Quick release the steam. Press Cancel. 4. Carefully remove the steamer basket from the pot and drain the water. If you steamed a full bunch of broccoli, pull the florets off the stem. (Chop the stem into bite-size pieces, it's surprisingly creamy.) 5. Turn the pot to Sauté mode. Add the cream and butter. Stir continuously while the butter melts and the cream warms up. 6. When the cream begins to bubble on the edges, add the Cheddar cheese, cheese spread, salt, and pepper. Whisk continuously until the cheeses are melted and a sauce consistency is reached, 1 to 2 minutes. 7. Top one-fourth of the broccoli with 2 tablespoons cheese sauce.

Red Wine Mushrooms

Prep time: 5 minutes | Cook time: 15 minutes | Serves 2

- 8 ounces (227 g) sliced mushrooms
- ¼ cup dry red wine
- 2 tablespoons beef broth
- ½ teaspoon garlic powder
- ¼ teaspoon Worcestershire sauce
- Pinch of salt
- Pinch of black pepper
- ¼ teaspoon xanthan gum

1. Add the mushrooms, wine, broth, garlic powder, Worcestershire sauce, salt, and pepper to the pot. 2. Close the lid and seal the vent. Cook on High Pressure for 13 minutes. Quick release the steam. Press Cancel. 3. Turn the pot to Sauté mode. Add the xanthan gum and whisk until the juices have thickened, 1 to 2 minutes.

Bok Choy Salad Boats with Shrimp

Prep time: 8 minutes | Cook time: 2 minutes | Serves 8

- 26 shrimp, cleaned and deveined
- 2 tablespoons fresh lemon juice
- 1 cup water
- Sea salt and ground black pepper, to taste
- 4 ounces (113 g) feta cheese, crumbled
- 2 tomatoes, diced
- ⅓ cup olives, pitted and sliced
- 4 tablespoons olive oil
- 2 tablespoons apple cider vinegar
- 8 Bok choy leaves
- 2 tablespoons fresh basil leaves, snipped
- 2 tablespoons chopped fresh mint leaves

1. Toss the shrimp and lemon juice in the Instant Pot until well coated. Pour in the water. 2. Lock the lid. Select the Manual mode and set the cooking time for 2 minutes at Low Pressure. 3. When the timer beeps, perform a quick pressure release. Carefully remove the lid. 4. Season the shrimp with salt and pepper to taste, then let them cool completely. 5. Toss the shrimp with the feta cheese, tomatoes, olives, olive oil, and vinegar until well incorporated. 6. Divide the salad evenly onto each Bok choy leaf and place them on a serving plate. Scatter the basil and mint leaves on top and serve immediately.

Brussels Sprouts with Aioli Sauce

Prep time: 5 minutes | Cook time: 7 minutes | Serves 4

- 1 tablespoon butter
- ½ cup chopped scallions
- ¾ pound (340 g) Brussels sprouts
- Aioli Sauce:
- ¼ cup mayonnaise
- 1 tablespoon fresh lemon juice
- 1 garlic clove, minced
- ½ teaspoon Dijon mustard

1. Set your Instant Pot to Sauté and melt the butter. 2. Add the scallions and sauté for 2 minutes until softened. Add the Brussels sprouts and cook for another 1 minute. 3. Lock the lid. Select the Manual mode and set the cooking time for 4 minutes at High Pressure. 4. Meanwhile, whisk together all the ingredients for the Aioli sauce in a small bowl until well incorporated. 5. When the timer beeps, perform a quick pressure release. Carefully remove the lid. 6. Serve the Brussels sprouts with the Aioli sauce on the side.

Cheese Stuffed Mushrooms

Prep time: 15 minutes | Cook time: 8 minutes | Serves 4

- 1 cup cremini mushroom caps
- 1 tablespoon chopped scallions
- 1 tablespoon chopped chives
- 1 teaspoon cream cheese
- 1 teaspoon sour cream
- 1 ounce (28 g) Monterey Jack cheese, shredded
- 1 teaspoon butter, softened
- ½ teaspoon smoked paprika
- 1 cup water, for cooking

1. Trim the mushroom caps if needed and wash them well. 2. After this, in the mixing bowl, mix up scallions, chives, cream cheese, sour cream, butter, and smoked paprika. 3. Then fill the mushroom caps with the cream cheese mixture and top with shredded Monterey Jack cheese. 4. Pour water and insert the trivet in the instant pot. 5. Arrange the stuffed mushrooms caps on the trivet and close the lid. 6. Cook the meal on Manual (High Pressure) for 8 minutes. 7. Then make a quick pressure release.

Blackberry Baked Brie

Prep time: 5 minutes | Cook time: 15 minutes | Serves 5

- 8-ounce round Brie
- 1 cup water
- ¼ cup sugar-free blackberry
- preserves
- 2 teaspoons chopped fresh mint

1. Slice a grid pattern into the top of the rind of the Brie with a knife. 2. In a 7-inch round baking dish, place the Brie, then cover the baking dish securely with foil. 3. Insert the trivet into the inner pot of the Instant Pot; pour in the water. 4. Make a foil sling and arrange it on top of the trivet. Place the baking dish on top of the trivet and foil sling. 5. Secure the lid to the locked position and turn the vent to sealing. 6. Press Manual and set the Instant Pot for 15 minutes on high pressure. 7. When cooking time is up, turn off the Instant Pot and do a quick release of the pressure. 8. When the valve has dropped, remove the lid, then remove the baking dish. 9. Remove the top rind of the Brie and top with the preserves. Sprinkle with the fresh mint.

Herbed Shrimp

Prep time: 5 minutes | Cook time: 5 minutes | Serves 4

- 2 tablespoons olive oil
- ¾ pound (340 g) shrimp, peeled and deveined
- 1 teaspoon paprika
- 1 teaspoon garlic powder
- 1 teaspoon onion powder
- 1 teaspoon dried parsley flakes
- ½ teaspoon dried oregano
- ½ teaspoon dried thyme
- ½ teaspoon dried basil
- ½ teaspoon dried rosemary
- ¼ teaspoon red pepper flakes
- Coarse sea salt and ground black pepper, to taste
- 1 cup chicken broth

1. Set your Instant Pot to Sauté and heat the olive oil. 2. Add the shrimp and sauté for 2 to 3 minutes. 3. Add the remaining ingredients to the Instant Pot and stir to combine. 4. Secure the lid. Select the Manual mode and set the cooking time for 2 minutes at Low Pressure. 5. When the timer beeps, perform a quick pressure release. Carefully remove the lid. 6. Transfer the shrimp to a plate and serve.

Crispy Brussels Sprouts with Bacon

Prep time: 5 minutes | Cook time: 10 minutes | Serves 4

- ½ pound (227 g) bacon
- 1 pound (454 g) Brussels sprouts
- 4 tablespoons butter
- 1 teaspoon salt
- ½ teaspoon pepper
- ½ cup water

1. Press the Sauté button and press the Adjust button to lower heat to Less. Add bacon to Instant Pot and fry for 3 to 5 minutes or until fat begins to render. Press the Cancel button. 2. Press the Sauté button, with heat set to Normal, and continue frying bacon until crispy. While bacon is frying, wash Brussels sprouts and remove damaged outer leaves. Cut in half or quarters. 3. When bacon is done, remove and set aside. Add Brussels sprouts to hot bacon grease and add butter. Sprinkle with salt and pepper. Sauté for 8 to 10 minutes until caramelized and crispy, adding a few tablespoons of water at a time as needed to deglaze pan. Serve warm.

Buffalo Chicken Meatballs

Prep time: 5 minutes | Cook time: 10 minutes | Serves 4

- 1 pound (454 g) ground chicken
- ½ cup almond flour
- 2 tablespoons cream cheese
- 1 packet dry ranch dressing mix
- ½ teaspoon salt
- ¼ teaspoon pepper
- ¼ teaspoon garlic powder
- 1 cup water
- 2 tablespoons butter, melted
- ⅓ cup hot sauce
- ¼ cup crumbled feta cheese
- ¼ cup sliced green onion

1. In large bowl, mix ground chicken, almond flour, cream cheese, ranch, salt, pepper, and garlic powder. Roll mixture into 16 balls. 2. Place meatballs on steam rack and add 1 cup water to Instant Pot. Click lid closed. Press the Meat/Stew button and set time for 10 minutes. 3. Combine butter and hot sauce. When timer beeps, remove meatballs and place in clean large bowl. Toss in hot sauce mixture. Top with sprinkled feta and green onions to serve.

Spinach and Artichoke Dip

Prep time: 5 minutes | Cook time: 4 minutes | Serves 11

- 8 ounces low-fat cream cheese
- 10-ounce box frozen spinach
- ½ cup no-sodium chicken broth
- 14-ounce can artichoke hearts, drained
- ½ cup low-fat sour cream
- ½ cup low-fat mayo
- 3 cloves of garlic, minced
- 1 teaspoon onion powder
- 16 ounces reduced-fat shredded Parmesan cheese
- 8 ounces reduced-fat shredded mozzarella

1. Put all ingredients in the inner pot of the Instant Pot, except the Parmesan cheese and the mozzarella cheese. 2. Secure the lid and set vent to sealing. Place on Manual high pressure for 4 minutes. 3. Do a quick release of steam. 4. Immediately stir in the cheeses.

Zucchini and Cheese Tots

Prep time: 15 minutes | Cook time: 10 minutes | Serves 6

- 4 ounces (113 g) Parmesan, grated
- 4 ounces (113 g) Cheddar cheese, grated
- 1 zucchini, grated
- 1 egg, beaten
- 1 teaspoon dried oregano
- 1 tablespoon coconut oil

1. In the mixing bowl, mix up Parmesan, Cheddar cheese, zucchini, egg, and dried oregano. 2. Make the small tots with the help of the fingertips. 3. Then melt the coconut oil in the instant pot on Sauté mode. 4. Put the prepared zucchini tots in the hot coconut oil and cook them for 3 minutes from each side or until they are light brown. Cool the zucchini tots for 5 minutes.

Chinese Spare Ribs

Prep time: 3 minutes | Cook time: 24 minutes | Serves 6

- 1½ pounds (680 g) spare ribs
- Salt and ground black pepper, to taste
- 2 tablespoons sesame oil
- ½ cup chopped green onions
- ½ cup chicken stock
- 2 tomatoes, crushed
- 2 tablespoons sherry
- 1 tablespoon coconut aminos
- 1 teaspoon ginger-garlic paste
- ½ teaspoon crushed red pepper flakes
- ½ teaspoon dried parsley
- 2 tablespoons sesame seeds, for serving

1. Season the spare ribs with salt and black pepper to taste. 2. Set your Instant Pot to Sauté and heat the sesame oil. 3. Add the seasoned spare ribs and sear each side for about 3 minutes. 4. Add the remaining ingredients except the sesame seeds to the Instant Pot and stir well. 5. Secure the lid. Select the Meat/Stew mode and set the cooking time for 18 minutes at High Pressure. 6. When the timer beeps, perform a natural pressure release for 10 minutes, then release any remaining pressure. Carefully remove the lid. 7. Serve topped with the sesame seeds.

Candied Pecans

Prep time: 5 minutes | Cook time: 20 minutes | Serves 10

- 4 cups raw pecans
- 1½ teaspoons liquid stevia
- ½ cup plus 1 tablespoon water, divided
- 1 teaspoon vanilla extract
- 1 teaspoon cinnamon
- ¼ teaspoon nutmeg
- ⅛ teaspoon ground ginger
- ⅛ teaspoon sea salt

1. Place the raw pecans, liquid stevia, 1 tablespoon water, vanilla, cinnamon, nutmeg, ground ginger, and sea salt into the inner pot of the Instant Pot. 2. Press the Sauté button on the Instant Pot and sauté the pecans and other ingredients until the pecans are soft. 3. Pour in the ½ cup water and secure the lid to the locked position. Set the vent to sealing. 4. Press Manual and set the Instant Pot for 15 minutes. 5. Preheat the oven to 350°F. 6. When cooking time is up, turn off the Instant Pot, then do a quick release. 7. Spread the pecans onto a greased, lined baking sheet. 8. Bake the pecans for 5 minutes or less in the oven, checking on them frequently so they do not burn.

Cheddar Chips

Prep time: 10 minutes | Cook time: 5 minutes | Serves 4

- 1 cup shredded Cheddar cheese
- 1 tablespoon almond flour

1. Mix up Cheddar cheese and almond flour. 2. Then preheat the instant pot on Sauté mode. 3. Line the instant pot bowl with baking paper. 4. After this, make the small rounds from the cheese in the instant pot (on the baking paper) and close the lid. 5. Cook them for 5 minutes on Sauté mode or until the cheese is melted. 6. Then switch off the instant pot and remove the baking paper with cheese rounds from it. 7. Cool the chips well and remove them from the baking paper.

Lemon-Butter Mushrooms

Prep time: 10 minutes | Cook time: 4 minutes | Serves 2

- 1 cup cremini mushrooms, sliced
- ½ cup water
- 1 tablespoon lemon juice
- 1 teaspoon almond butter
- 1 teaspoon grated lemon zest
- ½ teaspoon salt
- ½ teaspoon dried thyme

1. Combine all the ingredients in the Instant Pot. 2. Secure the lid. Select the Manual mode and set the cooking time for 4 minutes at High Pressure. 3. Once cooking is complete, do a natural pressure release for 5 minutes, then release any remaining pressure. Carefully open the lid. 4. Serve warm.

Herbed Zucchini Slices

Prep time: 5 minutes | Cook time: 5 minutes | Serves 4

- 2 tablespoons olive oil
- 2 garlic cloves, chopped
- 1 pound (454 g) zucchini, sliced
- ½ cup water
- ½ cup sugar-free tomato purée
- 1 teaspoon dried thyme
- ½ teaspoon dried rosemary
- ½ teaspoon dried oregano

1. Set your Instant Pot to Sauté and heat the olive oil. 2. Add the garlic and sauté for 2 minutes until fragrant. 3. Add the remaining ingredients to the Instant Pot and stir well. 4. Lock the lid. Select the Manual mode and set the cooking time for 3 minutes at Low Pressure. 5. When the timer beeps, perform a quick pressure release. Carefully remove the lid. 6. Serve warm.

Oregano Sausage Balls

Prep time: 10 minutes | Cook time: 16 minutes | Serves 10

- 15 ounces (425 g) ground pork sausage
- 1 teaspoon dried oregano
- 4 ounces (113 g) Mozzarella, shredded
- 1 cup coconut flour
- 1 garlic clove, grated
- 1 teaspoon coconut oil, melted

1. In the bowl mix up ground pork sausages, dried oregano, shredded Mozzarella, coconut flour, and garlic clove. 2. When the mixture is homogenous, make the balls. 3. After this, pour coconut oil in the instant pot. 4. Arrange the balls in the instant pot and cook them on Sauté mode for 8 minutes from each side.

Creamy Mashed Cauliflower

Prep time: 3 minutes | Cook time: 1 minute | Serves 4

- 1 head cauliflower, chopped into florets
- 1 cup water
- 1 clove garlic, finely minced
- 3 tablespoons butter

- 2 tablespoons sour cream
- ½ teaspoon salt
- ¼ teaspoon pepper

1. Place cauliflower on steamer rack. Add water and steamer rack to Instant Pot. Press the Steam button and adjust time to 1 minute. When timer beeps, quick-release the pressure. 2. Place cooked cauliflower into food processor and add remaining ingredients. Blend until smooth and creamy. Serve warm.

Porcupine Meatballs

Prep time: 20 minutes | Cook time: 15 minutes | Serves 8

- 1 pound ground sirloin or turkey
- ½ cup raw brown rice, parboiled
- 1 egg
- ¼ cup finely minced onion

- 1 or 2 cloves garlic, minced
- ¼ teaspoon dried basil and/or oregano, optional
- 10¾-ounce can reduced-fat condensed tomato soup
- ½ soup can of water

1. Mix all ingredients, except tomato soup and water, in a bowl to combine well. 2. Form into balls about 1½-inch in diameter. 3. Mix tomato soup and water in the inner pot of the Instant Pot, then add the meatballs. 4. Secure the lid and make sure the vent is turned to sealing. 5. Press the Meat button and set for 15 minutes on high pressure. 6. Allow the pressure to release naturally after cook time is up.

Pancetta Pizza Dip

Prep time: 10 minutes | Cook time: 4 minutes | Serves 10

- 10 ounces (283 g) Pepper Jack cheese
- 10 ounces (283 g) cream cheese
- 10 ounces (283 g) pancetta, chopped
- 1 pound (454 g) tomatoes, puréed
- 1 cup green olives, pitted and halved

- 1 teaspoon dried oregano
- ½ teaspoon garlic powder
- 1 cup chicken broth
- 4 ounces (113 g) Mozzarella cheese, thinly sliced

1. Mix together the Pepper Jack cheese, cream cheese, pancetta, tomatoes, olives, oregano, and garlic powder in the Instant Pot. Pour in the chicken broth. 2. Lock the lid. Select the Manual mode and set the cooking time for 4 minutes at High Pressure. 3. When the timer beeps, perform a quick pressure release. Carefully remove the lid. 4. Scatter the Mozzarella cheese on top. Cover and allow to sit in the residual heat. Serve warm.

Chapter 6

Vegetables and Sides

Chapter 6 Vegetables and Sides

Braised Fennel with radicchio, Pear, and Pecorino

Prep time: 20 minutes | Cook time: 12 minutes | Serves 4

- 6 tablespoons extra-virgin olive oil, divided
- 2 fennel bulbs (12 ounces / 340 g each), 2 tablespoons fronds chopped, stalks discarded, bulbs halved, each half cut into 1-inch-thick wedges
- ¾ teaspoon table salt, divided
- ½ teaspoon grated lemon zest plus 4 teaspoons juice
- 5 ounces (142 g) baby arugula
- 1 small head radicchio (6 ounces/ 170 g), shredded
- 1 Bosc or Bartlett pear, quartered, cored, and sliced thin
- ¼ cup whole almonds, toasted and chopped
- Shaved Pecorino Romano cheese

1. Using highest sauté function, heat 2 tablespoons oil in Instant Pot for 5 minutes (or until just smoking). Brown half of fennel, about 3 minutes per side; transfer to plate. Repeat with 1 tablespoon oil and remaining fennel; do not remove from pot. 2. Return first batch of fennel to pot along with ½ cup water and ½ teaspoon salt. Lock lid in place and close pressure release valve. Select high pressure cook function and cook for 2 minutes. Turn off Instant Pot and quick-release pressure. Carefully remove lid, allowing steam to escape away from you. Using slotted spoon, transfer fennel to plate; discard cooking liquid. 3. Whisk remaining 3 tablespoons oil, lemon zest and juice, and remaining ¼ teaspoon salt together in large bowl. Add arugula, radicchio, and pear and toss to coat. Transfer arugula mixture to serving dish and arrange fennel wedges on top. Sprinkle with almonds, fennel fronds, and Pecorino. Serve.

Best Brown Rice

Prep time: 5 minutes | Cook time: 22 minutes | Serves 6 to 12

- 2 cups brown rice
- 2½ cups water

1. Rinse brown rice in a fine-mesh strainer. 2. Add rice and water to the inner pot of the Instant Pot. 3. Secure the lid and make sure vent is on sealing. 4. Use Manual setting and select 22 minutes cooking time on high pressure. 5. When cooking time is done, let the pressure release naturally for 10 minutes, then press Cancel and manually release any remaining pressure.

Steamed Tomato with Halloumi Cheese

Prep time: 5 minutes | Cook time: 3 minutes | Serves 4

- 8 tomatoes, sliced
- 1 cup water
- ½ cup crumbled Halloumi cheese
- 2 tablespoons extra-virgin
- olive oil
- 2 tablespoons snipped fresh basil
- 2 garlic cloves, smashed

1. Pour the water into the Instant Pot and put the trivet in the pot. Place the tomatoes in the trivet. 2. Lock the lid. Select the Manual mode and set the cooking time for 3 minutes on High Pressure. When the timer goes off, perform a quick pressure release. Carefully open the lid. 3. Toss the tomatoes with the remaining ingredients and serve.

Cauliflower Mac and Cheese

Prep time: 6 minutes | Cook time: 3 minutes | Serves 6

- 1 cup water
- 1 large cauliflower, chopped into bite-size florets
- 1 cup heavy whipping cream
- ½ cup sour cream
- 1 cup shredded Gruyère or Mozzarella cheese
- 2½ cups shredded sharp Cheddar cheese
- 1 teaspoon ground mustard
- 1 teaspoon ground turmeric
- Sea salt, to taste
- Pinch of cayenne pepper (optional)

1. Pour the water into the Instant Pot. Place a metal steaming basket inside. Put the cauliflower florets in the basket. Secure the lid and set the steam release valve to Sealing. Press the Manual button and set the cook time to 3 minutes. When the Instant Pot beeps, carefully switch the steam release valve to Venting to quick-release the pressure. When fully released, open the lid. 2. Meanwhile, prepare the cheese sauce. In a large skillet, gently bring the cream to a simmer over medium to medium-low heat. Whisk in the sour cream until smooth, then gradually whisk in the Gruyère and 2 cups of the Cheddar until melted. Stir in the ground mustard and turmeric. Taste and adjust the salt. 3. Remove the cauliflower from the pot and toss it in the cheese sauce to coat. Serve warm, topped with the remaining Cheddar and a sprinkling of cayenne (if using).

Vegetable Medley

Prep time: 20 minutes | Cook time: 2 minutes | Serves 8

- 2 medium parsnips
- 4 medium carrots
- 1 turnip, about 4½ inches diameter
- 1 cup water

- 1 teaspoon salt
- 3 tablespoons sugar
- 2 tablespoons canola or olive oil
- ½ teaspoon salt

1. Clean and peel vegetables. Cut in 1-inch pieces. 2. Place the cup of water and 1 teaspoon salt into the Instant Pot's inner pot with the vegetables. 3. Secure the lid and make sure vent is set to sealing. Press Manual and set for 2 minutes. 4. When cook time is up, release the pressure manually and press Cancel. Drain the water from the inner pot. 5. Press Sauté and stir in sugar, oil, and salt. Cook until sugar is dissolved. Serve.

Lemon Broccoli

Prep time: 5 minutes | Cook time: 4 minutes | Serves 4

- 2 cups broccoli florets
- 1 tablespoon ground paprika
- 1 tablespoon lemon juice
- 1 teaspoon grated lemon

- zest
- 1 teaspoon olive oil
- ½ teaspoon chili powder
- 1 cup water

1. Pour the water in the Instant Pot and insert the trivet. 2. In the Instant Pot pan, stir together the remaining ingredients. 3. Place the pan on the trivet. 4. Set the lid in place. Select the Manual mode and set the cooking time for 4 minutes on High Pressure. When the timer goes off, do a quick pressure release. Carefully open the lid. 5. Serve immediately.

Vegetable Curry

Prep time: 25 minutes | Cook time: 3 minutes | Serves 10

- 16-ounce package baby carrots
- 3 medium potatoes, unpeeled, cubed
- 1 pound fresh or frozen green beans, cut in 2-inch pieces
- 1 medium green pepper, chopped
- 1 medium onion, chopped
- 1–2 cloves garlic, minced

- 15-ounce can garbanzo beans, drained
- 28-ounce can crushed tomatoes
- 3 teaspoons curry powder
- 1½ teaspoons chicken bouillon granules
- 1¾ cups boiling water
- 3 tablespoons minute tapioca

1. Combine carrots, potatoes, green beans, pepper, onion, garlic,

garbanzo beans, crushed tomatoes, and curry powder in the Instant Pot. 2. Dissolve bouillon in boiling water, then stir in tapioca. Pour over the contents of the Instant Pot and stir. 3. Secure the lid and make sure vent is set to sealing. Press Manual and set for 3 minutes. 4. When cook time is up, manually release the pressure.

Mushroom Stroganoff with Vodka

Prep time: 8 minutes | Cook time: 8 minutes | Serves 4

- 2 tablespoons olive oil
- ½ teaspoon crushed caraway seeds
- ½ cup chopped onion
- 2 garlic cloves, smashed
- ¼ cup vodka
- ¾ pound (340 g) button

- mushrooms, chopped
- 1 celery stalk, chopped
- 1 ripe tomato, puréed
- 1 teaspoon mustard seeds
- Sea salt and freshly ground pepper, to taste
- 2 cups vegetable broth

1. Press the Sauté button to heat up your Instant Pot. Now, heat the oil and sauté caraway seeds until fragrant, about 40 seconds. 2. Then, add the onion and garlic, and continue sautéing for 1 to 2 minutes more, stirring frequently. 3. After that, add the remaining ingredients and stir to combine. 4. Secure the lid. Choose Manual mode and High Pressure; cook for 5 minutes. Once cooking is complete, use a quick pressure release; carefully remove the lid. 5. Ladle into individual bowls and serve warm. Bon appétit!

Moroccan Zucchini

Prep time: 10 minutes | Cook time: 6 minutes | Serves 4

- 2 tablespoons avocado oil
- ½ medium onion, diced
- 1 clove garlic, minced
- ¼ teaspoon cayenne pepper
- ¼ teaspoon ground coriander
- ¼ teaspoon ground cumin
- ¼ teaspoon ground ginger
- Pinch of ground cinnamon

- 1 Roma (plum) tomato, diced
- 2 medium zucchini, cut into 1-inch pieces
- ½ tablespoon fresh lemon juice
- ¼ cup bone broth or vegetable stock

1. Set the Instant Pot to Sauté. When hot, add the oil. Add the onion and sauté, stirring frequently, until translucent, about 2 minutes. Add the garlic, cayenne, coriander, cumin, ginger, and cinnamon and cook until fragrant, about 1 minute. Stir in the tomato and zucchini and cook 2 minutes longer. 2. Press Cancel. Add the lemon juice and broth. Secure the lid and set the steam release valve to Sealing. Press the Manual button, adjust the pressure to Low, and set the cook time to 1 minute. 3. When the Instant Pot beeps, carefully switch the steam release valve to Venting to quick-release the pressure. When fully released, open the lid. Stir and serve warm.

Garlicky Broccoli with Roasted Almonds

Prep time: 10 minutes | Cook time: 4 minutes | Serves 4 to 6

- 6 cups broccoli florets
- 1 cup water
- 1½ tablespoons olive oil
- 8 garlic cloves, thinly sliced
- 2 shallots, thinly sliced
- ½ teaspoon crushed red pepper flakes
- Grated zest and juice of 1

- medium lemon
- ½ teaspoon kosher salt
- Freshly ground black pepper, to taste
- ¼ cup chopped roasted almonds
- ¼ cup finely slivered fresh basil

1. Pour the water into the Instant Pot. Place the broccoli florets in a steamer basket and lower into the pot. 2. Close and secure the lid. Select the Steam setting and set the cooking time for 2 minutes at Low Pressure. Once the timer goes off, use a quick pressure release. Carefully open the lid. 3. Transfer the broccoli to a large bowl filled with cold water and ice. Once cooled, drain the broccoli and pat dry. 4. Select the Sauté mode on the Instant Pot and heat the olive oil. Add the garlic to the pot and sauté for 30 seconds, tossing constantly. Add the shallots and pepper flakes to the pot and sauté for 1 minute. 5. Stir in the cooked broccoli, lemon juice, salt and black pepper. Toss the ingredients together and cook for 1 minute. 6. Transfer the broccoli to a serving platter and sprinkle with the chopped almonds, lemon zest and basil. Serve immediately.

Chanterelle Mushrooms with Cheddar Cheese

Prep time: 10 minutes | Cook time: 5 minutes | Serves 4

- 1 tablespoon olive oil
- 2 cloves garlic, minced
- 1 (1-inch) ginger root, grated
- 16 ounces (454 g) Chanterelle mushrooms, brushed clean and sliced
- ½ cup unsweetened tomato purée
- ½ cup water

- 2 tablespoons dry white wine
- 1 teaspoon dried basil
- ½ teaspoon dried thyme
- ½ teaspoon dried dill weed
- ⅓ teaspoon freshly ground black pepper
- Kosher salt, to taste
- 1 cup shredded Cheddar cheese

1. Press the Sauté button on the Instant Pot and heat the olive oil. Add the garlic and grated ginger to the pot and sauté for 1 minute, or until fragrant. Stir in the remaining ingredients, except for the cheese. 2. Lock the lid. Select the Manual mode and set the cooking time for 5 minutes on Low Pressure. When the timer goes off, perform a quick pressure release. Carefully open the lid.. 3. Serve topped with the shredded cheese.

Spaghetti Squash

Prep time: 5 minutes | Cook time: 7 minutes | Serves 4

- 1 spaghetti squash (about 2 pounds)

1. Cut the spaghetti squash in half crosswise and use a large spoon to remove the seeds. 2. Pour 1 cup of water into the electric pressure cooker and insert a wire rack or trivet. 3. Place the squash halves on the rack, cut-side up. 4. Close and lock the lid of the pressure cooker. Set the valve to sealing. 5. Cook on high pressure for 7 minutes. 6. When the cooking is complete, hit Cancel and quick release the pressure. 7. Once the pin drops, unlock and remove the lid. 8. With tongs, remove the squash from the pot and transfer it to a plate. When it is cool enough to handle, scrape the squash with the tines of a fork to remove the strands. Discard the skin.

Spaghetti Squash Noodles with Tomatoes

Prep time: 15 minutes | Cook time: 14 to 16 minutes | Serves 4

- 1 medium spaghetti squash
- 1 cup water
- 2 tablespoons olive oil
- 1 small yellow onion, diced
- 6 garlic cloves, minced
- 2 teaspoons crushed red pepper flakes
- 2 teaspoons dried oregano
- 1 cup sliced cherry tomatoes

- 1 teaspoon kosher salt
- ½ teaspoon freshly ground black pepper
- 1 (14.5-ounce / 411-g) can sugar-free crushed tomatoes
- ¼ cup capers
- 1 tablespoon caper brine
- ½ cup sliced olives

1. With a sharp knife, halve the spaghetti squash crosswise. Using a spoon, scoop out the seeds and sticky gunk in the middle of each half. 2. Pour the water into the Instant Pot and place the trivet in the pot with the handles facing up. Arrange the squash halves, cut side facing up, on the trivet. 3. Lock the lid. Select the Manual mode and set the cooking time for 7 minutes on High Pressure. When the timer goes off, use a quick pressure release. Carefully open the lid. 4. Remove the trivet and pour out the water that has collected in the squash cavities. Using the tines of a fork, separate the cooked strands into spaghetti-like pieces and set aside in a bowl. 5. Pour the water out of the pot. Select the Sauté mode and heat the oil. 6. Add the onion to the pot and sauté for 3 minutes. Add the garlic, pepper flakes and oregano to the pot and sauté for 1 minute. 7. Stir in the cherry tomatoes, salt and black pepper and cook for 2 minutes, or until the tomatoes are tender. 8. Pour in the crushed tomatoes, capers, caper brine and olives and bring the mixture to a boil. Continue to cook for 2 to 3 minutes to allow the flavors to meld. 9. Stir in the spaghetti squash noodles and cook for 1 to 2 minutes to warm everything through. 10. Transfer the dish to a serving platter and serve.

Cauliflower Rice Curry

Prep time: 5 minutes | Cook time: 2 minutes | Serves 4

- 1 (9-ounce / 255-g) head cauliflower, chopped
- ½ teaspoon garlic powder
- ½ teaspoon freshly ground black pepper
- ½ teaspoon ground turmeric
- ½ teaspoon curry powder
- ½ teaspoon kosher salt
- ½ teaspoon fresh paprika
- ¼ small onion, thinly sliced

1. Pour 1 cup of filtered water into the inner pot of the Instant Pot, then insert the trivet. In a well-greased, Instant Pot-friendly dish, add the cauliflower. Sprinkle the garlic powder, black pepper, turmeric, curry powder, salt, paprika, and onion over top. 2. Place the dish onto the trivet, and cover loosely with aluminum foil. Close the lid, set the pressure release to Sealing and select Manual. Set the Instant Pot to 2 minutes on High Pressure, and let cook. 3. Once cooked, perform a quick release. 4. Open the Instant Pot, and remove the dish. Serve, and enjoy!

Spiced Winter Squash with Halloumi and Shaved Brussels Sprouts

Prep time: 20 minutes | Cook time: 15 minutes | Serves 4

- 3 tablespoons extra-virgin olive oil, divided
- 2 tablespoons lemon juice
- 2 garlic cloves, minced, divided
- ⅛ teaspoon plus ½ teaspoon table salt, divided
- 8 ounces (227 g) Brussels sprouts, trimmed, halved, and sliced very thin
- 1 (8-ounce / 227-g) block halloumi cheese, sliced crosswise into ¾-inch-thick slabs
- 4 scallions, white parts
- minced, green parts sliced thin on bias
- ½ teaspoon ground cardamom
- ¼ teaspoon ground cumin
- ⅛ teaspoon cayenne pepper
- 2 pounds (907 g) butternut squash, peeled, seeded, and cut into 1-inch pieces
- ½ cup chicken or vegetable broth
- 2 teaspoons honey
- ¼ cup dried cherries
- 2 tablespoons roasted pepitas

1. Whisk 1 tablespoon oil, lemon juice, ¼ teaspoon garlic, and ⅛ teaspoon salt together in bowl. Add Brussels sprouts and toss to coat; let sit until ready to serve. 2. Using highest sauté function, heat remaining 2 tablespoons oil in Instant Pot until shimmering. Arrange halloumi around edges of pot and cook until browned, about 3 minutes per side; transfer to plate. Add scallion whites to fat left in pot and cook until softened, about 2 minutes. Stir in remaining garlic, cardamom, cumin, and cayenne and cook until fragrant, about 30 seconds. Stir in squash, broth, and remaining ½ teaspoon salt. Lock lid in place and close pressure release valve. Select high pressure cook function and cook for 6 minutes. 3.

Turn off Instant Pot and quick-release pressure. Carefully remove lid, allowing steam to escape away from you. Using highest sauté function, continue to cook squash mixture, stirring occasionally until liquid is almost completely evaporated, about 5 minutes. Turn off Instant Pot. Using potato masher, mash squash until mostly smooth. Season with salt and pepper to taste. 4. Spread portion of squash over bottom of individual serving plates. Top with Brussels sprouts and halloumi. Drizzle with honey and sprinkle with cherries, pepitas, and scallion greens. Serve.

Asparagus with Copoundy Cheese

Prep time: 5 minutes | Cook time: 1 minute | Serves 4

- 1½ pounds (680 g) fresh asparagus
- 1 cup water
- 2 tablespoons olive oil
- 4 garlic cloves, minced
- Sea salt, to taste
- ¼ teaspoon ground black pepper
- ½ cup shredded Copoundy cheese

1. Pour the water into the Instant Pot and put the steamer basket in the pot. 2. Place the asparagus in the steamer basket. Drizzle the asparagus with the olive oil and sprinkle with the garlic on top. Season with salt and black pepper. 3. Close and secure the lid. Select the Manual mode and set the cooking time for 1 minute at High Pressure. Once cooking is complete, do a quick pressure release. Carefully open the lid. 4. Transfer the asparagus to a platter and served topped with the shredded cheese.

Asparagus and Mushroom Soup

Prep time: 10 minutes | Cook time: 7 minutes | Serves 4

- 2 tablespoons coconut oil
- ½ cup chopped shallots
- 2 cloves garlic, minced
- 1 pound (454 g) asparagus, washed, trimmed, and chopped
- 4 ounces (113 g) button mushrooms, sliced
- 4 cups vegetable broth
- 2 tablespoons balsamic vinegar
- Himalayan salt, to taste
- ¼ teaspoon ground black pepper
- ¼ teaspoon paprika
- ¼ cup vegan sour cream

1. Press the Sauté button to heat up your Instant Pot. Heat the oil and cook the shallots and garlic for 2 to 3 minutes. 2. Add the remaining ingredients, except for sour cream, to the Instant Pot. 3. Secure the lid. Choose Manual mode and High Pressure; cook for 4 minutes. Once cooking is complete, use a quick pressure release; carefully remove the lid. 4. Spoon into four soup bowls; add a dollop of sour cream to each serving and serve immediately. Bon appétit!

Simple Cauliflower Gnocchi

Prep time: 5 minutes | Cook time: 2 minutes | Serves 4

- 2 cups cauliflower, boiled
- ½ cup almond flour
- 1 tablespoon sesame oil
- 1 teaspoon salt
- 1 cup water

1. In a bowl, mash the cauliflower until puréed. Mix it up with the almond flour, sesame oil and salt. 2. Make the log from the cauliflower dough and cut it into small pieces. 3. Pour the water in the Instant Pot and add the gnocchi. 4. Lock the lid. Select the Manual mode and set the cooking time for 2 minutes on High Pressure. Once the timer goes off, perform a natural pressure release for 5 minutes, then release any remaining pressure. Carefully open the lid. 5. Remove the cooked gnocchi from the water and serve.

Caramelized Onions

Prep time: 10 minutes | Cook time: 35 minutes | Serves 8

- 4 tablespoons margarine
- 6 large Vidalia or other sweet onions, sliced into
- thin half rings
- 10-ounce can chicken, or vegetable, broth

1. Press Sauté on the Instant Pot. Add in the margarine and let melt. 2. Once the margarine is melted, stir in the onions and sauté for about 5 minutes. Pour in the broth and then press Cancel. 3. Secure the lid and make sure vent is set to sealing. Press Manual and set time for 20 minutes. 4. When cook time is up, release the pressure manually. Remove the lid and press Sauté. Stir the onion mixture for about 10 more minutes, allowing extra liquid to cook off.

Potatoes with Parsley

Prep time: 10 minutes | Cook time: 5 minutes | Serves 4

- 3 tablespoons margarine, divided
- 2 pounds medium red potatoes (about 2 ounces each), halved lengthwise
- 1 clove garlic, minced
- ½ teaspoon salt
- ½ cup low-sodium chicken broth
- 2 tablespoons chopped fresh parsley

1. Place 1 tablespoon margarine in the inner pot of the Instant Pot and select Sauté. 2. After margarine is melted, add potatoes, garlic, and salt, stirring well. 3. Sauté 4 minutes, stirring frequently. 4. Add chicken broth and stir well. 5. Seal lid, make sure vent is on sealing, then select Manual for 5 minutes on high pressure. 6. When cooking time is up, manually release the pressure. 7. Strain potatoes, toss with remaining 2 tablespoons margarine and chopped parsley, and serve immediately.

Sesame Zoodles with Scallions

Prep time: 10 minutes | Cook time: 3 minutes | Serves 6

- 2 large zucchinis, trimmed and spiralized
- ¼ cup chicken broth
- 1 tablespoon chopped scallions
- 1 tablespoon coconut aminos
- 1 teaspoon sesame oil
- 1 teaspoon sesame seeds
- ¼ teaspoon chili flakes

1. Set the Instant Pot on the Sauté mode. Add the zucchini spirals to the pot and pour in the chicken broth. Sauté for 3 minutes and transfer to the serving bowls. 2. Sprinkle with the scallions, coconut aminos, sesame oil, sesame seeds and chili flakes. Gently stir the zoodles. 3. Serve immediately.

Spicy Cauliflower Head

Prep time: 5 minutes | Cook time: 7 minutes | Serves 4

- 13 ounces (369 g) cauliflower head
- 1 cup water
- 1 tablespoon coconut cream
- 1 tablespoon avocado oil
- 1 teaspoon ground paprika
- 1 teaspoon ground turmeric
- ½ teaspoon ground cumin
- ½ teaspoon salt

1. Pour the water in the Instant Pot and insert the trivet. 2. In the mixing bowl, stir together the coconut cream, avocado oil, paprika, turmeric, cumin and salt. 3. Carefully brush the cauliflower head with the coconut cream mixture. Sprinkle the remaining coconut cream mixture over the cauliflower. 4. Transfer the cauliflower head onto the trivet. 5. Lock the lid. Select the Manual mode and set the cooking time for 7 minutes at High Pressure. When the timer goes off, use a natural pressure release for 10 minutes, then release any remaining pressure. Carefully open the lid. 6. Serve immediately.

Parmesan Zoodles

Prep time: 5 minutes | Cook time: 5 minutes | Serves 2

- 1 large zucchini, trimmed and spiralized
- 1 tablespoon butter
- 1 garlic clove, diced
- ½ teaspoon chili flakes
- 3 ounces (85 g) Parmesan cheese, grated

1. Set the Instant Pot on the Sauté mode and melt the butter. Add the garlic and chili flakes to the pot. Sauté for 2 minutes, or until fragrant. 2. Stir in the zucchini spirals and sauté for 2 minutes, or until tender. 3. Add the grated Parmesan cheese to the pot and stir well. Continue to cook it for 1 minute, or until the cheese melts. 4. Transfer to a plate and serve immediately

Green Cabbage Turmeric Stew

Prep time: 5 minutes | Cook time: 4 minutes | Serves 4

- 2 tablespoons olive oil
- ½ cup sliced yellow onion
- 1 teaspoon crushed garlic
- Sea salt and freshly ground black pepper, to taste
- 1 teaspoon turmeric powder
- 1 serrano pepper, chopped
- 1 pound (454 g) green cabbage, shredded
- 1 celery stalk, chopped
- 2 tablespoons rice wine
- 1 cup roasted vegetable broth

1. Place all of the above ingredients in the Instant Pot. 2. Secure the lid. Choose Manual mode and High Pressure; cook for 4 minutes. Once cooking is complete, use a quick pressure release; carefully remove the lid. 3. Divide between individual bowls and serve warm. Bon appétit!

Instant Pot Zucchini Sticks

Prep time: 5 minutes | Cook time: 8 minutes | Serves 2

- 2 zucchinis, trimmed and cut into sticks
- 2 teaspoons olive oil
- ½ teaspoon white pepper
- ½ teaspoon salt
- 1 cup water

1. Place the zucchini sticks in the Instant Pot pan and sprinkle with the olive oil, white pepper and salt. 2. Pour the water and put the trivet in the pot. Place the pan on the trivet. 3. Lock the lid. Select the Manual setting and set the cooking time for 8 minutes at High Pressure. Once the timer goes off, use a quick pressure release. Carefully open the lid. 4. Remove the zucchinis from the pot and serve.

Italian Wild Mushrooms

Prep time: 30 minutes | Cook time: 3 minutes | Serves 10

- 2 tablespoons canola oil
- 2 large onions, chopped
- 4 garlic cloves, minced
- 3 large red bell peppers, chopped
- 3 large green bell peppers, chopped
- 12 ounces package oyster mushrooms, cleaned and
- chopped
- 3 fresh bay leaves
- 10 fresh basil leaves, chopped
- 1 teaspoon salt
- 1½ teaspoons pepper
- 28 ounces can Italian plum tomatoes, crushed or chopped

1. Press Sauté on the Instant Pot and add in the oil. Once the oil is heated, add the onions, garlic, peppers, and mushroom to the oil.

Sauté just until mushrooms begin to turn brown. 2. Add remaining ingredients. Stir well. 3. Secure the lid and make sure vent is set to sealing. Press Manual and set time for 3 minutes. 4. When cook time is up, release the pressure manually. Discard bay leaves.

Sauerkraut and Mushroom Casserole

Prep time: 6 minutes | Cook time: 15 minutes | Serves 6

- 1 tablespoon olive oil
- 1 celery rib, diced
- ½ cup chopped leeks
- 2 pounds (907 g) canned sauerkraut, drained
- 6 ounces (170 g) brown
- mushrooms, sliced
- 1 teaspoon caraway seeds
- 1 teaspoon brown mustard
- 1 bay leaf
- 1 cup dry white wine

1. Press the Sauté button to heat up your Instant Pot. Now, heat the oil and cook celery and leeks until softened. 2. Add the sauerkraut and mushrooms and cook for 2 minutes more. 3. Add the remaining ingredients and stir to combine well. 4. Secure the lid. Choose Manual mode and High Pressure; cook for 10 minutes. Once cooking is complete, use a natural pressure release; carefully remove the lid. Bon appétit!

Indian Okra

Prep time: 8 minutes | Cook time: 7 minutes | Serves 6

- 1 pound (454 g) young okra
- 4 tablespoons ghee or avocado oil
- ½ teaspoon cumin seeds
- ¼ teaspoon ground turmeric
- Pinch of ground cinnamon
- ½ medium onion, diced
- 2 cloves garlic, minced
- 2 teaspoons minced fresh
- ginger
- 1 serrano chile, seeded and ribs removed, minced
- 1 small tomato, diced
- ½ teaspoon sea salt
- ¼ teaspoon cayenne pepper (optional)
- 1 cup vegetable stock or filtered water

1. Rinse and thoroughly dry the okra. Slice it on a diagonal into slices ½ to ¾ inch thick, discarding the stems. 2. Set the Instant Pot to Sauté. Once hot, add the ghee and heat until melted. Stir in the cumin seeds, turmeric, and cinnamon and cook until they are fragrant, about 1 minute. This may cause the cumin seeds to jump and pop. Add the onion and cook, stirring frequently, until soft and translucent, about 3 minutes. Add the garlic, ginger, and serrano chile and sauté for an additional minute. Press Cancel. 3. Stir in the tomato, okra, salt, cayenne (if using), and stock. Secure the lid and set the steam release valve to Sealing. Press the Manual button and set the cook time to 2 minutes. 4. When the Instant Pot beeps, carefully switch the steam release valve to Venting to quick-release the pressure. When fully released, open the lid. Stir gently and allow the okra to rest on the Keep Warm setting for a few minutes before serving.

Braised Whole Cauliflower with North African Spices

Prep time: 15 minutes | Cook time: 10 minutes | Serves 4

- 2 tablespoons extra-virgin olive oil
- 6 garlic cloves, minced
- 3 anchovy fillets, rinsed and minced (optional)
- 2 teaspoons ras el hanout
- ⅛ teaspoon red pepper flakes
- 1 (28-ounce / 794-g) can whole peeled tomatoes,
- drained with juice reserved, chopped coarse
- 1 large head cauliflower (3 pounds / 1.4 kg)
- ½ cup pitted brine-cured green olives, chopped coarse
- ¼ cup golden raisins
- ¼ cup fresh cilantro leaves
- ¼ cup pine nuts, toasted

1. Using highest sauté function, cook oil, garlic, anchovies (if using), ras el hanout, and pepper flakes in Instant Pot until fragrant, about 3 minutes. Turn off Instant Pot, then stir in tomatoes and reserved juice. 2. Trim outer leaves of cauliflower and cut stem flush with bottom florets. Using paring knife, cut 4-inch-deep cross in stem. Nestle cauliflower stem side down into pot and spoon some of sauce over top. Lock lid in place and close pressure release valve. Select high pressure cook function and cook for 3 minutes. 3. Turn off Instant Pot and quick-release pressure. Carefully remove lid, allowing steam to escape away from you. Using tongs and slotted spoon, transfer cauliflower to serving dish and tent with aluminum foil. Stir olives and raisins into sauce and cook, using highest sauté function, until sauce has thickened slightly, about 5 minutes. Season with salt and pepper to taste. Cut cauliflower into wedges and spoon some of sauce over top. Sprinkle with cilantro and pine nuts. Serve, passing remaining sauce separately.

Savory and Rich Creamed Kale

Prep time: 10 minutes | Cook time: 5 minutes | Serves 4

- 2 tablespoons extra-virgin olive oil
- 2 cloves garlic, crushed
- 1 small onion, chopped
- 12 ounces (340 g) kale, finely chopped
- ½ cup chicken broth
- 1 teaspoon Herbes de Provence
- 4 ounces (113 g) cream cheese
- ½ cup full-fat heavy cream
- 1 teaspoon dried tarragon

1. Press the Sauté button on the Instant Pot and heat the olive oil. Add the garlic and onion to the pot and sauté for 2 minutes, or until the onion is soft. Stir in the kale, chicken broth and Herbes de Provence. 2. Lock the lid. Select the Manual mode and set the cooking time for 3 minutes at High Pressure. When the timer goes off, perform a quick pressure release. Carefully open the lid. 3. Stir in the cream cheese, heavy cream and tarragon. Stir well to thicken the dish. Serve immediately.

Lemony Brussels Sprouts with Poppy Seeds

Prep time: 10 minutes | Cook time: 2 minutes | Serves 4

- 1 pound (454 g) Brussels sprouts
- 2 tablespoons avocado oil, divided
- 1 cup vegetable broth or chicken bone broth
- 1 tablespoon minced garlic
- ½ teaspoon kosher salt
- Freshly ground black pepper, to taste
- ½ medium lemon
- ½ tablespoon poppy seeds

1. Trim the Brussels sprouts by cutting off the stem ends and removing any loose outer leaves. Cut each in half lengthwise (through the stem). 2. Set the electric pressure cooker to the Sauté/ More setting. When the pot is hot, pour in 1 tablespoon of the avocado oil. 3. Add half of the Brussels sprouts to the pot, cut-side down, and let them brown for 3 to 5 minutes without disturbing. Transfer to a bowl and add the remaining tablespoon of avocado oil and the remaining Brussels sprouts to the pot. Hit Cancel and return all of the Brussels sprouts to the pot. 4. Add the broth, garlic, salt, and a few grinds of pepper. Stir to distribute the seasonings. 5. Close and lock the lid of the pressure cooker. Set the valve to sealing. 6. Cook on high pressure for 2 minutes. 7. While the Brussels sprouts are cooking, zest the lemon, then cut it into quarters. 8. When the cooking is complete, hit Cancel and quick release the pressure. 9. Once the pin drops, unlock and remove the lid. 10. Using a slotted spoon, transfer the Brussels sprouts to a serving bowl. Toss with the lemon zest, a squeeze of lemon juice, and the poppy seeds. Serve immediately.

Parmesan Cauliflower Mash

Prep time: 7 minutes | Cook time: 5 minutes | Serves 4

- 1 head cauliflower, cored and cut into large florets
- ½ teaspoon kosher salt
- ½ teaspoon garlic pepper
- 2 tablespoons plain Greek yogurt
- ¾ cup freshly grated Parmesan cheese
- 1 tablespoon unsalted butter or ghee (optional)
- Chopped fresh chives

1. Pour 1 cup of water into the electric pressure cooker and insert a steamer basket or wire rack. 2. Place the cauliflower in the basket. 3. Close and lock the lid of the pressure cooker. Set the valve to sealing. 4. Cook on high pressure for 5 minutes. 5. When the cooking is complete, hit Cancel and quick release the pressure. 6. Once the pin drops, unlock and remove the lid. 7. Remove the cauliflower from the pot and pour out the water. Return the cauliflower to the pot and add the salt, garlic pepper, yogurt, and cheese. Use an immersion blender or potato masher to purée or mash the cauliflower in the pot. 8. Spoon into a serving bowl, and garnish with butter (if using) and chives.

Chinese-Style Pe-Tsai with Onion

Prep time: 5 minutes | Cook time: 8 minutes | Serves 4

- 2 tablespoons sesame oil
- 1 yellow onion, chopped
- 1 pound (454 g) pe-tsai cabbage, shredded
- ¼ cup rice wine vinegar
- 1 tablespoon coconut aminos
- 1 teaspoon finely minced garlic
- ½ teaspoon salt
- ¼ teaspoon Szechuan pepper

1. Set the Instant Pot on the Sauté mode and heat the sesame oil. Add the onion to the pot and sauté for 5 minutes, or until tender. Stir in the remaining ingredients. 2. Lock the lid. Select the Manual mode and set the cooking time for 3 minutes on High Pressure. When the timer goes off, perform a quick pressure release. Carefully open the lid. 3. Transfer the cabbage mixture to a bowl and serve immediately.

Falafel and Lettuce Salad

Prep time: 10 minutes | Cook time: 6 to 8 minutes | Serves 4

- 1 cup shredded cauliflower
- ⅓ cup coconut flour
- 1 teaspoon grated lemon zest
- 1 egg, beaten
- 2 tablespoons coconut oil
- 2 cups chopped lettuce
- 1 cucumber, chopped
- 1 tablespoon olive oil
- 1 teaspoon lemon juice
- ½ teaspoon cayenne pepper

1. In a bowl, combine the cauliflower, coconut flour, grated lemon zest and egg. Form the mixture into small balls. 2. Set the Instant Pot to the Sauté mode and melt the coconut oil. Place the balls in the pot in a single layer. Cook for 3 to 4 minutes per side, or until they are golden brown. 3. In a separate bowl, stir together the remaining ingredients. 4. Place the cooked balls on top and serve.

Vinegary Broccoli with Cheese

Prep time: 5 minutes | Cook time: 5 minutes | Serves 4

- 1 pound (454 g) broccoli, cut into florets
- 1 cup water
- 2 garlic cloves, minced
- 1 cup crumbled Cottage cheese
- 2 tablespoons balsamic vinegar
- 1 teaspoon cumin seeds
- 1 teaspoon mustard seeds
- Salt and pepper, to taste

1. Pour the water into the Instant Pot and put the steamer basket in the pot. Place the broccoli in the steamer basket. 2. Close and secure the lid. Select the Manual setting and set the cooking time for 5 minutes at High Pressure. Once the timer goes off, do a quick pressure release. Carefully open the lid. 3. Stir in the remaining ingredients. 4. Serve immediately.

Chapter
7

Desserts

Chapter 7 Desserts

Tapioca Berry Parfaits

Prep time: 10 minutes | Cook time: 6 minutes | Serves 4

- 2 cups unsweetened almond milk
- ½ cup small pearl tapioca, rinsed and still wet
- 1 teaspoon almond extract
- 1 tablespoon pure maple syrup
- 2 cups berries
- ¼ cup slivered almonds

1. Pour the almond milk into the electric pressure cooker. Stir in the tapioca and almond extract. 2. Close and lock the lid of the pressure cooker. Set the valve to sealing. 3. Cook on High pressure for 6 minutes. 4. When the cooking is complete, hit Cancel. Allow the pressure to release naturally for 10 minutes, then quick release any remaining pressure. 5. Once the pin drops, unlock and remove the lid. Remove the pot to a cooling rack. 6. Stir in the maple syrup and let the mixture cool for about an hour. 7. In small glasses, create several layers of tapioca, berries, and almonds. Refrigerate for 1 hour. 8. Serve chilled.

Coconut Almond Cream Cake

Prep time: 10 minutes | Cook time: 40 minutes | Serves 8

- Nonstick cooking spray
- 1 cup almond flour
- ½ cup unsweetened shredded coconut
- ⅓ cup Swerve
- 1 teaspoon baking powder
- 1 teaspoon apple pie spice
- 2 eggs, lightly whisked
- ¼ cup unsalted butter, melted
- ½ cup heavy (whipping) cream

1. Grease a 6-inch round cake pan with the cooking spray. 2. In a medium bowl, mix together the almond flour, coconut, Swerve, baking powder, and apple pie spice. 3. Add the eggs, then the butter, then the cream, mixing well after each addition. 4. Pour the batter into the pan and cover with aluminum foil. 5. Pour 2 cups of water into the inner cooking pot of the Instant Pot, then place a trivet in the pot. Place the pan on the trivet. 6. Lock the lid into place. Select Manual and adjust the pressure to High. Cook for 40 minutes. When the cooking is complete, let the pressure release naturally for 10 minutes, then quick-release any remaining pressure. Unlock the lid. 7. Carefully take out the pan and let it cool for 15 to 20 minutes. Invert the cake onto a plate. Sprinkle with shredded coconut, almond slices, or powdered sweetener, if desired, and serve.

Traditional Kentucky Butter Cake

Prep time: 5 minutes | Cook time: 35 minutes | Serves 4

- 2 cups almond flour
- ¾ cup granulated erythritol
- 1½ teaspoons baking powder
- 4 eggs
- 1 tablespoon vanilla extract
- ½ cup butter, melted
- Cooking spray
- ½ cup water

1. In a medium bowl, whisk together the almond flour, erythritol, and baking powder. Whisk well to remove any lumps. 2. Add the eggs and vanilla and whisk until combined. 3. Add the butter and whisk until the batter is mostly smooth and well combined. 4. Grease the pan with cooking spray and pour in the batter. Cover tightly with aluminum foil. 5. Add the water to the pot. Place the Bundt pan on the trivet and carefully lower it into the pot using. 6. Set the lid in place. Select the Manual mode and set the cooking time for 35 minutes on High Pressure. When the timer goes off, do a quick pressure release. Carefully open the lid. 7. Remove the pan from the pot. Let the cake cool in the pan before flipping out onto a plate.

Greek Yogurt Strawberry Pops

Prep time: 5 minutes | Cook time: 0 minutes | Serves 6

- 2 ripe bananas, peeled, cut into ½-inch pieces, and frozen
- ½ cup plain 2 percent Greek
- yogurt
- 1 cup chopped fresh strawberries

1. In a food processor, combine the bananas and yogurt and process at high speed for 2 minutes, until mostly smooth (it's okay if a few small chunks remain). Scrape down the sides of the bowl, add the strawberries, and process for 1 minute, until smooth. 2. Divide the mixture evenly among six ice-pop molds. Tap each mold on a countertop a few times to get rid of any air pockets, then place an ice-pop stick into each mold and transfer the molds to the freezer. Freeze for at least 4 hours, or until frozen solid. 3. To unmold each ice pop, run it under cold running water for 5 seconds, taking care not to get water inside the mold, then remove the ice pop from the mold. Eat the ice pops right away or store in a ziplock plastic freezer bag in the freezer for up to 2 months.

Deconstructed Tiramisu

Prep time: 5 minutes | Cook time: 9 minutes | Serves 4

- 1 cup heavy cream (or full-fat coconut milk for dairy-free)
- 2 large egg yolks
- 2 tablespoons brewed decaf espresso or strong brewed coffee
- 2 tablespoons Swerve, or more to taste
- 1 teaspoon rum extract
- 1 teaspoon unsweetened cocoa powder, or more to taste
- Pinch of fine sea salt
- 1 cup cold water
- 4 teaspoons Swerve, for topping

1. Heat the cream in a pan over medium-high heat until hot, about 2 minutes. 2. Place the egg yolks, coffee, sweetener, rum extract, cocoa powder, and salt in a blender and blend until smooth. 3. While the blender is running, slowly pour in the hot cream. Taste and adjust the sweetness to your liking. Add more cocoa powder, if desired. 4. Scoop the mixture into four ramekins with a spatula. Cover the ramekins with aluminum foil. 5. Place a trivet in the bottom of the Instant Pot and pour in the water. Place the ramekins on the trivet. 6. Lock the lid. Select the Manual mode and set the cooking time for 7 minutes at High Pressure. 7. When the timer beeps, use a quick pressure release. Carefully remove the lid. 8. Keep the ramekins covered with the foil and place in the refrigerator for about 2 hours until completely chilled. 9. Sprinkle 1 teaspoon of Swerve on top of each tiramisu. Use the oven broiler to melt the sweetener. 10. Put in the fridge to chill the topping, about 20 minutes. 11. Serve.

Pine Nut Mousse

Prep time: 5 minutes | Cook time: 35 minutes | Serves 8

- 1 tablespoon butter
- 1¼ cups pine nuts
- 1¼ cups full-fat heavy cream
- 2 large eggs
- 1 teaspoon vanilla extract
- 1 cup Swerve, reserve 1 tablespoon
- 1 cup water
- 1 cup full-fat heavy whipping cream

1. Butter the bottom and the side of a pie pan and set aside. 2. In a food processor, blend the pine nuts and heavy cream. Add the eggs, vanilla extract and Swerve and pulse a few times to incorporate. 3. Pour the batter into the pan and loosely cover with aluminum foil. Pour the water in the Instant Pot and place the trivet inside. Place the pan on top of the trivet. 4. Close the lid. Select Manual mode and set the timer for 35 minutes on High pressure. 5. In a small mixing bowl, whisk the heavy whipping cream and 1 tablespoon of Swerve until a soft peak forms. 6. When timer beeps, use a natural pressure release for 15 minutes, then release any remaining pressure and open the lid. 7. Serve immediately with whipped cream on top.

Daikon and Almond Cake

Prep time: 10 minutes | Cook time: 45 minutes | Serves 12

- 5 eggs, beaten
- ½ cup heavy cream
- 1 cup almond flour
- 1 daikon, diced
- 1 teaspoon ground
- cinnamon
- 2 tablespoon erythritol
- 1 tablespoon butter, melted
- 1 cup water

1. In the mixing bowl, mix up eggs, heavy cream, almond flour, ground cinnamon, and erythritol. 2. When the mixture is smooth, add daikon and stir it carefully with the help of the spatula. 3. Pour the mixture in the cake pan. 4. Then pour water and insert the trivet in the instant pot. 5. Place the cake in the instant pot. 6. Set the lid in place. Select the Manual mode and set the cooking time for 45 minutes on High Pressure. When the timer goes off, do a quick pressure release. Carefully open the lid. 7. Serve immediately.

Lemon-Ricotta Cheesecake

Prep time: 10 minutes | Cook time: 30 minutes | Serves 6

- Unsalted butter or vegetable oil, for greasing the pan
- 8 ounces (227 g) cream cheese, at room temperature
- ¼ cup plus 1 teaspoon Swerve, plus more as needed
- ⅓ cup full-fat or part-skim
- ricotta cheese, at room temperature
- Zest of 1 lemon
- Juice of 1 lemon
- ½ teaspoon lemon extract
- 2 eggs, at room temperature
- 2 tablespoons sour cream

1. Grease a 6-inch springform pan extremely well. I find this easiest to do with a silicone basting brush so I can get into all the nooks and crannies. Alternatively, line the sides of the pan with parchment paper. 2. In the bowl of a stand mixer, beat the cream cheese, ¼ cup of Swerve, the ricotta, lemon zest, lemon juice, and lemon extract on high speed until you get a smooth mixture with no lumps. 3. Taste to ensure the sweetness is to your liking and adjust if needed. 4. Add the eggs, reduce the speed to low and gently blend until the eggs are just incorporated. Overbeating at this stage will result in a cracked crust. 5. Pour the mixture into the prepared pan and cover with aluminum foil or a silicone lid. 6. Pour 2 cups of water into the inner cooking pot of the Instant Pot, then place a trivet in the pot. Place the covered pan on the trivet. 7. Lock the lid into place. Select Manual and adjust the pressure to High. Cook for 30 minutes. When the cooking is complete, let the pressure release naturally. Unlock the lid. 8. Carefully remove the pan from the pot, and remove the foil. 9. In a small bowl, mix together the sour cream and remaining 1 teaspoon of Swerve and spread this over the top of the warm cake. 10. Refrigerate the cheesecake for 6 to 8 hours. Do not be in a hurry! The cheesecake needs every bit of this time to be its best.

Cocoa Custard

Prep time: 5 minutes | Cook time: 7 minutes | Serves 4

- 2 cups heavy cream (or full-fat coconut milk for dairy-free)
- 4 large egg yolks
- ¼ cup Swerve, or more to taste
- 1 tablespoon plus 1 teaspoon unsweetened cocoa powder, or more to taste
- ½ teaspoon almond extract
- Pinch of fine sea salt
- 1 cup cold water

1. Heat the cream in a pan over medium-high heat until hot, about 2 minutes. 2. Place the remaining ingredients except the water in a blender and blend until smooth. 3. While the blender is running, slowly pour in the hot cream. Taste and adjust the sweetness to your liking. Add more cocoa powder, if desired. 4. Scoop the custard mixture into four ramekins with a spatula. Cover the ramekins with aluminum foil. 5. Place a trivet in the Instant Pot and pour in the water. Place the ramekins on the trivet. 6. Lock the lid. Select the Manual mode and set the cooking time for 5 minutes at High Pressure. 7. When the timer beeps, use a quick pressure release. Carefully remove the lid. 8. Remove the foil and set the foil aside. Let the custard cool for 15 minutes. Cover the ramekins with the foil again and place in the refrigerator to chill completely, about 2 hours. 9. Serve.

Espresso Cheesecake with Raspberries

Prep time: 5 minutes | Cook time: 35 minutes | Serves 8

- 1 cup blanched almond flour
- ½ cup plus 2 tablespoons Swerve
- 3 tablespoons espresso powder, divided
- 2 tablespoons butter
- 1 egg
- ½ cup full-fat heavy cream
- 16 ounces (454 g) cream
- cheese
- 1 cup water
- 6 ounces (170 g) dark chocolate (at least 80% cacao)
- 8 ounces (227 g) full-fat heavy whipping cream
- 2 cups raspberries

1. In a small mixing bowl, combine the almond flour, 2 tablespoons of Swerve, 1 tablespoon of espresso powder and the butter. 2. Line the bottom of a springform pan with parchment paper. Press the almond flour dough flat on the bottom and about 1 inch on the sides. Set aside. 3. In a food processor, mix the egg, heavy cream, cream cheese, remaining Swerve and remaining espresso powder until smooth. 4. Pour the cream cheese mixture into the springform pan. Loosely cover with aluminum foil. 5. Put the water in the Instant Pot and place the trivet inside. 6. Close the lid. Select Manual button and set the timer for 35 minutes on High pressure. 7. When timer beeps, use a natural pressure release for 15 minutes, then release any remaining pressure. Open the lid. 8. Remove the springform pan and place it on a cooling rack for 2 to 3 hours or until it reaches room temperature. Refrigerate overnight. 9. Melt the chocolate and heavy whipping cream in the double boiler. Cool for 15 minutes and drizzle on top of the cheesecake, allowing the chocolate to drip down the sides. 10. Add the raspberries on top of the cheesecake before serving.

Almond Pie with Coconut

Prep time: 5 minutes | Cook time: 41 minutes | Serves 8

- 1 cup almond flour
- ½ cup coconut milk
- 1 teaspoon vanilla extract
- 2 tablespoons butter,
- softened
- 1 tablespoon Truvia
- ¼ cup shredded coconut
- 1 cup water

1. In the mixing bowl, mix up almond flour, coconut milk, vanilla extract, butter, Truvia, and shredded coconut. 2. When the mixture is smooth, transfer it in the baking pan and flatten. 3. Pour water and insert the trivet in the instant pot. 4. Put the baking pan with cake on the trivet. 5. Lock the lid. Select the Manual mode and set the cooking time for 41 minutes on High Pressure. Once the timer goes off, perform a natural pressure release for 10 minutes, then release any remaining pressure. Carefully open the lid. 6. Serve immediately.

Chocolate Macadamia Bark

Prep time: 5 minutes | Cook time: 20 minutes | Serves 20

- 16 ounces (454 g) raw dark chocolate
- 3 tablespoons raw coconut butter
- 2 tablespoons coconut oil
- 2 cups chopped macadamia
- nuts
- 1 tablespoon almond butter
- ½ teaspoon salt
- ⅓ cup Swerve, or more to taste

1. In a large bowl, mix together the chocolate, coconut butter, coconut oil, macadamia nuts, almond butter, salt, and Swerve. Combine them very thoroughly, until a perfectly even mixture is obtained. 2. Pour 1 cup of filtered water into the Instant Pot, and insert the trivet. Transfer the mixture from the bowl into a well-greased, Instant Pot-friendly dish. 3. Place the dish onto the trivet, and cover loosely with aluminum foil. Close the lid, set the pressure release to Sealing, and select Manual. Set the Instant Pot to 20 minutes on High Pressure, and let cook. 4. Once cooked, let the pressure naturally disperse from the Instant Pot for about 10 minutes, then carefully switch the pressure release to Venting. 5. Open the Instant Pot and remove the dish. Cool in the refrigerator until set. Break into pieces, serve, and enjoy! Store remaining bark in the refrigerator or freezer.

Cocoa Cookies

Prep time: 15 minutes | Cook time: 25 minutes | Serves 4

- ½ cup coconut flour
- 3 tablespoons cream cheese
- 1 teaspoon cocoa powder
- 1 tablespoon erythritol
- ¼ teaspoon baking powder
- 1 teaspoon apple cider vinegar
- 1 tablespoon butter
- 1 cup water, for cooking

1. Make the dough: Mix up coconut flour, cream cheese, cocoa powder, erythritol, baking powder, apple cider vinegar, and butter. Knead the dough, 2. Then transfer the dough in the baking pan and flatten it in the shape of a cookie. 3. Pour water and insert the steamer rack in the instant pot. 4. Put the pan with a cookie in the instant pot. Close and seal the lid. 5. Cook the cookie on Manual (High Pressure) for 25 minutes. Make a quick pressure release. Cool the cookie well.

Lemon Vanilla Cheesecake

Prep time: 15 minutes | Cook time: 20 minutes | Serves 6

- 2 teaspoons freshly squeezed lemon juice
- 2 teaspoons vanilla extract or almond extract
- ½ cup sour cream, divided, at room temperature
- ½ cup plus 2 teaspoons Swerve
- 8 ounces (227 g) cream cheese, at room temperature
- 2 eggs, at room temperature

1. Pour 2 cups of water into the inner cooking pot of the Instant Pot, then place a trivet (preferably with handles) in the pot. Line the sides of a 6-inch springform pan with parchment paper. 2. In a food processor, put the lemon juice, vanilla, ¼ cup of sour cream, ½ cup of Swerve, and the cream cheese. 3. Gently but thoroughly blend all the ingredients, scraping down the sides of the bowl as needed. 4. Add the eggs and blend only as long as you need to in order to get them well incorporated, 20 to 30 seconds. Your mixture will be pourable by now. 5. Pour the mixture into the prepared pan. Cover the pan with aluminum foil and place on the trivet. (If your trivet doesn't have handles, you may wish to use a foil sling to make removing the pan easier.) 6. Lock the lid into place. Select Manual and adjust the pressure to High. Cook for 20 minutes. When the cooking is complete, let the pressure release naturally. Unlock the lid. 7. Meanwhile, in a small bowl, mix together the remaining ¼ cup of sour cream and 2 teaspoons of Swerve for the topping. 8. Take out the cheesecake and remove the foil. Spread the topping over the top. Doing this while the cheesecake is still hot helps melt the topping into the cheesecake. 9. Put the cheesecake in the refrigerator and leave it alone. Seriously. Leave it alone and let it chill for at least 6 to 8 hours. It won't taste right hot. 10. When you're ready to serve, open the sides of the pan and peel off the parchment paper. Slice and serve.

Cinnamon Roll Cheesecake

Prep time: 15 minutes | Cook time: 35 minutes | Serves 12

Crust:
- 3½ tablespoons unsalted butter or coconut oil
- 1½ ounces (43 g) unsweetened baking chocolate, chopped
- 1 large egg, beaten

Filling:
- 4 (8-ounce / 227-g) packages cream cheese, softened
- ¾ cup Swerve
- ½ cup unsweetened almond milk (or hemp milk for nut-

Cinnamon Swirl:
- 6 tablespoons (¾ stick) unsalted butter (or butter flavored coconut oil for dairy-free)
- ½ cup Swerve
- Seeds scraped from ½ vanilla bean (about 8 inches

- ⅓ cup Swerve
- 2 teaspoons ground cinnamon
- 1 teaspoon vanilla extract
- ¼ teaspoon fine sea salt

free)
- 1 teaspoon vanilla extract
- ¼ teaspoon almond extract (omit for nut-free)
- ¼ teaspoon fine sea salt
- 3 large eggs

long), or 1 teaspoon vanilla extract
- 1 tablespoon ground cinnamon
- ¼ teaspoon fine sea salt
- 1 cup cold water

1. Line a baking pan with two layers of aluminum foil. 2. Make the crust: Melt the butter in a pan over medium-low heat. Slowly add the chocolate and stir until melted. Stir in the egg, sweetener, cinnamon, vanilla extract, and salt. 3. Transfer the crust mixture to the prepared baking pan, spreading it with your hands to cover the bottom completely. 4. Make the filling: In the bowl of a stand mixer, add the cream cheese, sweetener, milk, extracts, and salt and mix until well blended. Add the eggs, one at a time, mixing on low speed after each addition just until blended. Then blend until the filling is smooth. Pour half of the filling over the crust. 5. Make the cinnamon swirl: Heat the butter over high heat in a pan until the butter froths and brown flecks appear, stirring occasionally. Stir in the sweetener, vanilla seeds, cinnamon, and salt. Remove from the heat and allow to cool slightly. 6. Spoon half of the cinnamon swirl on top of the cheesecake filling in the baking pan. Use a knife to cut the cinnamon swirl through the filling several times for a marbled effect. Top with the rest of the cheesecake filling and cinnamon swirl. Cut the cinnamon swirl through the cheesecake filling again several times. 7. Place a trivet in the bottom of the Instant Pot and pour in the water. Use a foil sling to lower the baking pan onto the trivet. Cover the cheesecake with 3 large sheets of paper towel to ensure that condensation doesn't leak onto it. Tuck in the sides of the sling. 8. Lock the lid. Select the Manual mode and set the cooking time for 26 minutes at High Pressure. 9. When the timer beeps, use a natural pressure release for 10 minutes. Carefully remove the lid. 10. Use the foil sling to lift the pan out of the Instant Pot. 11. Let the cheesecake cool, then place in the refrigerator for 4 hours to chill and set completely before slicing and serving.

Cardamom Rolls with Cream Cheese

Prep time: 20 minutes | Cook time: 18 minutes | Serves 5

- ½ cup coconut flour
- 1 tablespoon ground cardamom
- 2 tablespoon Swerve
- 1 egg, whisked
- ¼ cup almond milk
- 1 tablespoon butter, softened
- 1 tablespoon cream cheese
- ⅓ cup water

1. Combine together coconut flour, almond milk, and softened butter. 2. Knead the smooth dough. 3. Roll up the dough with the help of the rolling pin. 4. Then combine together Swerve and ground cardamom. 5. Sprinkle the surface of the dough with the ground cardamom mixture. 6. Roll the dough into one big roll and cut them into servings. 7. Place the rolls into the instant pot round mold. 8. Pour water in the instant pot (⅓ cup) and insert the mold inside. 9. Set Manual mode (High Pressure) for 18 minutes. 10. Then use the natural pressure release method for 15 minutes. 11. Chill the rolls to the room temperature and spread with cream cheese.

Caramelized Pumpkin Cheesecake

Prep time: 15 minutes | Cook time: 45 minutes | Serves 8

Crust:
- 1½ cups almond flour
- 4 tablespoons butter, melted
- 1 tablespoon Swerve
- 1 tablespoon granulated erythritol
- ½ teaspoon ground cinnamon
- Cooking spray

Filling:
- 16 ounces (454 g) cream cheese, softened
- ½ cup granulated erythritol
- 2 eggs
- ¼ cup pumpkin purée
- 3 tablespoons Swerve
- 1 teaspoon vanilla extract
- ¼ teaspoon pumpkin pie spice
- 1½ cups water

1. To make the crust: In a medium bowl, combine the almond flour, butter, Swerve, erythritol, and cinnamon. Use a fork to press it all together. 2. Spray the pan with cooking spray and line the bottom with parchment paper. 3. Press the crust evenly into the pan. Work the crust up the sides of the pan, about halfway from the top, and make sure there are no bare spots on the bottom. 4. Place the crust in the freezer for 20 minutes while you make the filling. 5. To make the filling: In a large bowl using a hand mixer on medium speed, combine the cream cheese and erythritol. Beat until the cream cheese is light and fluffy, 2 to 3 minutes. 6. Add the eggs, pumpkin purée, Swerve, vanilla, and pumpkin pie spice. Beat until well combined. 7. Remove the crust from the freezer and pour in the filling. Cover the pan with aluminum foil and place it on the trivet. 8.

Add the water to the pot and carefully lower the trivet into the pot. 9. Set the lid in place. Select the Manual mode and set the cooking time for 45 minutes on High Pressure. When the timer goes off, do a quick pressure release. Carefully open the lid. 10. Remove the trivet and cheesecake from the pot. Remove the foil from the pan. The center of the cheesecake should still be slightly jiggly. 11. Let the cheesecake cool for 30 minutes on the counter before placing it in the refrigerator to set. Leave the cheesecake in the refrigerator for at least 6 hours before removing the sides and serving.

Hearty Crème Brûlée

Prep time: 5 minutes | Cook time: 30 minutes | Serves 4

- 5 egg yolks
- 5 tablespoons powdered erythritol
- 1½ cups heavy cream
- 2 teaspoons vanilla extract
- 2 cups water

1. In a small bowl, use a fork to break up the egg yolks. Stir in the erythritol. 2. Pour the cream into a small saucepan over medium-low heat and let it warm up for 3 to 4 minutes. Remove the saucepan from the heat. 3. Temper the egg yolks by slowly adding a small spoonful of the warm cream, keep whisking. Do this three times to make sure the egg yolks are fully tempered. 4. Slowly add the tempered eggs to the cream, whisking the whole time. Add the vanilla and whisk again. 5. Pour the cream mixture into the ramekins. Each ramekin should have ½ cup liquid. Cover each with aluminum foil. 6. Place the trivet inside the Instant Pot. Add the water. Carefully place the ramekins on top of the trivet. 7. Close the lid. Select Manual mode and set cooking time for 11 minutes on High Pressure. 8. When timer beeps, use a natural release for 15 minutes, then release any remaining pressure. Open the lid. 9. Carefully remove a ramekin from the pot. Remove the foil and check for doneness. The custard should be mostly set with a slightly jiggly center. 10. Place all the ramekins in the fridge for 2 hours to chill and set. Serve chilled.

Chocolate Pecan Clusters

Prep time: 5 minutes | Cook time: 5 minutes | Makes 8 clusters

- 3 tablespoons butter
- ¼ cup heavy cream
- 1 teaspoon vanilla extract
- 1 cup chopped pecans
- ¼ cup low-carb chocolate chips

1. Press the Sauté button and add butter to Instant Pot. Allow butter to melt and begin to turn golden brown. Once it begins to brown, immediately add heavy cream. Press the Cancel button. 2. Add vanilla and chopped pecans to Instant Pot. Allow to cool for 10 minutes, stirring occasionally. Spoon mixture onto parchment-lined baking sheet to form eight clusters, and scatter chocolate chips over clusters. Place in fridge to cool.

Strawberry Cheesecake

Prep time: 20 minutes | Cook time: 10 minutes | Serves 2

- 1 tablespoon gelatin
- 4 tablespoon water (for gelatin)
- 4 tablespoon cream cheese
- 1 strawberry, chopped
- ¼ cup coconut milk
- 1 tablespoon Swerve

1. Mix up gelatin and water and leave the mixture for 10 minutes. 2. Meanwhile, pour coconut milk in the instant pot. 3. Bring it to boil on Sauté mode, about 10 minutes. 4. Meanwhile, mash the strawberry and mix it up with cream cheese. 5. Add the mixture in the hot coconut milk and stir until smooth. 6. Cool the liquid for 10 minutes and add gelatin. Whisk it until gelatin is melted. 7. Then pour the cheesecake in the mold and freeze in the freezer for 3 hours.

Spiced Pear Applesauce

Prep time: 15 minutes | Cook time: 5 minutes | Makes: 3½ cups

- 1 pound pears, peeled, cored, and sliced
- 2 teaspoons apple pie spice
- or cinnamon
- Pinch kosher salt
- Juice of ½ small lemon

1. In the electric pressure cooker, combine the apples, pears, apple pie spice, salt, lemon juice, and ¼ cup of water. 2. Close and lock the lid of the pressure cooker. Set the valve to sealing. 3. Cook on high pressure for 5 minutes. 4. When the cooking is complete, hit Cancel and let the pressure release naturally. 5. Once the pin drops, unlock and remove the lid. 6. Mash the apples and pears with a potato masher to the consistency you like. 7. Serve warm, or cool to room temperature and refrigerate.

Egg Custard Tarts

Prep time: 10 minutes | Cook time: 20 minutes | Serves 2

- ¼ cup almond flour
- 1 tablespoon coconut oil
- 2 egg yolks
- ¼ cup coconut milk
- 1 tablespoon erythritol
- 1 teaspoon vanilla extract
- 1 cup water, for cooking

1. Make the dough: Mix up almond flour and coconut oil. 2. Then place the dough into 2 mini tart molds and flatten well in the shape of cups. 3. Pour water in the instant pot. Insert the steamer rack. 4. Place the tart mold in the instant pot. Close and seal the lid. 5. Cook them for 3 minutes on Manual mode (High Pressure). Make a quick pressure release. 6. Then whisk together vanilla extract, erythritol, coconut milk, and egg yolks. 7. Pour the liquid in the tart molds and

close the lid. 8. Cook the dessert for 7 minutes on Manual mode (High Pressure). 9. Then allow the natural pressure release for 10 minutes more.

Nutmeg Cupcakes

Prep time: 5 minutes | Cook time: 30 minutes | Serves 7

Cake:
- 2 cups blanched almond flour
- 2 tablespoons grass-fed butter, softened
- 2 eggs
- ½ cup unsweetened almond
- milk
- ½ cup Swerve, or more to taste
- ½ teaspoon ground nutmeg
- ½ teaspoon baking powder

Frosting:
- 4 ounces (113 g) full-fat cream cheese, softened
- 4 tablespoons grass-fed butter, softened
- 2 cups heavy whipping cream
- 1 teaspoon vanilla extract
- ½ cup Swerve, or more to taste
- 6 tablespoons sugar-free chocolate chips (optional)

1. Pour 1 cup of filtered water into the inner pot of the Instant Pot, then insert the trivet. In a large bowl, combine the flour, butter, eggs, almond milk, Swerve, nutmeg, and baking powder. Mix thoroughly. Working in batches if needed, transfer this mixture into a well-greased, Instant Pot-friendly muffin (or egg bites) mold. 2. Place the molds onto the trivet, and cover loosely with aluminum foil. Close the lid, set the pressure release to Sealing, and select Manual. Set the Instant Pot to 30 minutes on High Pressure, and let cook. 3. While you wait, in a large bowl, combine the cream cheese, butter, whipping cream, vanilla, Swerve, and chocolate chips. Use an electric hand mixer until you achieve a light and fluffy texture. Place frosting in refrigerator. 4. Once the cupcakes are cooked, let the pressure release naturally, for about 10 minutes. Then, switch the pressure release to Venting. Open the Instant Pot, and remove the food. Let cool, top each cupcake evenly with a scoop of frosting.

Coconut Squares

Prep time: 15 minutes | Cook time: 4 minutes | Serves 2

- ⅓ cup coconut flakes
- 1 tablespoon butter
- 1 egg, beaten
- 1 cup water, for cooking

1. Mix up together coconut flakes, butter, and egg. 2. Then put the mixture into the square shape mold and flatten well. 3. Pour water and insert the steamer rack in the instant pot. 4. Put the mold with dessert on the rack. Close and seal the lid. 5. Cook the meal on Manual mode (High Pressure) for 4 minutes. Make a quick pressure release. 6. Cool the cooked dessert little and cut into the squares.

Chipotle Black Bean Brownies

Prep time: 15 minutes | Cook time: 30 minutes | Serves 8

- Nonstick cooking spray
- ½ cup dark chocolate chips, divided
- ¾ cup cooked calypso beans or black beans
- ½ cup extra-virgin olive oil
- 2 large eggs
- ¼ cup unsweetened dark chocolate cocoa powder
- ⅓ cup honey
- 1 teaspoon vanilla extract
- ⅓ cup white wheat flour
- ½ teaspoon chipotle chili powder
- ½ teaspoon ground cinnamon
- ½ teaspoon baking powder
- ½ teaspoon kosher salt

1. Spray a 7-inch Bundt pan with nonstick cooking spray. 2. Place half of the chocolate chips in a small bowl and microwave them for 30 seconds. Stir and repeat, if necessary, until the chips have completely melted. 3. In a food processor, blend the beans and oil together. Add the melted chocolate chips, eggs, cocoa powder, honey, and vanilla. Blend until the mixture is smooth. 4. In a large bowl, whisk together the flour, chili powder, cinnamon, baking powder, and salt. Pour the bean mixture from the food processor into the bowl and stir with a wooden spoon until well combined. Stir in the remaining chocolate chips. 5. Pour the batter into the prepared Bundt pan. Cover loosely with foil. 6. Pour 1 cup of water into the electric pressure cooker. 7. Place the Bundt pan onto the wire rack and lower it into the pressure cooker. 8. Close and lock the lid of the pressure cooker. Set the valve to sealing. 9. Cook on high pressure for 30 minutes. 10. When the cooking is complete, hit Cancel and quick release the pressure. 11. Once the pin drops, unlock and remove the lid. 12. Carefully transfer the pan to a cooling rack for about 10 minutes, then invert the cake onto the rack and let it cool completely. 13. Cut into slices and serve.

Pumpkin Pie Pudding

Prep time: 10 minutes | Cook time: 20 minutes | Serves 6

- Nonstick cooking spray
- 2 eggs
- ½ cup heavy (whipping) cream or almond milk (for dairy-free)
- ¾ cup Swerve
For Serving:
- ½ cup heavy (whipping) cream
- 1 (15-ounce / 425-g) can pumpkin purée
- 1 teaspoon pumpkin pie spice
- 1 teaspoon vanilla extract

1. Grease a 6-by-3-inch pan extremely well with the cooking spray, making sure it gets into all the nooks and crannies. 2. In a medium bowl, whisk the eggs. Add the cream, Swerve, pumpkin purée, pumpkin pie spice, and vanilla, and stir to mix thoroughly. 3. Pour the mixture into the prepared pan and cover it with a silicone lid or aluminum foil. 4. Pour 2 cups of water into the inner cooking pot of

the Instant Pot, then place a trivet in the pot. Place the covered pan on the trivet. 5. Lock the lid into place. Select Manual and adjust the pressure to High. Cook for 20 minutes. When the cooking is complete, let the pressure release naturally for 10 minutes, then quick-release any remaining pressure. Unlock the lid. 6. Remove the pan and place it in the refrigerator. Chill for 6 to 8 hours. 8. When ready to serve, finish by making the whipped cream. Using a hand mixer, beat the heavy cream until it forms soft peaks. Do not overbeat and turn it to butter. Serve each pudding with a dollop of whipped cream.

Vanilla Cream Pie

Prep time: 20 minutes | Cook time: 35 minutes | Serves 12

- 1 cup heavy cream
- 3 eggs, beaten
- 1 teaspoon vanilla extract
- ¼ cup erythritol
- 1 cup coconut flour
- 1 tablespoon butter, melted
- 1 cup water, for cooking

1. In the mixing bowl, mix up coconut flour, erythritol, vanilla extract, eggs, and heavy cream. 2. Grease the baking pan with melted butter. 3. Pour the coconut mixture in the baking pan. 4. Pour water and insert the steamer rack in the instant pot. 5. Place the pie on the rack. Close and seal the lid. 6. Cook the pie on Manual mode (High Pressure) for 35 minutes. 7. Allow the natural pressure release for 10 minutes.

Pumpkin Pie Spice Pots De Crème

Prep time: 5 minutes | Cook time: 7 minutes | Serves 4

- 2 cups heavy cream (or full-fat coconut milk for dairy-free)
- 4 large egg yolks
- ¼ cup Swerve, or more to taste
- 2 teaspoons pumpkin pie spice
- 1 teaspoon vanilla extract
- Pinch of fine sea salt
- 1 cup cold water

1. Heat the cream in a pan over medium-high heat until hot, about 2 minutes. 2. Place the remaining ingredients except the water in a medium bowl and stir until smooth. 3. Slowly pour in the hot cream while stirring. Taste and adjust the sweetness to your liking. Scoop the mixture into four ramekins with a spatula. Cover the ramekins with aluminum foil. 4. Place a trivet in the Instant Pot and pour in the water. Place the ramekins on the trivet. 5. Lock the lid. Select the Manual mode and set the cooking time for 5 minutes at High Pressure. 6. When the timer beeps, use a quick pressure release. Carefully remove the lid. 7. Remove the foil and set the foil aside. Let the pots de crème cool for 15 minutes. Cover the ramekins with the foil again and place in the refrigerator to chill completely, about 2 hours. 8. Serve.

Thai Pandan Coconut Custard

Prep time: 10 minutes | Cook time: 30 minutes | Serves 4

- Nonstick cooking spray
- 1 cup unsweetened coconut milk
- 3 eggs
- ⅓ cup Swerve
- 3 to 4 drops pandan extract, or use vanilla extract if you must

1. Grease a 6-inch heatproof bowl with the cooking spray. 2. In a large bowl, whisk together the coconut milk, eggs, Swerve, and pandan extract. Pour the mixture into the prepared bowl and cover it with aluminum foil. 3. Pour 2 cups of water into the inner cooking pot of the Instant Pot, then place a trivet in the pot. Place the bowl on the trivet. 4. Lock the lid into place. Select Manual and adjust the pressure to High. Cook for 30 minutes. When the cooking is complete, let the pressure release naturally. Unlock the lid. 5. Remove the bowl from the pot and remove the foil. A knife inserted into the custard should come out clean. Cool in the refrigerator for 6 to 8 hours, or until the custard is set.

Traditional Cheesecake

Prep time: 30 minutes | Cook time: 45 minutes | Serves 8

For Crust:
- 1½ cups almond flour
- 4 tablespoons butter, melted
- 1 tablespoon Swerve
- 1 tablespoon granulated

For Filling:
- 16 ounces (454 g) cream cheese, softened
- ½ cup granulated erythritol
- 2 eggs

- erythritol
- ½ teaspoon ground cinnamon

- 1 teaspoon vanilla extract
- ½ teaspoon lemon extract
- 1½ cups water

1. To make the crust: In a medium bowl, combine the almond flour, butter, Swerve, erythritol, and cinnamon. Use a fork to press it all together. When completed, the mixture should resemble wet sand. 2. Spray the springform pan with cooking spray and line the bottom with parchment paper. 3. Press the crust evenly into the pan. Work the crust up the sides of the pan, about halfway from the top, and make sure there are no bare spots on the bottom. 4. Place the crust in the freezer for 20 minutes while you make the filling. 5. To make the filling: In the bowl of a stand mixer using the whip attachment, combine the cream cheese and erythritol on medium speed until the cream cheese is light and fluffy, 2 to 3 minutes. 6. Add the eggs, vanilla extract, and lemon extract. Mix until well combined. 7. Remove the crust from the freezer and pour in the filling. Cover the pan tightly with aluminum foil and place it on the trivet. 8. Add the water to the pot and carefully lower the trivet into the pot. 9. Close the lid. Select Manual mode and set cooking time for 45 minutes on

High Pressure. 10. When timer beeps, use a quick pressure release and open the lid. 11. Remove the trivet and cheesecake from the pot. Remove the foil from the pan. The center of the cheesecake should still be slightly jiggly. If the cheesecake is still very jiggly in the center, cook for an additional 5 minutes on High pressure until the appropriate doneness is reached. 12. Let the cheesecake cool for 30 minutes on the counter before placing it in the refrigerator to set. Leave the cheesecake in the refrigerator for at least 6 hours before removing the sides of the pan, slicing, and serving.

Candied Mixed Nuts

Prep time: 5 minutes | Cook time: 15 minutes | Serves 8

- 1 cup pecan halves
- 1 cup chopped walnuts
- ⅓ cup Swerve, or more to taste
- ⅓ cup grass-fed butter
- 1 teaspoon ground cinnamon

1. Preheat your oven to 350ºF (180ºC), and line a baking sheet with aluminum foil. 2. While your oven is warming, pour ½ cup of filtered water into the inner pot of the Instant Pot, followed by the pecans, walnuts, Swerve, butter, and cinnamon. Stir nut mixture, close the lid, and then set the pressure valve to Sealing. Use the Manual mode to cook at High Pressure, for 5 minutes. 3. Once cooked, perform a quick release by carefully switching the pressure valve to Venting, and strain the nuts. Pour the nuts onto the baking sheet, spreading them out in an even layer. Place in the oven for 5 to 10 minutes (or until crisp, being careful not to overcook). Cool before serving. Store leftovers in the refrigerator or freezer.

Vanilla Poppy Seed Cake

Prep time: 10 minutes | Cook time: 25 minutes | Serves 6

- 1 cup almond flour
- 2 eggs
- ½ cup erythritol
- 2 teaspoons vanilla extract
- 1 teaspoon lemon extract
- 1 tablespoon poppy seeds
- 4 tablespoons melted butter
- ¼ cup heavy cream
- ⅛ cup sour cream
- ½ teaspoon baking powder
- 1 cup water
- ¼ cup powdered erythritol, for garnish

1. In large bowl, mix almond flour, eggs, erythritol, vanilla, lemon, and poppy seeds. 2. Add butter, heavy cream, sour cream, and baking powder. 3. Pour into 7-inch round cake pan. Cover with foil. 4. Pour water into Instant Pot and place steam rack in bottom. Place baking pan on steam rack and click lid closed. Press the Cake button and press the Adjust button to set heat to Less. Set time for 25 minutes. 5. When timer beeps, allow a 15-minute natural release, then quick-release the remaining pressure. Let cool completely. Sprinkle with powdered erythritol for serving.

Chocolate Chip Banana Cake

Prep time: 15 minutes | Cook time: 25 minutes | Serves 8

- Nonstick cooking spray
- 3 ripe bananas
- ½ cup buttermilk
- 3 tablespoons honey
- 1 teaspoon vanilla extract
- 2 large eggs, lightly beaten
- 3 tablespoons extra-virgin olive oil
- 1½ cups whole wheat pastry flour
- ⅛ teaspoon ground nutmeg
- 1 teaspoon ground cinnamon
- ¼ teaspoon salt
- 1 teaspoon baking soda
- ⅓ cup dark chocolate chips

1. Spray a 7-inch Bundt pan with nonstick cooking spray. 2. In a large bowl, mash the bananas. Add the buttermilk, honey, vanilla, eggs, and olive oil, and mix well. 3. In a medium bowl, whisk together the flour, nutmeg, cinnamon, salt, and baking soda. 4. Add the flour mixture to the banana mixture and mix well. Stir in the chocolate chips. Pour the batter into the prepared Bundt pan. Cover the pan with foil. 5. Pour 1 cup of water into the electric pressure cooker. Place the pan on the wire rack and lower it into the pressure cooker. 6. Close and lock the lid of the pressure cooker. Set the valve to sealing. 7. Cook on high pressure for 25 minutes. 8. When the cooking is complete, hit Cancel and quick release the pressure. 9. Once the pin drops, unlock and remove the lid. 10. Carefully transfer the pan to a cooling rack, uncover, and let it cool for 10 minutes. 11. Invert the cake onto the rack and let it cool for about an hour. 12. Slice and serve the cake.

Chocolate Cake with Walnuts

Prep time: 10 minutes | Cook time: 20 minutes | Serves 6

- 1 cup almond flour
- ⅔ cup Swerve
- ¼ cup unsweetened cocoa powder
- ¼ cup chopped walnuts
- 1 teaspoon baking powder
- 3 eggs
- ⅓ cup heavy (whipping) cream
- ¼ cup coconut oil
- Nonstick cooking spray

1. Put the flour, Swerve, cocoa powder, walnuts, baking powder, eggs, cream, and coconut oil in a large bowl. Using a hand mixer on high speed, combine the ingredients until the mixture is well incorporated and looks fluffy. This will keep the cake from being too dense. 2. With the cooking spray, grease a heatproof pan, such as a 3-cup Bundt pan, that fits inside your Instant Pot. Pour the cake batter into the pan and cover with aluminum foil. 3. Pour 2 cups of water into the inner cooking pot of the Instant Pot, then place a trivet in the pot. Place the pan on the trivet. 4. Lock the lid into place. Select Manual and adjust the pressure to High. Cook for 20 minutes. When the cooking is complete, let the pressure release naturally for 10 minutes, then quick-release any remaining

pressure. 5. Carefully take out the pan and let it cool for 15 to 20 minutes. Invert the cake onto a plate. It can be served hot or at room temperature. Serve with a dollop of whipped cream, if desired.

Goat Cheese–Stuffed Pears

Prep time: 6 minutes | Cook time: 2 minutes | Serves 4

- 2 ounces goat cheese, at room temperature
- 2 teaspoons pure maple syrup
- 2 ripe, firm pears, halved lengthwise and cored
- 2 tablespoons chopped pistachios, toasted

1. Pour 1 cup of water into the electric pressure cooker and insert a wire rack or trivet. 2. In a small bowl, combine the goat cheese and maple syrup. 3. Spoon the goat cheese mixture into the cored pear halves. Place the pears on the rack inside the pot, cut-side up. 4. Close and lock the lid of the pressure cooker. Set the valve to sealing. 5. Cook on high pressure for 2 minutes. 6. When the cooking is complete, hit Cancel and quick release the pressure. 7. Once the pin drops, unlock and remove the lid. 8. Using tongs, carefully transfer the pears to serving plates. 9. Sprinkle with pistachios and serve immediately.

Flourless Chocolate Tortes

Prep time: 7 minutes | Cook time: 10 minutes | Serves 8

- 7 ounces (198 g) unsweetened baking chocolate, finely chopped
- ¾ cup plus 2 tablespoons unsalted butter (or butter-flavored coconut oil for dairy-free)
- 1¼ cups Swerve, or more to taste
- 5 large eggs
- 1 tablespoon coconut flour
- 2 teaspoons ground cinnamon
- Seeds scraped from 1 vanilla bean (about 8 inches long), or 2 teaspoons vanilla extract
- Pinch of fine sea salt

1. Grease 8 ramekins. Place the chocolate and butter in a pan over medium heat and stir until the chocolate is completely melted, about 3 minutes. 2. Remove the pan from the heat, then add the remaining ingredients and stir until smooth. Taste and adjust the sweetness to your liking. Pour the batter into the greased ramekins. 3. Place a trivet in the bottom of the Instant Pot and pour in 1 cup of cold water. Place four of the ramekins on the trivet. 4. Lock the lid. Select the Manual mode and set the cooking time for 7 minutes at High Pressure. 5. When the timer beeps, use a quick pressure release. Carefully remove the lid. 6. Use tongs to remove the ramekins. Repeat with the remaining ramekins. 7. Serve the tortes warm or chilled.

Vanilla Crème Brûlée

Prep time: 7 minutes | Cook time: 9 minutes | Serves 4

- 1 cup heavy cream (or full-fat coconut milk for dairy-free)
- 2 large egg yolks
- 2 tablespoons Swerve, or more to taste
- Seeds scraped from ½

- vanilla bean (about 8 inches long), or 1 teaspoon vanilla extract
- 1 cup cold water
- 4 teaspoons Swerve, for topping

1. Heat the cream in a pan over medium-high heat until hot, about 2 minutes. 2. Place the egg yolks, Swerve, and vanilla seeds in a blender and blend until smooth. 3. While the blender is running, slowly pour in the hot cream. Taste and adjust the sweetness to your liking. 4. Scoop the mixture into four ramekins with a spatula. Cover the ramekins with aluminum foil. 5. Add the water to the Instant Pot and insert a trivet. Place the ramekins on the trivet. 6. Lock the lid. Select the Manual mode and set the cooking time for 7 minutes at High Pressure. 7. When the timer beeps, perform a quick pressure release. Carefully remove the lid. 8. Keep the ramekins covered with the foil and place in the refrigerator for about 2 hours until completely chilled. 9. Sprinkle 1 teaspoon of Swerve on top of each crème brûlée. Use the oven broiler to melt the sweetener. 10. Allow the topping to cool in the fridge for 5 minutes before serving.

Lemon and Ricotta Torte

Prep time: 15 minutes | Cook time: 35 minutes | Serves 12

- Cooking spray

Torte:
- 1⅓ cups Swerve
- ½ cup (1 stick) unsalted butter, softened
- 2 teaspoons lemon or vanilla extract
- 5 large eggs, separated

Lemon Glaze:
- ½ cup (1 stick) unsalted butter
- ¼ cup Swerve
- 2 tablespoons lemon juice

- 2½ cups blanched almond flour
- 1¼ (10-ounce / 284-g) cups whole-milk ricotta cheese
- ¼ cup lemon juice
- 1 cup cold water

- 2 ounces (57 g) cream cheese (¼ cup)
- Grated lemon zest and lemon slices, for garnish

1. Line a baking pan with parchment paper and spray with cooking spray. Set aside. 2. Make the torte: In the bowl of a stand mixer, place the Swerve, butter, and extract and blend for 8 to 10 minutes until well combined. Scrape down the sides of the bowl as needed. 3. Add the egg yolks and continue to blend until fully combined. Add the almond flour and mix until smooth, then stir in the ricotta and lemon juice. 4. Whisk the egg whites in a separate medium bowl until stiff peaks form. Add the whites to the batter and stir

well. Pour the batter into the prepared pan and smooth the top. 5. Place a trivet in the bottom of your Instant Pot and pour in the water. Use a foil sling to lower the baking pan onto the trivet. Tuck in the sides of the sling. 6. Seal the lid, press Pressure Cook or Manual, and set the timer for 30 minutes. Once finished, let the pressure release naturally. 7. Lock the lid. Select the Manual mode and set the cooking time for 30 minutes at High Pressure. 8. When the timer beeps, perform a natural pressure release for 10 minutes. Carefully remove the lid. 9. Use the foil sling to lift the pan out of the Instant Pot. Place the torte in the fridge for 40 minutes to chill before glazing. 10. Meanwhile, make the glaze: Place the butter in a large pan over high heat and cook for about 5 minutes until brown, stirring occasionally. Remove from the heat. While stirring the browned butter, add the Swerve. 11. Carefully add the lemon juice and cream cheese to the butter mixture. Allow the glaze to cool for a few minutes, or until it starts to thicken. 12. Transfer the chilled torte to a serving plate. Pour the glaze over the torte and return it to the fridge to chill for an additional 30 minutes. 13. Scatter the lemon zest on top of the torte and arrange the lemon slices on the plate around the torte. 14. Serve.

Apple Crunch

Prep time: 13 minutes | Cook time: 2 minutes | Serves 4

- 3 apples, peeled, cored, and sliced (about 1½ pounds)
- 1 teaspoon pure maple syrup
- 1 teaspoon apple pie spice

- or ground cinnamon
- ¼ cup unsweetened apple juice, apple cider, or water
- ¼ cup low-sugar granola

1. In the electric pressure cooker, combine the apples, maple syrup, apple pie spice, and apple juice. 2. Close and lock the lid of the pressure cooker. Set the valve to sealing. 3. Cook on high pressure for 2 minutes. 4. When the cooking is complete, hit Cancel and quick release the pressure. 5. Once the pin drops, unlock and remove the lid. 6. Spoon the apples into 4 serving bowls and sprinkle each with 1 tablespoon of granola.

Vanilla Butter Curd

Prep time: 5 minutes | Cook time: 6 hours | Serves 3

- 4 egg yolks, whisked
- 2 tablespoon butter
- 1 tablespoon erythritol

- ½ cup organic almond milk
- 1 teaspoon vanilla extract

1. Set the instant pot to Sauté mode and when the "Hot" is displayed, add butter. 2. Melt the butter but not boil it and add whisked egg yolks, almond milk, and vanilla extract. 3. Add erythritol. Whisk the mixture. 4. Cook the meal on Low for 6 hours.

Chapter 8

Stews and Soups

Chapter 8 Stews and Soups

Chicken Zucchini Soup

Prep time: 8 minutes | Cook time: 14 minutes | Serves 6

- ¼ cup coconut oil or unsalted butter
- 1 cup chopped celery
- ¼ cup chopped onions
- 2 cloves garlic, minced
- 1 pound (454 g) boneless, skinless chicken breasts, cut into 1-inch cubes
- 6 cups chicken broth
- 1 tablespoon dried parsley
- 1 teaspoon fine sea salt
- ½ teaspoon dried marjoram
- ½ teaspoon ground black pepper
- 1 bay leaf
- 2 cups zucchini noodles

1. Place the coconut oil in the Instant Pot and press Sauté. Once melted, add the celery, onions, and garlic and cook, stirring occasionally, for 4 minutes, or until the onions are soft. Press Cancel to stop the Sauté. 2. Add the cubed chicken, broth, parsley, salt, marjoram, pepper, and bay leaf. Seal the lid, press Manual, and set the timer for 10 minutes. Once finished, let the pressure release naturally. 3. Remove the lid and stir well. Place the noodles in bowls, using ⅓ cup per bowl. Ladle the soup over the noodles and serve immediately; if it sits too long, the noodles will get too soft.

Ground Turkey Stew

Prep time: 5 minutes | Cook time: 25 minutes | Serves 5

- 1 tablespoon olive oil
- 1 onion, chopped
- 1 pound ground turkey
- ½ teaspoon garlic powder
- 1 teaspoon chili powder
- ¾ teaspoon cumin
- 2 teaspoons coriander
- 1 teaspoon dried oregano
- ½ teaspoon salt
- 1 green pepper, chopped
- 1 red pepper, chopped
- 1 tomato, chopped
- 1½ cups reduced-sodium tomato sauce
- 1 tablespoon low-sodium soy sauce
- 1 cup water
- 2 handfuls cilantro, chopped
- 15-ounce can reduced-salt black beans

1. Press the Sauté function on the control panel of the Instant Pot. 2. Add the olive oil to the inner pot and let it get hot. Add onion and sauté for a few minutes, or until light golden. 3. Add ground turkey. Break the ground meat using a wooden spoon to avoid formation of lumps. Sauté for a few minutes, until the pink color has faded. 4. Add garlic powder, chili powder, cumin, coriander, dried oregano, and salt. Combine well. Add green pepper, red pepper, and chopped tomato. Combine well. 5. Add tomato sauce, soy sauce, and water; combine well. 6. Close and secure the lid. Click on the Cancel key to cancel the Sauté mode. Make sure the pressure release valve on the lid is in the sealing position. 7. Click on Manual function first and then select high pressure. Click the + button and set the time to 15 minutes. 8. You can either have the steam release naturally (it will take around 20 minutes) or, after 10 minutes, turn the pressure release valve on the lid to venting and release steam. Be careful as the steam is very hot. After the pressure has released completely, open the lid. 9. If the stew is watery, turn on the Sauté function and let it cook for a few more minutes with the lid off. 10. Add cilantro and can of black beans, combine well, and let cook for a few minutes.

Southwestern Bean Soup with Corn Dumplings

Prep time: 50 minutes | Cook time: 4 to 12 hours | Serves 8

- 15½ ounces can red kidney beans, rinsed and drained
- 15½ ounces can black beans, pinto beans, or great northern beans, rinsed and drained
- 3 cups water
- 14½ ounces can Mexican-style stewed tomatoes
- 10 ounces package frozen whole-kernel corn, thawed
- 1 cup sliced carrots
- 1 cup chopped onions
- 4 ounces can chopped green chilies
- 3 teaspoons sodium-free instant bouillon powder (any flavor)
- 1 to 2 teaspoons chili powder
- 2 cloves garlic, minced

Sauce:

- ⅓ cup flour
- ¼ cup yellow cornmeal
- 1 teaspoon baking powder
- Dash of pepper
- 1 egg white, beaten
- 2 tablespoons milk
- 1 tablespoon oil

1. Combine the 11 soup ingredients in inner pot of the Instant Pot. 2. Secure the lid and cook on the Low Slow Cook setting for 10 to 12 hours or high for 4 to 5 hours. 3. Make dumplings by mixing together flour, cornmeal, baking powder, and pepper. 4. Combine egg white, milk, and oil. Add to flour mixture. Stir with fork until just combined. 5. At the end of the soup's cooking time, turn the Instant Pot to Slow Cook function high if you don't already have it there. Remove the lid and drop dumpling mixture by rounded teaspoonfuls to make 8 mounds atop the soup. 6. Secure the lid once more and cook for an additional 30 minutes.

Unstuffed Cabbage Soup

Prep time: 15 minutes | Cook time: 20 minutes | Serves 5

- 2 tablespoons coconut oil
- 1 pound ground sirloin or turkey
- 1 medium onion, diced
- 2 cloves garlic, minced
- 1 small head cabbage, chopped, cored, cut into roughly 2-inch pieces.
- 6-ounce can low-sodium tomato paste
- 32-ounce can low-sodium diced tomatoes, with liquid
- 2 cups low-sodium beef broth
- 1½ cups water
- ¾ cup brown rice
- 1–2 teaspoons salt
- ½ teaspoon black pepper
- 1 teaspoon oregano
- 1 teaspoon parsley

1. Melt coconut oil in the inner pot of the Instant Pot using Sauté function. Add ground meat. Stir frequently until meat loses color, about 2 minutes. 2. Add onion and garlic and continue to sauté for 2 more minutes, stirring frequently. 3. Add chopped cabbage. 4. On top of cabbage layer tomato paste, tomatoes with liquid, beef broth, water, rice, and spices. 5. Secure the lid and set vent to sealing. Using Manual setting, select 20 minutes. 6. When time is up, let the pressure release naturally for 10 minutes, then do a quick release.

Thai Shrimp and Mushroom Soup

Prep time: 15 minutes | Cook time: 10 minutes | Serves 6

- 2 tablespoons unsalted butter, divided
- ½ pound (227 g) medium uncooked shrimp, shelled and deveined
- ½ medium yellow onion, diced
- 2 cloves garlic, minced
- 1 cup sliced fresh white mushrooms
- 1 tablespoon freshly grated ginger root
- 4 cups chicken broth
- 2 tablespoons fish sauce
- 2½ teaspoons red curry
- paste
- 2 tablespoons lime juice
- 1 stalk lemongrass, outer stalk removed, crushed, and finely chopped
- 2 tablespoons coconut aminos
- 1 teaspoon sea salt
- ½ teaspoon ground black pepper
- 13½ ounces (383 g) can unsweetened, full-fat coconut milk
- 3 tablespoons chopped fresh cilantro

1. Select the Instant Pot on Sauté mode. Add 1 tablespoon butter. 2. Once the butter is melted, add the shrimp and sauté for 3 minutes or until opaque. Transfer the shrimp to a medium bowl. Set aside. 3. Add the remaining butter to the pot. Once the butter is melted, add the onions and garlic and sauté for 2 minutes or until the garlic is fragrant and the onions are softened. 4. Add the mushrooms, ginger root, chicken broth, fish sauce, red curry paste, lime juice, lemongrass, coconut aminos, sea salt, and black pepper to the pot. Stir to combine. 5. Lock the lid. Select Manual mode and set cooking time for 5 minutes on High Pressure. 6. When cooking is complete, allow the pressure to release naturally for 5 minutes, then release the remaining pressure. 7. Open the lid. Stir in the cooked shrimp and coconut milk. 8. Select Sauté mode. Bring the soup to a boil and then press Keep Warm / Cancel. Let the soup rest in the pot for 2 minutes. 9. Ladle the soup into bowls and sprinkle the cilantro over top. Serve hot.

Buffalo Chicken Soup

Prep time: 7 minutes | Cook time: 10 minutes | Serves 2

- 1 ounce (28 g) celery stalk, chopped
- 4 tablespoons coconut milk
- ¾ teaspoon salt
- ¼ teaspoon white pepper
- 1 cup water
- 2 ounces (57 g) Mozzarella, shredded
- 6 ounces (170 g) cooked chicken, shredded
- 2 tablespoons keto-friendly Buffalo sauce

1. Place the chopped celery stalk, coconut milk, salt, white pepper, water, and Mozzarella in the Instant Pot. Stir to mix well. 2. Set the Manual mode and set timer for 7 minutes on High Pressure. 3. When timer beeps, use a quick pressure release and open the lid. 4. Transfer the soup on the bowls. Stir in the chicken and Buffalo sauce. Serve warm.

Broccoli Brie Soup

Prep time: 5 minutes | Cook time: 14 minutes | Serves 6

- 1 tablespoon coconut oil or unsalted butter
- 1 cup finely diced onions
- 1 head broccoli, cut into small florets
- 2½ cups chicken broth or vegetable broth
- 8 ounces (227 g) Brie cheese, cut off rind and cut
- into chunks
- 1 cup unsweetened almond milk or heavy cream, plus more for drizzling
- Fine sea salt and ground black pepper, to taste
- Extra-virgin olive oil, for drizzling
- Coarse sea salt, for garnish

1. Place the coconut oil in the Instant Pot and press Sauté. Once hot, add the onions and sauté for 4 minutes, or until soft. Press Cancel to stop the Sauté. 2. Add the broccoli and broth. Seal the lid, press Manual, and set the timer for 10 minutes. Once finished, let the pressure release naturally. 3. Remove the lid and add the Brie and almond milk to the pot. Transfer the soup to a food processor or blender and process until smooth, or purée the soup right in the pot with a stick blender. 4. Season with salt and pepper to taste. Ladle the soup into bowls and drizzle with almond milk and olive oil. Garnish with coarse sea salt and freshly ground pepper.

Curried Chicken Soup

Prep time: 10 minutes | Cook time: 10 minutes | Serves 6

- 1 pound (454 g) boneless, skinless chicken thighs
- 1½ cups unsweetened coconut milk
- ½ onion, finely diced
- 3 or 4 garlic cloves, crushed
- 1 (2-inch) piece ginger, finely chopped
- 1 cup sliced mushrooms,

- such as cremini and shiitake
- 4 ounces (113 g) baby spinach
- 1 teaspoon salt
- ½ teaspoon ground turmeric
- ½ teaspoon cayenne
- 1 teaspoon garam masala
- ¼ cup chopped fresh cilantro

1. In the inner cooking pot of your Instant Pot, add the chicken, coconut milk, onion, garlic, ginger, mushrooms, spinach, salt, turmeric, cayenne, garam masala, and cilantro. 2. Lock the lid into place. Select Manual and adjust the pressure to High. Cook for 10 minutes. When the cooking is complete, let the pressure release naturally. Unlock the lid. 3. Use tongs to transfer the chicken to a bowl. Shred the chicken, then stir it back into the soup. 4. Eat and rejoice.

Chicken Brunswick Stew

Prep time: 0 minutes | Cook time: 30 minutes | Serves 6

- 2 tablespoons extra-virgin olive oil
- 2 garlic cloves, chopped
- 1 large yellow onion, diced
- 2 pounds boneless, skinless chicken (breasts, tenders, or thighs), cut into bite-size pieces
- 1 teaspoon dried thyme
- 1 teaspoon smoked paprika
- 1 teaspoon fine sea salt
- ½ teaspoon freshly ground black pepper
- 1 cup low-sodium chicken

- broth
- 1 tablespoon hot sauce (such as Tabasco or Crystal)
- 1 tablespoon raw apple cider vinegar
- 1½ cups frozen corn
- 1½ cups frozen baby lima beans
- One 14½ ounces can fire-roasted diced tomatoes and their liquid
- 2 tablespoons tomato paste
- Cornbread, for serving

1. Select the Sauté setting on the Instant Pot and heat the oil and garlic for 2 minutes, until the garlic is bubbling but not browned. Add the onion and sauté for 3 minutes, until it begins to soften. Add the chicken and sauté for 3 minutes more, until mostly opaque. The chicken does not have to be cooked through. Add the thyme, paprika, salt, and pepper and sauté for 1 minute more. 2. Stir in the broth, hot sauce, vinegar, corn, and lima beans. Add the diced tomatoes and their liquid in an even layer and dollop the tomato paste on top. Do not stir them in. 3. Secure the lid and set the Pressure Release to Sealing. Press the Cancel button to reset the cooking program, then select the Pressure Cook or Manual setting

and set the cooking time for 5 minutes at high pressure. (The pot will take about 15 minutes to come up to pressure before the cooking program begins.) 4. When the cooking program ends, let the pressure release naturally for at least 10 minutes, then move the Pressure Release to Venting to release any remaining steam. Open the pot and stir the stew to mix all of the ingredients. 5. Ladle the stew into bowls and serve hot, with cornbread alongside.

Turkey Barley Vegetable Soup

Prep time: 5 minutes | Cook time: 20 minutes | Serves 8

- 2 tablespoons avocado oil
- 1 pound ground turkey
- 4 cups Chicken Bone Broth, low-sodium store-bought chicken broth, or water
- 1 (28-ounce) carton or can diced tomatoes
- 2 tablespoons tomato paste
- 1 (15-ounce) package frozen chopped carrots (about 2½

- cups)
- 1 (15-ounce) package frozen peppers and onions (about 2½ cups)
- ⅓ cup dry barley
- 1 teaspoon kosher salt
- ¼ teaspoon freshly ground black pepper
- 2 bay leaves

1. Set the electric pressure cooker to the Sauté/More setting. When the pot is hot, pour in the avocado oil. 2. Add the turkey to the pot and sauté, stirring frequently to break up the meat, for about 7 minutes or until the turkey is no longer pink. Hit Cancel. 3. Add the broth, tomatoes and their juices, and tomato paste. Stir in the carrots, peppers and onions, barley, salt, pepper, and bay leaves. 4. Close and lock the lid of the pressure cooker. Set the valve to sealing. 5. Cook on high pressure for 20 minutes. 6. When the cooking is complete, hit Cancel and allow the pressure to release naturally for 10 minutes, then quick release any remaining pressure. 7. Once the pin drops, unlock and remove the lid. Discard the bay leaves. 8. Spoon into bowls and serve.

Bacon Curry Soup

Prep time: 10 minutes | Cook time: 20 minutes | Serves 4

- 3 ounces (85 g) bacon, chopped
- 1 tablespoon chopped scallions
- 1 teaspoon curry powder

- 1 cup coconut milk
- 3 cups beef broth
- 1 cup Cheddar cheese, shredded

1. Heat the the Instant Pot on Sauté mode for 3 minutes and add bacon. Cook for 5 minutes. Flip constantly. 2. Add the scallions and curry powder. Sauté for 5 minutes more. 3. Pour in the coconut milk and beef broth. Add the Cheddar cheese and stir to mix well. 4. Select Manual mode and set cooking time for 10 minutes on High Pressure. 5. When timer beeps, use a quick pressure release. Open the lid. 6. Blend the soup with an immersion blender until smooth. Serve warm.

Vegetable and Chickpea Stew

Prep time: 25 minutes | Cook time: 30 minutes | Serves 6 to 8

- ¼ cup extra-virgin olive oil, plus extra for drizzling
- 2 red bell peppers, stemmed, seeded, and cut into 1-inch pieces
- 1 onion, chopped fine
- ½ teaspoon table salt
- ½ teaspoon pepper
- 1½ tablespoons baharat
- 4 garlic cloves, minced
- 1 tablespoon tomato paste
- 4 cups vegetable or chicken broth
- 1 (28-ounce / 794-g) can whole peeled tomatoes, drained with juice reserved, chopped
- 1 pound (454 g) Yukon Gold potatoes, peeled and cut into ½-inch pieces
- 2 zucchini, quartered lengthwise and sliced 1 inch thick
- 1 (15-ounce / 425-g) can chickpeas, rinsed
- ⅓ cup chopped fresh mint

1. Using highest sauté function, heat oil in Instant Pot until shimmering. Add bell pepper, onion, salt, and pepper and cook until vegetables are softened and lightly browned, 5 to 7 minutes. Stir in baharat, garlic, and tomato paste and cook until fragrant, about 1 minute. Stir in broth and tomatoes and reserved juice, scraping up any browned bits, then stir in potatoes. 2. Lock lid in place and close pressure release valve. Select high pressure cook function and cook for 9 minutes. Turn off Instant Pot and quick-release pressure. Carefully remove lid, allowing steam to escape away from you. 3. Stir zucchini and chickpeas into stew and cook, using highest sauté function, until zucchini is tender, 10 to 15 minutes. Turn off multicooker. Season with salt and pepper to taste. Drizzle individual portions with extra oil, and sprinkle with mint before serving.

All-Purpose Chicken Broth

Prep time: 10 minutes | Cook time: 1 hour 25 minutes | Makes 3 quarts

- 3 pounds (1.4 kg) chicken wings
- 1 tablespoon vegetable oil
- 1 onion, chopped
- 3 garlic cloves, lightly
- crushed and peeled
- 12 cups water, divided
- ½ teaspoon table salt
- 3 bay leaves

1. Pat chicken wings dry with paper towels. Using highest sauté function, heat oil in Instant Pot for 5 minutes (or until just smoking). Brown half of chicken wings on all sides, about 10 minutes; transfer to bowl. Repeat with remaining chicken wings; transfer to bowl. 2. Add onion to fat left in pot and cook until softened and well browned, 8 to 10 minutes. Stir in garlic and cook until fragrant, about 30 seconds. Stir in 1 cup water, scraping up any browned bits. Stir in remaining 11 cups water, salt, bay leaves, and chicken and any accumulated juices. 3. Lock lid in place and close pressure release valve. Select high pressure cook function and cook for 1 hour. Turn off Instant Pot and let pressure release naturally for 15 minutes. Quick-release any remaining pressure, then carefully remove lid, allowing steam to escape away from you. 4. Strain broth through fine-mesh strainer into large container, pressing on solids to extract as much liquid as possible; discard solids. Using wide, shallow spoon, skim excess fat from surface of broth. (Broth can be refrigerated for up to 4 days or frozen for up to 2 months.)

Savory Beef Stew with Mushrooms and Turnips

Prep time: 0 minutes | Cook time: 55 minutes | Serves 6

- 1½ pounds beef stew meat
- ¾ teaspoon fine sea salt
- ¾ teaspoon freshly ground black pepper
- 1 tablespoon cold-pressed avocado oil
- 3 garlic cloves, minced
- 1 yellow onion, diced
- 2 celery stalks, diced
- 8 ounces cremini mushrooms, quartered
- 1 cup low-sodium roasted beef bone broth
- 2 tablespoons
- Worcestershire sauce
- 1 tablespoon Dijon mustard
- 1 teaspoon dried rosemary, crumbled
- 1 bay leaf
- 3 tablespoons tomato paste
- 8 ounces carrots, cut into 1-inch-thick rounds
- 1 pound turnips, cut into 1-inch pieces
- 1 pound parsnips, halved lengthwise, then cut crosswise into 1-inch pieces

1. Sprinkle the beef all over with the salt and pepper. 2. Select the Sauté setting on the Instant Pot and heat the oil and garlic for 2 minutes, until the garlic is bubbling but not browned. Add the onion, celery, and mushrooms and sauté for 5 minutes, until the onion begins to soften and the mushrooms are giving up their liquid. Stir in the broth, Worcestershire sauce, mustard, rosemary, and bay leaf. Stir in the beef. Add the tomato paste in a dollop on top. Do not stir it in. 3. Secure the lid and set the Pressure Release to Sealing. Press the Cancel button to reset the cooking program, then select the Meat/Stew, Pressure Cook, or Manual setting and set the cooking time for 20 minutes at high pressure. (The pot will take about 10 minutes to come up to pressure before the cooking program begins.) 4. When the cooking program ends, perform a quick pressure release by moving the Pressure Release to Venting, or let the pressure release naturally. Open the pot, remove and discard the bay leaf, and stir in the tomato paste. Place the carrots, turnips, and parsnips on top of the meat. 5. Secure the lid and set the Pressure Release to Sealing. Press the Cancel button to reset the cooking program, then select the Pressure Cook or Manual setting and set the cooking time for 3 minutes at low pressure. (The pot will take about 15 minutes to come up to pressure before the cooking program begins.) 6. When the cooking program ends, perform a quick pressure release by moving the Pressure Release to Venting. Open the pot and stir to combine all of the ingredients. 7. Ladle the stew into bowls and serve hot.

Nancy's Vegetable Beef Soup

Prep time: 25 minutes | Cook time: 8 hours | Serves 8

- 2 pounds roast, cubed, or 2 pounds stewing meat
- 15 ounces can corn
- 15 ounces can green beans
- 1 pound bag frozen peas
- 40 ounces can no-added-salt stewed tomatoes
- 5 teaspoons salt-free beef bouillon powder
- Tabasco, to taste
- ½ teaspoons salt

1. Combine all ingredients in the Instant Pot. Do not drain vegetables. 2. Add water to fill inner pot only to the fill line. 3. Secure the lid, or use the glass lid and set the Instant Pot on Slow Cook mode, Low for 8 hours, or until meat is tender and vegetables are soft.

Hot and Sour Soup

Prep time: 0 minutes | Cook time: 30 minutes | Serves 6

- 4 cups boiling water
- 1 ounce dried shiitake mushrooms
- 2 tablespoons cold-pressed avocado oil
- 3 garlic cloves, chopped
- 4 ounces cremini or button mushrooms, sliced
- 1 pound boneless pork loin, sirloin, or tip, thinly sliced against the grain into ¼-inch-thick, ½-inch-wide, 2-inch-long strips
- 1 teaspoon ground ginger
- ½ teaspoon ground white pepper
- 2 cups low-sodium chicken broth or vegetable broth
- One 8-ounce can sliced
- bamboo shoots, drained and rinsed
- 2 tablespoons low-sodium soy sauce
- 1 tablespoon chile garlic sauce
- 1 teaspoon toasted sesame oil
- 2 teaspoons Lakanto Monkfruit Sweetener Classic
- 2 large eggs
- ¼ cup rice vinegar
- 2 tablespoons cornstarch
- 4 green onions, white and green parts, thinly sliced
- ¼ cup chopped fresh cilantro

1. In a large liquid measuring cup or heatproof bowl, pour the boiling water over the shiitake mushrooms. Cover and let soak for 30 minutes. Drain the mushrooms, reserving the soaking liquid. Remove and discard the stems and thinly slice the caps. 2. Select the Sauté setting on the Instant Pot and heat the avocado oil and garlic for 2 minutes, until the garlic is bubbling but not browned. Add the cremini and shiitake mushrooms and sauté for 3 minutes, until the mushrooms are beginning to wilt. Add the pork, ginger, and white pepper and sauté for about 5 minutes, until the pork is opaque and cooked through. 3. Pour the mushroom soaking liquid into the pot, being careful to leave behind any sediment at the bottom of the measuring cup or bowl. Using a wooden spoon, nudge any browned bits from the bottom of the pot. Stir in the broth, bamboo shoots, soy sauce, chile garlic sauce, sesame oil, and sweetener. 4. Secure the lid and set the Pressure Release to Sealing. Press the Cancel button to reset the cooking program, then select the Pressure Cook or Manual setting and set the cooking time for 5 minutes at high pressure. (The pot will take about 10 minutes to come up to pressure before the cooking program begins.) 5. While the soup is cooking, in a small bowl, beat the eggs until no streaks of yolk remain. 6. When the cooking program ends, let the pressure release naturally for at least 15 minutes, then move the Pressure Release to Venting to release any remaining steam. 7. In a small bowl, stir together the vinegar and cornstarch until the cornstarch dissolves. Open the pot and stir the vinegar mixture into the soup. Press the Cancel button to reset the cooking program, then select the Sauté setting. Bring the soup to a simmer and cook, stirring occasionally, for about 3 minutes, until slightly thickened. While stirring the soup constantly, pour in the beaten eggs in a thin stream. Press the Cancel button to turn off the pot and then stir in the green onions and cilantro. 8. Ladle the soup into bowls and serve hot.

Venison and Tomato Stew

Prep time: 12 minutes | Cook time: 42 minutes | Serves 8

- 1 tablespoon unsalted butter
- 1 cup diced onions
- 2 cups button mushrooms, sliced in half
- 2 large stalks celery, cut into ¼-inch pieces
- Cloves squeezed from 2 heads roasted garlic or 4 cloves garlic, minced
- 2 pounds (907 g) boneless venison or beef roast, cut into 4 large pieces
- 5 cups beef broth
- 1 (14½-ounce / 411-g) can diced tomatoes
- 1 teaspoon fine sea salt
- 1 teaspoon ground black pepper
- ½ teaspoon dried rosemary, or 1 teaspoon fresh rosemary, finely chopped
- ½ teaspoon dried thyme leaves, or 1 teaspoon fresh thyme leaves, finely chopped
- ½ head cauliflower, cut into large florets
- Fresh thyme leaves, for garnish

1. Place the butter in the Instant Pot and press Sauté. Once melted, add the onions and sauté for 4 minutes, or until soft. 2. Add the mushrooms, celery, and garlic and sauté for another 3 minutes, or until the mushrooms are golden brown. Press Cancel to stop the Sauté. Add the roast, broth, tomatoes, salt, pepper, rosemary, and thyme. 3. Seal the lid, press Manual, and set the timer for 30 minutes. Once finished, turn the valve to venting for a quick release. 4. Add the cauliflower. Seal the lid, press Manual, and set the timer for 5 minutes. Once finished, let the pressure release naturally. 5. Remove the lid and shred the meat with two forks. Taste the liquid and add more salt, if needed. Ladle the stew into bowls. Garnish with thyme leaves.

Broccoli and Red Feta Soup

Prep time: 10 minutes | Cook time: 25 minutes | Serves 4

- 1 cup broccoli, chopped
- ½ cup coconut cream
- 1 teaspoon unsweetened tomato purée
- 4 cups beef broth
- 1 teaspoon chili flakes
- 6 ounces (170 g) feta, crumbled

1. Put broccoli, coconut cream, tomato purée, and beef broth in the Instant Pot. Sprinkle with chili flakes and stir to mix well. 2. Close the lid and select Manual mode. Set cooking time for 8 minutes on High Pressure. 3. When timer beeps, make a quick pressure release and open the lid. 4. Add the feta cheese and stir the soup on Sauté mode for 5 minutes or until the cheese melt. 5. Serve immediately.

Hearty Hamburger and Lentil Stew

Prep time: 0 minutes | Cook time: 55 minutes | Serves 8

- 2 tablespoons cold-pressed avocado oil
- 2 garlic cloves, chopped
- 1 large yellow onion, diced
- 2 carrots, diced
- 2 celery stalks, diced
- 2 pounds 95 percent lean ground beef
- ½ cup small green lentils
- 2 cups low-sodium roasted beef bone broth or vegetable broth
- 1 tablespoon Italian seasoning
- 1 tablespoon paprika
- 1½ teaspoons fine sea salt
- 1 extra-large russet potato, diced
- 1 cup frozen green peas
- 1 cup frozen corn
- One 14½-ounce can no-salt petite diced tomatoes and their liquid
- ¼ cup tomato paste

1. Select the Sauté setting on the Instant Pot and heat the oil and garlic for 3 minutes, until the garlic is bubbling but not browned. Add the onion, carrots, and celery and sauté for 5 minutes, until the onion begins to soften. Add the beef and sauté, using a wooden spoon or spatula to break up the meat as it cooks, for 6 minutes, until cooked through and no streaks of pink remain. 2. Stir in the lentils, broth, Italian seasoning, paprika, and salt. Add the potato, peas, corn, and tomatoes and their liquid in layers on top of the lentils and beef, then add the tomato paste in a dollop on top. Do not stir in the vegetables and tomato paste. 3. Secure the lid and set the Pressure Release to Sealing. Press the Cancel button to reset the cooking program, then select the Pressure Cook or Manual setting and set the cooking time for 20 minutes at high pressure. (The pot will take about 20 minutes to come up to pressure before the cooking program begins.) 4. When the cooking program ends, let the pressure release naturally for at least 15 minutes, then move the Pressure Release to Venting to release any remaining steam. Open the pot and stir the stew to mix all of the ingredients. 5. Ladle the stew into bowls and serve hot.

Chicken and Asparagus Soup

Prep time: 7 minutes | Cook time: 11 minutes | Serves 8

- 1 tablespoon unsalted butter (or coconut oil for dairy-free)
- ¼ cup finely chopped onions
- 2 cloves garlic, minced
- 1 (14-ounce / 397-g) can full-fat coconut milk
- 1 (14-ounce / 397-g) can sugar-free tomato sauce
- 1 cup chicken broth
- 1 tablespoon red curry paste
- 1 teaspoon fine sea salt
- ½ teaspoon ground black pepper
- 2 pounds (907 g) boneless, skinless chicken breasts, cut into ½-inch chunks
- 2 cups asparagus, trimmed and cut into 2-inch pieces
- Fresh cilantro leaves, for garnish
- Lime wedges, for garnish

1. Place the butter in the Instant Pot and press Sauté. Once melted, add the onions and garlic and sauté for 4 minutes, or until the onions are soft. Press Cancel to stop the Sauté. 2. Add the coconut milk, tomato sauce, broth, curry paste, salt, and pepper and whisk to combine well. Stir in the chicken and asparagus. 3. Seal the lid, press Manual, and set the timer for 7 minutes. Once finished, turn the valve to venting for a quick release. 4. Remove the lid and stir well. Taste and adjust the seasoning to your liking. Ladle the soup into bowls and garnish with cilantro. Serve with lime wedges or a squirt of lime juice.

Chicken Enchilada Soup

Prep time: 10 minutes | Cook time: 40 minutes | Serves 6

- 2 (6-ounce / 170-g) boneless, skinless chicken breasts
- ½ tablespoon chili powder
- ½ teaspoon salt
- ½ teaspoon garlic powder
- ¼ teaspoon pepper
- ½ cup red enchilada sauce
- ½ medium onion, diced
- 1 (4-ounce / 113-g) can green chilies
- 2 cups chicken broth
- ⅛ cup pickled jalapeños
- 4 ounces (113 g) cream cheese
- 1 cup uncooked cauliflower rice
- 1 avocado, diced
- 1 cup shredded mild Cheddar cheese
- ½ cup sour cream

1. Sprinkle seasoning over chicken breasts and set aside. Pour enchilada sauce into Instant Pot and place chicken on top. 2. Add onion, chilies, broth, and jalapeños to the pot, then place cream cheese on top of chicken breasts. Click lid closed. Adjust time for 25 minutes. When timer beeps, quick-release the pressure and shred chicken with forks. 3. Mix soup together and add cauliflower rice, with pot on Keep Warm setting. Replace lid and let pot sit for 15 minutes, still on Keep Warm. This will cook cauliflower rice. Serve with avocado, Cheddar, and sour cream.

Swiss Chard and Chicken Soup

Prep time: 10 minutes | Cook time: 5 minutes | Serves 4

- 1 onion, chopped
- 6 garlic cloves, peeled
- 1 (2-inch) piece fresh ginger, chopped
- 1 (10-ounce / 283-g) can tomatoes with chiles
- 1½ cups full-fat coconut milk, divided
- 1 tablespoon powdered chicken broth base
- 1 pound (454 g) boneless chicken thighs, cut into large bite-size pieces
- 1½ cups chopped celery
- 2 cups chopped Swiss chard
- 1 teaspoon ground turmeric

1. To a blender jar, add the onion, garlic, ginger, tomatoes, ½ cup of coconut milk, and chicken broth base. Purée the ingredients into a sauce. 2. Pour the mixture into the inner cooking pot of the Instant Pot. Add the chicken, celery, and chard. 3. Lock the lid into place. Select Manual and adjust the pressure to High. Cook for 5 minutes. When the cooking is complete, let the pressure release naturally for 10 minutes, then quick-release any remaining pressure. 4. Unlock the lid and add the remaining 1 cup of coconut milk and turmeric. Stir to heat through and serve.

Beef Meatball Minestrone

Prep time: 5 minutes | Cook time: 35 minutes | Serves 6

- 1 pound (454 g) ground beef
- 1 large egg
- 1½ tablespoons golden flaxseed meal
- ⅓ cup shredded Mozzarella cheese
- ¼ cup unsweetened tomato purée
- 1½ tablespoons Italian seasoning, divided
- 1½ teaspoons garlic powder, divided
- 1½ teaspoons sea salt, divided
- 1 tablespoon olive oil
- 2 garlic cloves, minced
- ½ medium yellow onion, minced
- ¼ cup pancetta, diced
- 1 cup sliced yellow squash
- 1 cup sliced zucchini
- ½ cup sliced turnips
- 4 cups beef broth
- 14 ounces (397 g) can diced tomatoes
- ½ teaspoon ground black pepper
- 3 tablespoons shredded Parmesan cheese

1. Preheat the oven to 400°F (205°C) and line a large baking sheet with aluminum foil. 2. In a large bowl, combine the ground beef, egg, flaxseed meal, Mozzarella, unsweetened tomato purée, ½ tablespoon of Italian seasoning, ½ teaspoon of garlic powder, and ½ teaspoon of sea salt. Mix the ingredients until well combined. 3. Make the meatballs by shaping 1 heaping tablespoon of the ground beef mixture into a meatball. Repeat with the remaining mixture and then transfer the meatballs to the prepared baking sheet. 4. Place the meatballs in the oven and bake for 15 minutes. When the baking time is complete, remove from the oven and set aside.

5. Select Sauté mode of the Instant Pot. Once the pot is hot, add the olive oil, garlic, onion, and pancetta. Sauté for 2 minutes or until the garlic becomes fragrant and the onions begin to soften. 6. Add the yellow squash, zucchini, and turnips to the pot. Sauté for 3 more minutes. 7. Add the beef broth, diced tomatoes, black pepper, and remaining garlic powder, sea salt, and Italian seasoning to the pot. Stir to combine and then add the meatballs. 8. Lock the lid. Select Manual mode and set cooking time for 15 minutes on High Pressure. 9. When cooking is complete, allow the pressure to release naturally for 10 minutes and then release the remaining pressure. 10. Open the lid and gently stir the soup. Ladle into serving bowls and top with Parmesan. Serve hot.

Beef and Mushroom Stew

Prep time: 15 minutes | Cook time: 30 minutes | Serves 4

- 2 tablespoons coconut oil
- 1 pound (454 g) cubed chuck roast
- 1 cup sliced button mushrooms
- ½ medium onion, chopped
- 2 cups beef broth
- ½ cup chopped celery
- 1 tablespoon sugar-free tomato paste
- 1 teaspoon thyme
- 2 garlic cloves, minced
- ½ teaspoon xanthan gum

1. Press the Sauté button and add coconut oil to Instant Pot. Brown cubes of chuck roast until golden, working in batches if necessary. (If the pan is overcrowded, they will not brown properly.) Set aside after browning is completed. 2. Add mushrooms and onions to pot. Sauté until mushrooms begin to brown and onions are translucent. Press the Cancel button. 3. Add broth to Instant Pot. Use wooden spoon to scrape bits from bottom if necessary. Add celery, tomato paste, thyme, and garlic. Click lid closed. Press the Manual button and adjust time for 35 minutes. When timer beeps, allow a natural release. 4. When pressure valve drops, stir in xanthan gum and allow to thicken. Serve warm.

Kale Curry Soup

Prep time: 10 minutes | Cook time: 15 minutes | Serves 3

- 2 cups kale
- 1 teaspoon almond butter
- 1 tablespoon fresh cilantro
- ½ cup ground chicken
- 1 teaspoon curry paste
- ½ cup heavy cream
- 1 cup chicken stock
- ½ teaspoon salt

1. Put the kale in the Instant Pot. 2. Add the almond butter, cilantro, and ground chicken. Sauté the mixture for 5 minutes. 3. Meanwhile, mix the curry paste and heavy cream in the Instant Pot until creamy. 4. Add chicken stock and salt, and close the lid. 5. Select Manual mode and set cooking time for 10 minutes on High Pressure. 6. When timer beeps, make a quick pressure release. Open the lid. 7. Serve warm.

Buttercup Squash Soup

Prep time: 15 minutes | Cook time: 10 minutes | Serves 6

- 2 tablespoons extra-virgin olive oil
- 1 medium onion, chopped
- 4 to 5 cups Vegetable Broth or Chicken Bone Broth
- 1½ pounds buttercup

- squash, peeled, seeded, and cut into 1-inch chunks
- ½ teaspoon kosher salt
- ¼ teaspoon ground white pepper
- Whole nutmeg, for grating

1. Set the electric pressure cooker to the Sauté setting. When the pot is hot, pour in the olive oil. 2. Add the onion and sauté for 3 to 5 minutes, until it begins to soften. Hit Cancel. 3. Add the broth, squash, salt, and pepper to the pot and stir. (If you want a thicker soup, use 4 cups of broth. If you want a thinner, drinkable soup, use 5 cups.) 4. Close and lock the lid of the pressure cooker. Set the valve to sealing. 5. Cook on high pressure for 10 minutes. 6. When the cooking is complete, hit Cancel and allow the pressure to release naturally. 7. Once the pin drops, unlock and remove the lid. 8. Use an immersion blender to purée the soup right in the pot. If you don't have an immersion blender, transfer the soup to a blender or food processor and purée. (Follow the instructions that came with your machine for blending hot foods.) 9. Pour the soup into serving bowls and grate nutmeg on top.

Pasta e Fagioli with Ground Beef

Prep time: 0 minutes | Cook time: 30 minutes | Serves 8

- 2 tablespoons extra-virgin olive oil
- 4 garlic cloves, minced
- 1 yellow onion, diced
- 2 large carrots, diced
- 4 celery stalks, diced
- 1½ pounds 95 percent extra-lean ground beef
- 4 cups low-sodium vegetable broth
- 2 teaspoons Italian seasoning
- ½ teaspoon freshly ground

- black pepper
- 1¼ cups chickpea-based elbow pasta or whole-wheat elbow pasta
- 1½ cups drained cooked kidney beans, or one 15-ounce can kidney beans, rinsed and drained
- One 28-ounce can whole San Marzano tomatoes and their liquid
- 2 tablespoons chopped fresh flat-leaf parsley

1. Select the Sauté setting on the Instant Pot and heat the oil and garlic for 2 minutes, until the garlic is bubbling but not browned. Add the onion, carrots, and celery and sauté for 5 minutes, until the onion begins to soften. Add the beef and sauté, using a wooden spoon or spatula to break up the meat as it cooks, for 5 minutes; it's fine if some streaks of pink remain, the beef does not need to be cooked through. 2. Stir in the broth, Italian seasoning, pepper, and pasta, making sure all of the pasta is submerged in the liquid.

Add the beans and stir to mix. Add the tomatoes and their liquid, crushing the tomatoes with your hands as you add them to the pot. Do not stir them in. 3. Secure the lid and set the Pressure Release to Sealing. Press the Cancel button to reset the cooking program, then select the Pressure Cook or Manual setting and set the cooking time for 2 minutes at low pressure. (The pot will take about 15 minutes to come up to pressure before the cooking program begins.) 4. When the cooking program ends, let the pressure release naturally for 10 minutes, then move the Pressure Release to Venting to release any remaining steam. Open the pot and stir the soup to mix all of the ingredients. 5. Ladle the soup into bowls, sprinkle with the parsley, and serve right away.

Blue Cheese Mushroom Soup

Prep time: 15 minutes | Cook time: 20 minutes | Serves 4

- 2 cups chopped white mushrooms
- 3 tablespoons cream cheese
- 4 ounces (113 g) scallions, diced
- 4 cups chicken broth

- 1 teaspoon olive oil
- ½ teaspoon ground cumin
- 1 teaspoon salt
- 2 ounces (57 g) blue cheese, crumbled

1. Combine the mushrooms, cream cheese, scallions, chicken broth, olive oil, and ground cumin in the Instant Pot. 2. Seal the lid. Select Manual mode and set cooking time for 20 minutes on High Pressure. 3. When timer beeps, use a quick pressure release and open the lid. 4. Add the salt and blend the soup with an immersion blender. 5. Ladle the soup in the bowls and top with blue cheese. Serve warm.

Chicken and Kale Soup

Prep time: 5 minutes | Cook time: 5 minutes | Serves 4

- 2 cups chopped cooked chicken breast
- 12 ounces (340 g) frozen kale
- 1 onion, chopped
- 2 cups water
- 1 tablespoon powdered chicken broth base

- ½ teaspoon ground cinnamon
- Pinch ground cloves
- 2 teaspoons minced garlic
- 1 teaspoon freshly ground black pepper
- 1 teaspoon salt
- 2 cups full-fat coconut milk

1. Put the chicken, kale, onion, water, chicken broth base, cinnamon, cloves, garlic, pepper, and salt in the inner cooking pot of the Instant Pot. 2. Lock the lid into place. Select Manual and adjust the pressure to High. Cook for 5 minutes. When the cooking is complete, let the pressure release naturally for 10 minutes, then quick-release any remaining pressure. Unlock the lid. 3. Stir in the coconut milk. Taste and adjust any seasonings as needed before serving.

Broccoli Cheddar Soup

Prep time: 5 minutes | Cook time: 10 minutes | Serves 4

- 2 tablespoons butter
- ⅛ cup onion, diced
- ½ teaspoon garlic powder
- ½ teaspoon salt
- ¼ teaspoon pepper
- 2 cups chicken broth
- 1 cup chopped broccoli
- 1 tablespoon cream cheese, softened
- ¼ cup heavy cream
- 1 cup shredded Cheddar cheese

1. Press the Sauté button and add butter to Instant Pot. Add onion and sauté until translucent. Press the Cancel button and add garlic powder, salt, pepper, broth, and broccoli to pot. 2. Click lid closed. Press the Soup button and set time for 5 minutes. When timer beeps, stir in heavy cream, cream cheese, and Cheddar.

Beef and Okra Stew

Prep time: 15 minutes | Cook time: 25 minutes | Serves 3

- 8 ounces (227 g) beef sirloin, chopped
- ¼ teaspoon cumin seeds
- 1 teaspoon dried basil
- 1 tablespoon avocado oil
- ¼ cup coconut cream
- 1 cup water
- 6 ounces (170 g) okra, chopped

1. Sprinkle the beef sirloin with cumin seeds and dried basil and put in the Instant Pot. 2. Add avocado oil and roast the meat on Sauté mode for 5 minutes. Flip occasionally. 3. Add coconut cream, water, and okra. 4. Close the lid and select Manual mode. Set cooking time for 25 minutes on High Pressure. 5. When timer beeps, use a natural pressure release for 10 minutes, the release any remaining pressure. Open the lid. 6. Serve warm.

Avocado and Serrano Chile Soup

Prep time: 10 minutes | Cook time: 7 minutes | Serves 4

- 2 avocados
- 1 small fresh tomatillo, quartered
- 2 cups chicken broth
- 2 tablespoons avocado oil
- 1 tablespoon butter
- 2 tablespoons finely minced onion
- 1 clove garlic, minced
- ½ Serrano chile, deseeded and ribs removed, minced, plus thin slices for garnish
- ¼ teaspoon sea salt
- Pinch of ground white pepper
- ½ cup full-fat coconut milk
- Fresh cilantro sprigs, for garnish

1. Scoop the avocado flesh into a food processor. Add the tomatillo and chicken broth and purée until smooth. Set aside. 2. Set the Instant Pot to Sauté mode and add the avocado oil and butter. When the butter melts, add the onion and garlic and sauté for a minute or until softened. Add the Serrano chile and sauté for 1 minute more. 3. Pour the puréed avocado mixture into the pot, add the salt and pepper, and stir to combine. 4. Secure the lid. Press the Manual button and set cooking time for 5 minutes on High Pressure. 5. When timer beeps, use a quick pressure release. Open the lid and stir in the coconut milk. 6. Serve hot topped with thin slices of Serrano chile, and cilantro sprigs.

French Onion Soup

Prep time: 10 minutes | Cook time: 20 minutes | Serves 10

- ½ cup light, soft tub margarine
- 8–10 large onions, sliced
- 3 14-ounce cans 98% fat-free, lower-sodium beef broth
- 2½ cups water
- 3 teaspoons sodium-free chicken bouillon powder
- 1½ teaspoons Worcestershire sauce
- 3 bay leaves
- 10 (1-ounce) slices French bread, toasted

1. Turn the Instant Pot to the Sauté function and add in the margarine and onions. Cook about 5 minutes, or until the onions are slightly soft. Press Cancel. 2. Add the beef broth, water, bouillon powder, Worcestershire sauce, and bay leaves and stir. 3. Secure the lid and make sure vent is set to sealing. Cook on Manual mode for 20 minutes. 4. Let the pressure release naturally for 15 minutes, then do a quick release. Open the lid and discard bay leaves. 5. Ladle into bowls. Top each with a slice of bread and some cheese if you desire.

Vegetarian Chili

Prep time: 25 minutes | Cook time: 10 minutes | Serves 6

- 2 teaspoons olive oil
- 3 garlic cloves, minced
- 2 onions, chopped
- 1 green bell pepper, chopped
- 1 cup textured vegetable protein (T.V.P.)
- 1-pound can beans of your choice, drained
- 1 jalapeño pepper, seeds removed, chopped
- 28-ounce can diced Italian tomatoes
- 1 bay leaf
- 1 tablespoon dried oregano
- ½ teaspoons salt
- ¼ teaspoons pepper

1. Set the Instant Pot to the Sauté function. As it's heating, add the olive oil, garlic, onions, and bell pepper. Stir constantly for about 5 minutes as it all cooks. Press Cancel. 2. Place all of the remaining ingredients into the inner pot of the Instant pot and stir. 3. Secure the lid and make sure vent is set to sealing. Cook on Manual mode for 10 minutes. 4. When cook time is up, let the steam release naturally for 5 minutes and then manually release the rest.

Chicken Vegetable Soup

Prep time: 12 to 25 minutes | Cook time: 4 minutes | Serves 6

- 1 to 2 raw chicken breasts, cubed
- ½ medium onion, chopped
- 4 cloves garlic, minced
- ½ sweet potato, small cubes
- 1 large carrot, peeled and cubed
- 4 stalks celery, chopped, leaves included
- ½ cup frozen corn
- ¼ cup frozen peas
- ¼ cup frozen lima beans
- 1 cup frozen green beans
- (bite-sized)
- ¼ to ½ cup chopped savoy cabbage
- 14½ ounces can low-sodium petite diced tomatoes
- 3 cups low-sodium chicken bone broth
- ½ teaspoon black pepper
- 1 teaspoon garlic powder
- ¼ cup chopped fresh parsley
- ¼ to ½ teaspoon red pepper flakes

1. Add all of the ingredients, in the order listed, to the inner pot of the Instant Pot. 2. Lock the lid in place, set the vent to sealing, press Manual, and cook at high pressure for 4 minutes. 3. Release the pressure manually as soon as cooking time is finished.

Spanish-Style Turkey Meatball Soup

Prep time: 10 minutes | Cook time: 15 minutes | Serves 6 to 8

- 1 slice hearty white sandwich bread, torn into quarters
- ¼ cup whole milk
- 1 ounce (28 g) Manchego cheese, grated (½ cup), plus extra for serving
- 5 tablespoons minced fresh parsley, divided
- ½ teaspoon table salt
- 1 pound (454 g) ground turkey
- 1 tablespoon extra-virgin olive oil
- 1 onion, chopped
- 1 red bell pepper, stemmed, seeded, and cut into ¾-inch pieces
- 4 garlic cloves, minced
- 2 teaspoons smoked paprika
- ½ cup dry white wine
- 8 cups chicken broth
- 8 ounces (227 g) kale, stemmed and chopped

1. Using fork, mash bread and milk together into paste in large bowl. Stir in Manchego, 3 tablespoons parsley, and salt until combined. Add turkey and knead mixture with your hands until well combined. Pinch off and roll 2-teaspoon-size pieces of mixture into balls and arrange on large plate (you should have about 35 meatballs); set aside. 2. Using highest sauté function, heat oil in Instant Pot until shimmering. Add onion and bell pepper and cook until softened and lightly browned, 5 to 7 minutes. Stir in garlic and paprika and cook until fragrant, about 30 seconds. Stir in wine, scraping up any browned bits, and cook until almost completely evaporated, about 5 minutes. Stir in broth and kale, then gently submerge meatballs. 3. Lock lid in place and close pressure release valve. Select high pressure cook function and cook for 3 minutes. Turn off Instant Pot and quick-release pressure. Carefully remove lid, allowing steam to escape away from you. 4. Stir in remaining 2 tablespoons parsley and season with salt and pepper to taste. Serve, passing extra Manchego separately.

Turkey and Pinto Chili

Prep time: 0 minutes | Cook time: 60 minutes | Serves 8

- 2 tablespoons cold-pressed avocado oil
- 4 garlic cloves, diced
- 1 large yellow onion, diced
- 4 jalapeño chiles, seeded and diced
- 2 carrots, diced
- 4 celery stalks, diced
- 2 teaspoons fine sea salt
- 2 pounds 93 percent lean ground turkey
- Two 4-ounce cans fire-roasted diced green chiles
- 4 tablespoons chili powder
- 2 teaspoons ground cumin
- 2 teaspoons ground coriander
- 1 teaspoon dried oregano
- 1 teaspoon dried sage
- 1 cup low-sodium chicken broth
- 3 cups drained cooked pinto beans, or two 15-ounce cans pinto beans, drained and rinsed
- Two 14½-ounce cans no-salt petite diced tomatoes and their liquid
- ¼ cup tomato paste

1. Select the Sauté setting on the Instant Pot and heat the oil and garlic for 3 minutes, until the garlic is bubbling but not browned. Add the onion, jalapeños, carrots, celery, and salt and sauté for 5 minutes, until the onion begins to soften. Add the turkey and sauté, using a wooden spoon or spatula to break up the meat as it cooks, for 6 minutes, until cooked through and no streaks of pink remain. Stir in the green chiles, chili powder, cumin, coriander, oregano, sage, and broth, using a wooden spoon or spatula to nudge any browned bits from the bottom of the pot. 2. Pour in the beans in a layer on top of the turkey. Pour in the tomatoes and their liquid and add the tomato paste in a dollop on top. Do not stir in the beans, tomatoes, or tomato paste. 3. Secure the lid and set the Pressure Release to Sealing. Press the Cancel button to reset the cooking program, then select the Pressure Cook or Manual setting and set the cooking time for 15 minutes at high pressure. (The pot will take about 15 minutes to come up to pressure before the cooking program begins.) 4. When the cooking program ends, let the pressure release naturally for at least 20 minutes, then move the Pressure Release to Venting to release any remaining steam. Open the pot and stir the chili to mix all of the ingredients. 5. Press the Cancel button to reset the cooking program, then select the Sauté setting and set the cooking time for 10 minutes. Allow the chili to reduce and thicken. Do not stir the chili while it is cooking, as this will cause it to sputter more. 6. When the cooking program ends, the pot will turn off. Wearing heat-resistant mitts, remove the inner pot from the housing. Wait for about 2 minutes to allow the chili to stop simmering, then give it a final stir. 7. Ladle the chili into bowls and serve hot.

Spicy Moroccan Lamb and Lentil Soup

Prep time: 10 minutes | Cook time: 28 minutes | Serves 6 to 8

- 1 pound (454 g) lamb shoulder chops (blade or round bone), 1 to 1½ inches thick, trimmed and halved
- ¾ teaspoon table salt, divided
- ⅛ teaspoon pepper
- 1 tablespoon extra-virgin olive oil
- 1 onion, chopped fine
- ¼ cup harissa, plus extra for serving
- 1 tablespoon all-purpose flour
- 8 cups chicken broth
- 1 cup French green lentils, picked over and rinsed
- 1 (15-ounce / 425-g) can chickpeas, rinsed
- 2 tomatoes, cored and cut into ¼-inch pieces
- ½ cup chopped fresh cilantro

1. Pat lamb dry with paper towels and sprinkle with ¼ teaspoon salt and pepper. Using highest sauté function, heat oil in Instant Pot for 5 minutes (or until just smoking). Place lamb in pot and cook until well browned on first side, about 4 minutes; transfer to plate. 2. Add onion and remaining ½ teaspoon salt to fat left in pot and cook, using highest sauté function, until softened, about 5 minutes. Stir in harissa and flour and cook until fragrant, about 30 seconds. Slowly whisk in broth, scraping up any browned bits and smoothing out any lumps. Stir in lentils, then nestle lamb into multicooker and add any accumulated juices. 3. Lock lid in place and close pressure release valve. Select high pressure cook function and cook for 10 minutes. Turn off Instant Pot and quick-release pressure. Carefully remove lid, allowing steam to escape away from you. 4. Transfer lamb to cutting board, let cool slightly, then shred into bite-size pieces using 2 forks; discard excess fat and bones. Stir lamb and chickpeas into soup and let sit until heated through, about 3 minutes. Season with salt and pepper to taste. Top individual portions with tomatoes and sprinkle with cilantro. Serve, passing extra harissa separately.

Easy Southern Brunswick Stew

Prep time: 20 minutes | Cook time: 8 minutes | Serves 12

- 2 pounds pork butt, visible fat removed
- 17-ounce can white corn
- 1¼ cups ketchup
- 2 cups diced, cooked potatoes
- 10-ounce package frozen peas
- 2 10¾-ounce cans reduced-sodium tomato soup
- Hot sauce to taste, optional

1. Place pork in the Instant Pot and secure the lid. 2. Press the Slow Cook setting and cook on low 6–8 hours. 3. When cook time is over, remove the meat from the bone and shred, removing and discarding all visible fat. 4. Combine all the meat and remaining ingredients (except the hot sauce) in the inner pot of the Instant Pot. 5. Secure the lid once more and cook in Slow Cook mode on low for 30 minutes more. Add hot sauce if you wish.

Lamb and Broccoli Soup

Prep time: 10 minutes | Cook time: 25 minutes | Serves 4

- 7 ounces (198 g) lamb fillet, chopped
- 1 tablespoon avocado oil
- ½ cup broccoli, roughly chopped
- ¼ daikon, chopped
- 2 bell peppers, chopped
- ¼ teaspoon ground cumin
- 5 cups beef broth

1. Sauté the lamb fillet with avocado oil in the Instant Pot for 5 minutes. 2. Add the broccoli, daikon, bell peppers, ground cumin, and beef broth. 3. Close the lid. Select Manual mode and set cooking time for 20 minutes on High Pressure. 4. When timer beeps, use a natural pressure release for 10 minutes, then release any remaining pressure. Open the lid. 5. Serve warm.

Garlic Beef Soup

Prep time: 12 minutes | Cook time: 42 minutes | Serves 8

- 10 strips bacon, chopped
- 1 medium white onion, chopped
- Cloves squeezed from 3 heads roasted garlic, or 6 cloves garlic, minced
- 1 to 2 jalapeño peppers, seeded and chopped (optional)
- 2 pounds (907 g) boneless

For Garnish:
- 1 avocado, peeled, pitted, and diced
- 2 radishes, very thinly sliced

- beef chuck roast, cut into 4 equal-sized pieces
- 5 cups beef broth
- 1 cup chopped fresh cilantro, plus more for garnish
- 2 teaspoons fine sea salt
- 1 teaspoon ground black pepper

- 2 tablespoons chopped fresh chives

1. Place the bacon in the Instant Pot and press Sauté. Cook, stirring occasionally, for 4 minutes, or until the bacon is crisp. Remove the bacon with a slotted spoon, leaving the drippings in the pot. Set the bacon on a paper towel-lined plate to drain. 2. Add the onion, garlic, and jalapeños, if using, to the Instant Pot and sauté for 3 minutes, or until the onion is soft. Press Cancel to stop the Sauté. 3. Add the beef, broth, cilantro, salt, and pepper. Stir to combine. 4. Seal the lid, press Manual, and set the timer for 35 minutes. Once finished, let the pressure release naturally. 5. Remove the lid and shred the beef with two forks. Taste the liquid and add more salt, if needed. 6. Ladle the soup into bowls. Garnish with the reserved bacon, avocado, radishes, chives, and more cilantro.

Beef Oxtail Soup with White Beans, Tomatoes, and Aleppo Pepper

Prep time: 20 minutes | Cook time: 1 hour 10 minutes | Serves 6 to 8

- 4 pounds (1.8 kg) oxtails, trimmed
- 1 teaspoon table salt
- 1 tablespoon extra-virgin olive oil
- 1 onion, chopped fine
- 2 carrots, peeled and chopped fine
- ¼ cup ground dried Aleppo pepper
- 6 garlic cloves, minced
- 2 tablespoons tomato paste
- ¾ teaspoon dried oregano

- ½ teaspoon ground cinnamon
- ½ teaspoon ground cumin
- 6 cups water
- 1 (28-ounce / 794-g) can diced tomatoes, drained
- 1 (15-ounce / 425-g) can navy beans, rinsed
- 1 tablespoon sherry vinegar
- ¼ cup chopped fresh parsley
- ½ preserved lemon, pulp and white pith removed, rind rinsed and minced (2 tablespoons)

1. Pat oxtails dry with paper towels and sprinkle with salt. Using highest sauté function, heat oil in Instant Pot for 5 minutes (or until just smoking). Brown half of oxtails, 4 to 6 minutes per side; transfer to plate. Set aside remaining uncooked oxtails. 2. Add onion and carrots to fat left in pot and cook, using highest sauté function, until softened, about 5 minutes. Stir in Aleppo pepper, garlic, tomato paste, oregano, cinnamon, and cumin and cook until fragrant, about 30 seconds. Stir in water, scraping up any browned bits, then stir in tomatoes. Nestle remaining uncooked oxtails into pot along with browned oxtails and add any accumulated juices. 3. Lock lid in place and close pressure release valve. Select high pressure cook function and cook for 45 minutes. Turn off Instant Pot and quick-release pressure. Carefully remove lid, allowing steam to escape away from you. 4. Transfer oxtails to cutting board, let cool slightly, then shred into bite-size pieces using 2 forks; discard bones and excess fat. Strain broth through fine-mesh strainer into large container; return solids to now-empty pot. Using wide, shallow spoon, skim excess fat from surface of liquid; return to pot. 5. Stir shredded oxtails and any accumulated juices and beans into pot. Using highest sauté function, cook until soup is heated through, about 5 minutes. Stir in vinegar and parsley and season with salt and pepper to taste. Serve, passing preserved lemon separately.

French Market Soup

Prep time: 20 minutes | Cook time: 1 hour | Serves 8

- 2 cups mixed dry beans, washed with stones removed
- 7 cups water
- 1 ham hock, all visible fat removed
- 1 teaspoon salt
- ¼ teaspoon pepper

- 16-ounce can low-sodium tomatoes
- 1 large onion, chopped
- 1 garlic clove, minced
- 1 chile, chopped, or 1 teaspoon chili powder
- ¼ cup lemon juice

1. Combine all ingredients in the inner pot of the Instant Pot. 2. Secure the lid and make sure vent is set to sealing. Using Manual, set the Instant Pot to cook for 60 minutes. 3. When cooking time is over, let the pressure release naturally. When the Instant Pot is ready, unlock the lid, then remove the bone and any hard or fatty pieces. Pull the meat off the bone and chop into small pieces. Add the ham back into the Instant Pot.

Cauliflower Rice and Chicken Thigh Soup

Prep time: 15 minutes | Cook time: 13 minutes | Serves 5

- 2 cups cauliflower florets
- 1 pound (454 g) boneless, skinless chicken thighs
- 4½ cups chicken broth
- ½ yellow onion, chopped
- 2 garlic cloves, minced
- 1 tablespoon unflavored gelatin powder
- 2 teaspoons sea salt
- ½ teaspoon ground black pepper

- ½ cup sliced zucchini
- ⅓ cup sliced turnips
- 1 teaspoon dried parsley
- 3 celery stalks, chopped
- 1 teaspoon ground turmeric
- ½ teaspoon dried marjoram
- 1 teaspoon dried thyme
- ½ teaspoon dried oregano

1. Add the cauliflower florets to a food processor and pulse until a ricelike consistency is achieved. Set aside. 2. Add the chicken thighs, chicken broth, onions, garlic, gelatin powder, sea salt, and black pepper to the pot. Gently stir to combine. 3. Lock the lid. Select Manual mode and set cooking time for 10 minutes on High Pressure. 4. When cooking is complete, quick release the pressure and open the lid. 5. Transfer the chicken thighs to a cutting board. Chop the chicken into bite-sized pieces and then return the chopped chicken to the pot. 6. Add the cauliflower rice, zucchini, turnips, parsley, celery, turmeric, marjoram, thyme, and oregano to the pot. Stir to combine. 7. Lock the lid. Select Manual mode and set cooking time for 3 minutes on High Pressure. 8. When cooking is complete, quick release the pressure. 9. Open the lid. Ladle the soup into serving bowls. Serve hot.

Beef and Cauliflower Soup

Prep time: 10 minutes | Cook time: 14 minutes | Serves 4

- 1 cup ground beef
- ½ cup cauliflower, shredded
- 1 teaspoon unsweetened tomato purée
- ¼ cup coconut milk

- 1 teaspoon minced garlic
- 1 teaspoon dried oregano
- ½ teaspoon salt
- 4 cups water

1. Put all ingredients in the Instant Pot and stir well. 2. Close the lid. Select Manual mode and set cooking time for 14 minutes on High Pressure. 3. When timer beeps, make a quick pressure release and open the lid. 4. Blend with an immersion blender until smooth. 5. Serve warm.

Appendix 1: Instant Pot Cooking Timetable

Dried Beans, Legumes and Lentils

Dried Beans and Legume	Dry (Minutes)	Soaked (Minutes)
Soy beans	25 – 30	20 – 25
Scarlet runner	20 – 25	10 – 15
Pinto beans	25 – 30	20 – 25
Peas	15 – 20	10 – 15
Navy beans	25 – 30	20 – 25
Lima beans	20 – 25	10 – 15
Lentils, split, yellow (moong dal)	15 – 18	N/A
Lentils, split, red	15 – 18	N/A
Lentils, mini, green (brown)	15 – 20	N/A
Lentils, French green	15 – 20	N/A
Kidney white beans	35 – 40	20 – 25
Kidney red beans	25 – 30	20 – 25
Great Northern beans	25 – 30	20 – 25
Pigeon peas	20 – 25	15 – 20
Chickpeas (garbanzo bean chickpeas)	35 – 40	20 – 25
Cannellini beans	35 – 40	20 – 25
Black-eyed peas	20 – 25	10 – 15
Black beans	20 – 25	10 – 15

Fish and Seafood

Fish and Seafood	Fresh (minutes)	Frozen (minutes)
Shrimp or Prawn	1 to 2	2 to 3
Seafood soup or stock	6 to 7	7 to 9
Mussels	2 to 3	4 to 6
Lobster	3 to 4	4 to 6
Fish, whole (snapper, trout, etc.)	5 to 6	7 to 10
Fish steak	3 to 4	4 to 6
Fish fillet,	2 to 3	3 to 4
Crab	3 to 4	5 to 6

Fruits

Fruits	Fresh (in Minutes)	Dried (in Minutes)
Raisins	N/A	4 to 5
Prunes	2 to 3	4 to 5
Pears, whole	3 to 4	4 to 6
Pears, slices or halves	2 to 3	4 to 5
Peaches	2 to 3	4 to 5
Apricots, whole or halves	2 to 3	3 to 4
Apples, whole	3 to 4	4 to 6
Apples, in slices or pieces	2 to 3	3 to 4

Meat

Meat and Cuts	Cooking Time (minutes)	Meat and Cuts	Cooking Time (minutes)
Veal, roast	35 to 45	Duck, with bones, cut up	10 to 12
Veal, chops	5 to 8	Cornish Hen, whole	10 to 15
Turkey, drumsticks (leg)	15 to 20	Chicken, whole	20 to 25
Turkey, breast, whole, with bones	25 to 30	Chicken, legs, drumsticks, or thighs	10 to 15
Turkey, breast, boneless	15 to 20	Chicken, with bones, cut up	10 to 15
Quail, whole	8 to 10	Chicken, breasts	8 to 10
Pork, ribs	20 to 25	Beef, stew	15 to 20
Pork, loin roast	55 to 60	Beef, shanks	25 to 30
Pork, butt roast	45 to 50	Beef, ribs	25 to 30
Pheasant	20 to 25	Beef, steak, pot roast, round, rump, brisket or blade, small chunks, chuck,	25 to 30
Lamb, stew meat	10 to 15		
Lamb, leg	35 to 45	Beef, pot roast, steak, rump, round, chuck, blade or brisket, large	35 to 40
Lamb, cubes,	10 t0 15		
Ham slice	9 to 12	Beef, ox-tail	40 to 50
Ham picnic shoulder	25 to 30	Beef, meatball	10 to 15
Duck, whole	25 to 30	Beef, dressed	20 to 25

Appendix 2: Recipes Index

Made in the USA
Middletown, DE
08 September 2024

60625494R00057